CORE CONCEPTS IN CULTURAL ANTHROPOLOGY

FIFTH EDITION

Robert H. Lavenda

Emily A. Schultz

St. Cloud State University

The McGraw·Hill Companies

Connect
Learn
Succeed™

CORE CONCEPTS IN CULTURAL ANTHROPOLOGY, FIFTH EDITION

Published by McGraw-Hill, a business unit of The McGraw-Hill Companies, Inc., 1221 Avenue of the Americas, New York, NY 10020. Copyright © 2013 by The McGraw-Hill Companies, Inc. All rights reserved. Printed in the United States of America. Previous editions © 2010 and 2007. Copyright © 2007 by Robert H. Lavenda and Emily A. Schultz. No part of this publication may be reproduced or distributed in any form or by any means, or stored in a database or retrieval system, without the prior written consent of The McGraw-Hill Companies, Inc., including, but not limited to, in any network or other electronic storage or transmission, or broadcast for distance learning.

Some ancillaries, including electronic and print components, may not be available to customers outside the United States.

This book is printed on acid-free paper.

1 2 3 4 5 6 7 8 9 0 DOC/DOC 1 0 9 8 7 6 5 4 3 2

ISBN: 978-0-07-803493-0
MHID: 0-07-803493-0

Vice President & Editor-in-Chief: *Michael Ryan*
Vice President of Specialized Publishing: *Janice M. Roerig-Blong*
Publisher: *William Glass*
Sponsoring Editor: *Gina Boedeker*
Marketing Manager: *Patrick Brown*
Project Manager: *Melissa M. Leick*
Design Coordinator: *Brenda A. Rolwes*
Cover Image: © *Photodisc/ Getty Images*
Cover Design: *Studio Montage, St. Louis, Missouri*
Buyer: *Louis Swaim*
Media Project Manager: *Sridevi Palani*
Compositor: *Laserwords Private Limited*
Typeface: *11/14 Sabon*
Printer: *R.R Donnelley*

All credits appearing on page or at the end of the book are considered to be an extension of the copyright page.

Library of Congress Cataloging-in-Publication Data

Lavenda, Robert H.
   Core concepts in cultural anthropology/Robert H. Lavenda, Emily A. Schultz.—5th ed.
   p. cm.
   ISBN 978-0-07-803493-0 (alk. paper)
   1. Ethnology. 2. Ethnology—Bibliography. I. Schultz, Emily A. (Emily Ann)- II. Title.
   GN316.L39 2012
   306—dc23
                               2011046294

www.mhhe.com

To Jan Beatty

Contents

⬦ Preface ⬦

THIS BOOK IS A CONCISE introduction to the fundamental key terms and issues of contemporary cultural anthropology. It is not a condensed version of the eighth edition of our textbook, *Cultural Anthropology: A Perspective on the Human Condition*; this is something different. Our goal is to provide students with a rapid sketch of the basic ideas and practices of cultural anthropology in a style analogous to an expanded glossary. A good glossary supports beginners in a discipline by expanding the analytic vocabulary at their command and situating this new terminology in the theoretical and practical history of the field. So, too, we hope, with this volume: We introduce the core concepts and key terms in cultural anthropology and indicate briefly where they come from and how they are related to one another in order to provide students with a context for understanding anthropological writing, especially ethnographic writing, when they turn to it.

Our expectation is that this text will be used in conjunction with ethnographies and/or collections of readings during the term. For that reason, we have omitted extended ethnographic examples and other kinds of details found in our textbook *Cultural Anthropology* (and most introductory texts), and we have concentrated on providing a scaffolding on which students can rely as they begin to read more conventional anthropological texts.

Features

- *Flexibility*. This text can be used in many different ways. It can be used by itself as a concise introduction to cultural

anthropology when the course time that can be devoted
to covering the discipline is limited. It can also be used
very successfully in conjunction with other readings, either
anthologies or ethnographies, or both. *Core Concepts
in Cultural Anthropology* may be assigned at the beginning of the term to go along with introductory lectures
and be referred to as needed. Another approach, popular
with users of earlier editions of *Core Concepts in Cultural
Anthropology,* is to assign specific chapters to be read
along with particular ethnographies or course topics. To
accommodate various uses, we have made each chapter as
self-contained as possible. Each chapter has numbered section headings to make it easier for students to navigate the
text and to give instructors additional flexibility should
they wish to assign segments of chapters in novel ways
best suited for the organization of their courses. We have
included cross-references to related topics in other chapters
wherever possible. If the order of our chapters does not fit
your arrangement of topics in your course, we invite you to
rearrange the chapters and sections in any order that works
for you. We think our order makes sense, but there are
many different ways to arrange a course, and instructors
should feel free to assign (or omit) the chapters and sections in whatever way best suits their approach to teaching
anthropology.

◆ *Brief and affordable.* What you have in your hands is an
unadorned framework for teaching cultural anthropology.
This book was written to be brief and to be affordable. Quite
intentionally, there are no photographs, no lavish graphics,
no elaborate text boxes, no extended ethnographic examples.
A consequence of writing a concise introduction is that many
of the details and nuances of the field are left out. We assume
that instructors will provide favorite ethnographic examples
both in class and in other readings to illustrate the issues they
raise in class. It is our hope that the brevity and affordability
of this text will allow the assignment of additional course

readings and will engender lectures and class discussions that bring back the nuance and subtlety that are a part of every human endeavor, including anthropology, teaching, and learning.

- *Provides useful study aids.* Each chapter opens with a list of key terms discussed in that chapter. Each chapter ends with a list of suggested readings, which—along with an extensive end-of-book bibliography—directs students to more detailed discussions. The index allows students to quickly find the key terms they need.

- *Includes a chapter on theory.* Because all anthropological writing is theoretically situated, we have included a chapter on theory in cultural anthropology. We think it is important for students to get a sense of how the texts they are reading fit into a broader theoretical context of the discipline. We also think they need some intellectual tools for interpreting what they are reading: Ethnographic writing often refers to alternative theoretical positions, and it is useful for students to know the issues those positions have raised in the course of ongoing anthropological discussion and debate.

- *Provides a unique appendix on reading ethnography.* Chapters 1 and 2 provide discussion of ethnographic *methods.* This distinctive appendix provides students with a set of tools for effectively reading ethnographic *writing.* It looks at how ethnographies are put together and how they are written; it also offers students strategies for getting the most from their reading.

As we put the book together, we had to decide whether some concepts would be addressed in one place in the text or needed to be referenced in several chapters. Where concepts are discussed in different places in the text (for example, discussion of gender issues, ecological anthropology, and field methods), we have cross-referenced the discussions.

What's New in the Fifth Edition?

There are two major changes in the structure and coverage of the fifth edition:

- We have added a new chapter on the anthropology of science, technology, and medicine to take account of this increasingly important part of anthropology.

- To make room for the new chapter, we have eliminated the chapter on culture and the individual. We have taken the material on socialization and enculturation and inserted it into the Chapter 2 discussion of learning culture and have taken the material on social suffering, structural violence, and trauma and worked it into the discussion of medical anthropology in Chapter 11.

While we have reviewed and edited every chapter, several chapters have been significantly revised:

- As noted earlier, Chapter 2 now includes a discussion of socialization and enculturation as part of the discussion of the learned nature of culture.

- Chapter 4 now has a new title—Making Meaning: Worldview, Religion, and Art—in order to highlight the connections among those elements of culture. There is a major new section on secularism, fundamentalism, and new religious movements. The section on anthropology and media has been substantially increased with a discussion of computer-facilitated media—the Internet and international migration, social media, and such virtual worlds as *Second Life* and *World of Warcraft*. The chapter also features a substantially revised definition of religion, following John Bowen's approach to the topic. The definition of myth has been expanded, as has the discussion of shamanism.

- Chapter 6, Political Anthropology, now contains a discussion of agency and a substantial discussion of biopower and governmentality.

- Chapter 7, Economic Anthropology, contains a new section on the anthropology of food and nutrition.

- Chapter 10, Globalization and the Culture of Capitalism, features a new discussion of tourism and a greatly expanded discussion of global assemblages with an emphasis on the anthropology of the environment.

- Chapter 11, The Anthropology of Science, Technology, and Medicine, is completely new.

- In all chapters, the suggested readings have been reviewed and updated.

Acknowledgments

For valuable suggestions on the appendix, we would like to thank Tom O'Toole and Katherine Woodhouse Beyer. It has been a pleasure to work with executive editor Gina Boedeker and developmental editor Craig Leonard. We also want to thank the reviewers of the text. Reviewers are extremely important to authors, even when we disagree, because they enable us to look at what we are doing from a wide variety of perspectives. This makes for a much better book. So, our thanks for their generous and careful comments to Warren Anderson, Southeast Missouri State University; Antonio Chiareli, Covenant College; Matthew Durington, Towson University; Cynthia Fowler, Wofford College; William Hope, Knox College; Douglas Hume, Northern Kentucky University; Steven Kane, Rhode Island College; Tracy Kopecky, College of DuPage; Clive McClelland, Liberty University; James Preston, Sonoma State University; Jennifer Price, Foothill College; Jeffrey Ratcliffe, Penn State Abington College; Brian Silverstein, University of Arizona; Linta Varghese, Vassar College; and Amelia Weinreb, University of Texas at Austin.

Finally, we would like to thank Jan Beatty, who suggested a book like this to us in the first place. This continues to be an interesting and valuable project for us as it pushes us to think about the different ways in which cultural anthropology might be presented. We hope that you find it to be an effective tool for teaching anthropology to new generations of students.

1 Anthropology

The key terms and concepts to be covered in this chapter, in the order in which they appear:

anthropology
holistic
comparative
evolutionary

biological anthropology
primatologists
paleoanthropologists
forensic anthropologists
medical anthropology

cultural anthropology
culture

fieldwork
informants
participant-observation
monograph

ethnography
ethnology

anthropological linguistics
linguistic anthropology
language
archaeology
prehistory

applied anthropology
development anthropology
objective knowledge

positivism
modernism
postmodernism
reflexive
multisited fieldwork

ANTHROPOLOGY IS A DISCIPLINE that exists at the borders of the social sciences, the humanities, and the biological sciences. The term comes from two Greek words: *anthropos*, meaning "human beings," and *logia*, "the study of." The "study of human beings" would seem to be a rather broad topic for any one field, but anthropologists take the name of their discipline seriously, and anything that has to do with human beings probably is of potential interest to anthropologists. Indeed, **anthropology** can be formally defined as the study of human nature, human society, and the human past. This means that some anthropologists study human origins, others try to understand diverse contemporary ways of life, and some excavate the past or try to understand why we speak the ways we do.

1.1 An Anthropological Perspective

Given its breadth, what coherence anthropology has as a discipline comes from its perspective. Anthropology is holistic, comparative, field based, and evolutionary. For anthropologists, being **holistic** means trying to fit together all that is known about human beings. That is, anthropologists draw on the findings of many different disciplines that study human beings (human biology, economics, and religion, for example), as well as data on similar topics that they have collected, and attempt to produce an encompassing picture of human life. In the same way, when an anthropologist studies a specific group of people, the goal is to produce a holistic portrait of that people's way of life by bringing together information about many different facets of their lives—social, religious, economic, political, linguistic, and so forth—in order to provide a nuanced context for understanding who they are and why they do what they do.

However, to generalize about human nature, human society, and the human past requires information from as wide a range of human groups as possible. Anthropologists realized long ago

2

that the patterns of life common in their own societies were not necessarily followed in other societies. And so, anthropology is a **comparative** discipline: Anthropologists must consider similarities and differences in as wide a range of human societies as possible before generalizing about what it means to be human.

Because anthropology is interested in human beings in all places and at all times, anthropologists are curious about how we got to be what we are today. For this reason, anthropology is **evolutionary**. A major branch of anthropology is concerned with the study of the biological evolution of the human species over time, including the study of human origins and genetic variety and inheritance in living human populations. Some anthropologists have also been interested in cultural evolution, looking for patterns of orderly change over time in socially acquired behavior that is not carried in the genes.

1.2 The Subfields of Anthropology

Anthropology in North America historically has been divided into four major subfields: biological anthropology, cultural anthropology, linguistic anthropology, and archaeology.

Biological anthropology is the subfield of anthropology that looks at human beings as biological organisms. Biological anthropologists are interested in many different aspects of human biology, including our similarities to and differences from other living organisms. Those who study the closest living relatives of human beings—the nonhuman primates (chimpanzees and gorillas, for example)—are called **primatologists**. Those who specialize in the study of the fossilized bones and teeth of our earliest ancestors are called **paleoanthropologists**. Other biological anthropologists examine the genetic variation among and within different human populations or investigate variation in human skeletal biology (for example, measuring and comparing the shapes and sizes of bones or teeth using skeletal remains from different human populations). Newer specialties focus on human adaptability in different ecological settings, on human growth and development, and on the connections between a population's evolutionary history and its susceptibility to disease. **Forensic anthropologists** use their knowledge of human anatomy to aid law-enforcement and human rights investigators by assisting in the identification of skeletal material found at crime or accident sites or at sites associated with possible human rights violations.

Overlapping biological anthropology and cultural anthropology is the vibrant and relatively new field of **medical anthropology**. Medical anthropologists study the factors that contribute to human disease or illness as well as the ways in which human groups respond to them. Medical anthropological research covers a vast range of topics, ranging from alcohol use in various societies, to the dimensions of the AIDS pandemic cross-culturally, to social aspects of medical care, to the effects of stress, violence, and social suffering. (See Chapter 11 for a fuller discussion of medical anthropology.)

Cultural anthropology (sometimes called *social anthropology* in Great Britain) is another major subfield of anthropology. Cultural anthropologists investigate how variation in the beliefs and behaviors of members of different human groups is shaped by **culture**, sets of learned behaviors and ideas that human beings acquire as members of society. (For a fuller discussion of the concept of culture, see Chapter 2.) Cultural anthropologists specialize in specific domains of human cultural activity. Some study the ways people organize themselves to carry out collective tasks, whether economic, political, or spiritual. Others focus on the forms and meanings of expressive behavior in human societies—language, art, music, ritual, religion, and the like. Still others examine material culture—the things people make and use, such as clothing, housing, and tools, and the techniques they employ to get food and produce material goods. They may also study the ways in which technologies and environments shape each other. For some time, cultural anthropologists have been interested in the way non-Western peoples have responded to the political and economic challenges of European colonialism and the capitalist industrial technology that came with it. They investigate contemporary issues of gender and sexuality, transnational labor migration, and the post–Cold War resurgence of ethnicity and nationalism around the world. And some cultural anthropologists have begun to examine the ways in which forms of science and technology that originated in the West—biotechnology, computers, and the

Internet, for example—have been incorporated into and continue to modify the cultural practices of peoples throughout the world.

In all of these cases, the comparative nature of anthropology requires that what is taken for granted by members of a specific society—the anthropologist's own, as much as any other—must be examined, or "problematized." As a result, there is a double movement in anthropology: Anthropologists study other ways of life not only to understand them in their own terms but also to put the anthropologists' own ways of life in perspective. In fact, in recent years, some anthropologists have concentrated on studying their own society, or aspects of it.

To make their discipline comparative, cultural anthropologists immerse themselves in the lives of other peoples. Traditionally, cultural anthropology is rooted in **fieldwork**, an anthropologist's personal, long-term experience with a specific group of people and their way of life. Where possible, anthropologists try to live for a year or more with the people whose way of life is of concern to them. The result is a fine-grained knowledge of the everyday details of life. Cultural anthropologists get to know people as individuals, not as "data sets." They remember the names and faces of people who, over the course of a year or more, have become familiar to them as complex and complicated men, women, and children. They remember the feel of the noonday sun, the sounds of the morning, the smells of food cooking, the pace and rhythm of life. In this sense, anthropology traditionally has been an *experiential* discipline. This approach does, of course, have drawbacks as well as advantages: Anthropologists are not usually able to make macrolevel generalizations about an entire nation or society, and their attention is not usually directed toward national or international policy-making or data collection. They are often, however, well aware of the *effects* of national or international decisions on the local level. In fact, in recent years, a number of anthropologists have done illuminating work about nations, refugees and migrations, and international and global processes.

People who share information about their way of life with anthropologists traditionally have been called **informants**. In recent years, however, a number of anthropologists have become uncomfortable with that term, which to some conjures up images of police informers and to others seems to reduce fully rounded individuals to the information they provide. But anthropologists have not been able to agree on an expression that might replace "informant"; some prefer "respondent" or "teacher" or "friend" or simply refer to "the people with whom I work." Regardless of the term, fieldworkers gain insight into another way of life by taking part as fully as they can in a group's social activities as well as by observing those activities as outsiders. This research method, known as **participant-observation,** is central to cultural anthropology. Cultural anthropologists also use a variety of other research methods including interviews, censuses, surveys, and even statistical sampling techniques when appropriate.

Cultural anthropologists write about what they have learned in scholarly articles or in books, and sometimes they document the lives of their research subjects on film. A book written about a single culture or way of life is often called a **monograph,** from the Greek *mono* ("single") and *graph* ("write"). An ethnographic monograph is more commonly referred to as an **ethnography. Ethnology** is the comparative study of two or more ways of life. Thus, cultural anthropologists who write ethnographies are sometimes called *ethnographers,* and anthropologists who compare ethnographic information on many different ways of life are sometimes called *ethnologists.* The prefix "ethno-" comes from the Greek *ethnos* ("people") and is used a great deal by anthropologists to mean "of (or about) a people" or "of (or about) an ethnic group." Increasing numbers of cultural anthropologists and their field consultants work closely together not only in the course of field research but also in the writing of ethnography based on that research, a practice called *collaborative ethnography.*

A third major subfield of anthropology, called **anthropological linguistics** or **linguistic anthropology,** is the branch of anthropology concerned with the study of human languages. For many people, the most striking cultural feature of human beings is **language,** the system of arbitrary vocal symbols we use to encode our experience of the world and of one another. Anthropological linguists were some of the first people to transcribe non-Western languages and to produce grammars and dictionaries of those languages. They also have worked to show the ways in which a people's language (or languages) serves as the main carrier of important cultural information. In tracing the relationships between language and culture, these anthropologists have investigated a range of topics (see Chapter 3 for details).

In all their research, linguistic anthropologists seek to understand language in relation to the broader cultural, historical, or biological contexts that make it possible. Modern linguistic anthropologists are trained in both formal linguistics and anthropology, and some cultural anthropologists study linguistics as part of their professional preparation.

Archaeology, the fourth traditional subfield of North American anthropology, can be defined as a cultural anthropology of the human past, involving the analysis of the material remains of earlier human societies. Through archaeology, anthropologists discover much about human history, particularly **prehistory**, the long stretch of time before the development of writing. Archaeologists look for evidence of past human cultural activity such as post-holes, garbage heaps, and settlement patterns. Depending on the locations and ages of the sites they are digging, archaeologists may also have to be experts in stone-tool manufacture, metallurgy, or ancient pottery. Because archaeological excavations frequently uncover remains such as bones or plant pollen, archaeologists often work in teams with other scientists who specialize in the analysis of those remains.

The work that archaeologists do complements the work done by other kinds of anthropologists. For example, paleontologists may find that archaeological information about successive stone-tool traditions in a particular region may correlate with fossil evidence of prehistoric occupation of that region by ancient human populations. Cultural anthropologists may use the work of archaeologists to help them interpret contemporary patterns of land use or forms of subsistence technology.

Although the popular media often portray archaeologists as concerned primarily with exotic ancient "stuff" (the "Indiana Jones syndrome," we might call it), archaeologists are usually more interested in seeking answers to cultural questions that can only be addressed properly by considering the passage of time. For example, archaeologists can use dating techniques to establish the ages of artifacts, which then allows them to hypothesize about patterns of

TABLE 1.1   The Traditional Subfields of Anthropology

SUBFIELD	DEFINITION
Biological anthropology	The study of human beings as biological organisms
Cultural anthropology	The study of how variation in the beliefs and behavior of members of different human groups is shaped by culture
Linguistic anthropology	The study of human language in cultural context
Archaeology	A cultural anthropology of the past

sociocultural change in ancient societies. That is, tracing the spread of cultural inventions over time from one site to another allows them to hypothesize about the nature and degree of social contact between different peoples. Some contemporary archaeologists even dig through layers of garbage deposited by people within the past two or three decades, often uncovering surprising information about modern consumption patterns. (Table 1.1 lists the four traditional subfields of anthropology.)

In recent decades, increasing numbers of anthropologists have been using the methods and findings from every subfield of anthropology to address problems in the contemporary world, in what is called **applied anthropology**. This subfield has grown rapidly as an area of involvement and employment for anthropologists. Some applied anthropologists may use a particular group's ideas about illness and health to introduce new public-health practices in a way that makes sense to, and will be accepted by, members of that group. Others may apply knowledge of traditional social organization to ease the problems of refugees trying to settle in a new land. Still others may tap their knowledge of traditional and Western methods of cultivation to help farmers increase their crop yields. Taken together, these activities are sometimes called **development anthropology** because their aim is to improve people's capacities to maintain their health, produce their food, and otherwise adapt to the challenges of life in the contemporary world.

Applied anthropologists with a background in archaeology may be involved with contract or salvage archaeology, or they may work in cultural resource management to ensure that the human past is not destroyed by, say, the construction of new buildings, highways, or dams. Biological anthropologists may become involved in forensic work, such as the determination of social characteristics of crime or accident victims, or in nutrition. Linguistic anthropologists, in partnership with local activists and social institutions striving to protect threatened cultural heritages, have worked to preserve indigenous languages on the verge of extinction. Applied anthropology has drawn cultural anthropologists into ever wider and more varied collaborations with scholars from other scholarly disciplines. For example, cultural anthropologists with interests in the ways that human cultural practices articulate with the wider physical environment have, over the years, established working relationships with ecologists and economists, historians and political scientists, geographers and soil scientists, botanists and zoologists. These collaborations have produced specialties ranging from *cultural ecology* (see Chapters 6 and 7) to *political ecology* (see Chapter 6) to *environmental anthropology*, an area of expertise that unites anthropologists with others who are concerned about ecology, the environment, and environmentalism (see Chapter 6).

In recent years, the number of new anthropologists with doctorate degrees who take up jobs in applied settings outside universities has grown steadily. As a result, increasing numbers of anthropologists have come to view applied anthropology as a separate field of professional specialization—related to the other four fields but with its own techniques and theoretical questions. More and more universities in the United States have begun to develop courses and programs in applied anthropology.

Anthropology may have begun in western Europe and the United States more than a century ago, but over the course of its history it has become an international discipline. Universities and research institutions in many countries around the world have established anthropology departments, offer courses and degrees, and carry out research, both theoretical and applied. Anthropologists in different countries have established national anthropological associations, and there are also international associations of anthropologists for the dissemination of anthropological research.

1.3 Is Anthropology a Science? Modernism, Postmodernism, and Beyond

At the beginning of the twentieth century, most anthropologists viewed their growing discipline as a science. They agreed that the truth about the world was accessible through the five senses; that a properly disciplined rational mind could derive universal, objective truths from material evidence; and that a single scientific method could be applied to any dimension of reality, from the movement of the planets to human sexual behavior. Such investigation was supposed to produce **objective knowledge:** undistorted, and thus universally valid, knowledge about the world. Anthropologists felt free to apply scientific methods in any area of anthropological interest, from stone tools to religion, confident that the combined results of these efforts would produce a genuine "Science of Man" (as it was then called). This set of ideas and practices is known as **positivism.**

Today, many critical observers of the natural and social sciences connect these ideas to a complex Western cultural ideology called **modernism.** Modernism can be (and has been) viewed in terms of liberation from outdated traditions that prevent people from building better lives for themselves and their children. Critics have argued, however, that modern Western science, rather than being a universal path to objective truth, is itself a culture-bound enterprise connected to a specific definition of progress. (For additional discussion of science, see Chapter 11.) Many members of non-Western societies agree with these critics that, in their experience, modernist ideas have been used by powerful Western states to dominate them and to undermine their traditional beliefs and practices. From their perspective, Western-style "progress" has meant the loss of political autonomy, an increase in economic impoverishment and environmental degradation, and destruction of systems of social relations and values that clash with the "modern" way of life.

This criticism of modernism, accompanied by an active questioning of all the boundaries and categories that modernists set up as objectively true, has come to be called **postmodernism.** Its plausibility as an intellectual position increased after the end of the Cold War in 1989 when many previously unquestioned cultural and political "truths" about the world seemed to crumble overnight. To be postmodern is to question the universalizing tendencies of modernism, including modernist understandings of science. Postmodernists point out that people occupying powerful social positions often can pass off their own cultural or political prejudices as universal truths while dismissing or ignoring alternative views held by powerless groups.

Anthropologists had long considered themselves to be debunkers of distorting Western stereotypes about non-Western peoples. Having frequently defended the integrity of indigenous societies against the onslaughts of modernizing missionaries and "development" experts, they had come to assume that they were on the side of those whose ways of life they studied. From the perspective of some members of those societies, however, as well as from the viewpoint of postmodernists, anthropologists looked just like another group of outside "experts" making their own universal claims about human cultures, behaving no differently from chemists making universal, "expert" claims about molecules.

1.4 Reflexive Anthropology

Postmodern criticism prompted anthropologists to engage in a reappraisal of their discipline and, in particular, to rethink what was involved in fieldwork and the writing of ethnography. While cultural anthropologists continue to value careful observational methods and accurate, systematic data gathering, many of them also take seriously certain parts of the postmodern critique. For example, modeling ethnographers in the field on natural scientists in their laboratories appears problematic once ethnographers grant that the subject matter of anthropology, unlike that of chemistry, consists of human beings, members of the same species as the scientists studying them. Rather than a relationship between a curious human being and inert matter, anthropological fieldwork always involved a social relationship between at least two curious individuals. This meant that the cultural identity and personal characteristics of fieldworkers had to be taken into account when attempting to make sense of their ethnographic writing. Put another way, fieldwork had to become a **reflexive** activity in which anthropologists carefully scrutinized both their own contribution to fieldwork interactions and the responses these interactions elicited from informants. That is, rather than assuming that they were, for all intents and purposes, invisible to the people they were studying, anthropologists began to consider the effect that they had on the people with whom they were living. They began to recognize that who they were as individuals and as socially situated actors had an effect on their research. Many contemporary cultural anthropologists have accepted the challenges of doing reflexive fieldwork and are persuaded that such fieldwork produces better, more accurate ethnography than modernist methods ever did. Reflexive fieldworkers are much more explicit about the limitations of their own knowledge and much more generous in the credit they give to their informants. Some have written their ethnographies in new, experimental styles that often read more like novels than scientific texts.

Indeed, some ethnographers today have taken up the challenge of doing participant-observation in cultural settings in which they are insiders. They are conscious of potential pitfalls but are convinced that their professional training will help them provide a unique and valuable perspective. Many ethnographers have also chosen to engage in **multisited fieldwork** in which the goal is to follow people, or objects, or cultural processes that are not contained by social, national, ethnic, or religious boundaries (see Chapter 2). Working in more than one place and with persons or institutions that have not traditionally been the focus of ethnographic analysis, they are also revealing interconnections and influences that in the past would have escaped the fieldworker's attention. These ethnographers see their task as finding a way to combine the most valuable elements of the postmodern critique of ethnography with a continuing respect for empirical evidence. The challenge of such a task is great and perhaps as paradoxical as the notion of participant-observation, but many ethnographers believe that research undertaken within and across uncomfortable middle ground can yield important insights into human cultural practices, insights that can be secured in no other way. Such disciplinary commitments make anthropological research and writing of ongoing, vital importance to human self-understanding.

At the beginning of the twenty-first century, many ethnographers (as well as many members of the societies in which they work) have moved beyond the opposition between modernism and postmodernism. They draw attention to the ways in which members of non-Western societies selectively incorporate "modern" or "scientific" practices originating in the Western world in order to help them develop their own *alternative modernities*. At the same time, a reconsideration of the nature of "science" by anthropologists and others has shown that the positivist understanding of science may in fact offer an incomplete account of scientific successes and failures, not only in the social sciences but also in physical sciences such as physics and biology (see Chapters 11 and 12). This development opens up new and exciting possibilities for alternative understandings of science—and of anthropology as a science—that are yet to be developed.

For Further Reading

BIOLOGICAL ANTHROPOLOGY
Marks 2011; Park 2009; Relethford 2009

ARCHAEOLOGY
Ashmore and Sharer 2009

APPLIED ANTHROPOLOGY
Ervin 2004; Gwynne 2003; Kedia and van Willigen 2006; McDonald 2001; van Willigen 2002

DEVELOPMENT ANTHROPOLOGY
Gardner and Lewis 1996

MEDICAL ANTHROPOLOGY
See *For Further Reading* in Chapter 11

FIELD RESEARCH
Agar 1996; Bernard 2011; Bradburd 1998; DeWalt and DeWalt 2010; Marcus 1995; Rabinow 1977; Wolcott 2004, 2008

POLITICAL ECOLOGY
Berglund et al. 2006

2 Culture

The key terms and concepts covered in this chapter, in the order in which they appear:

culture
race
socialization
enculturation
cultural universals

symbols
ethnocentrism
cultural relativism
cultural hybridization
indigenization

C ULTURE HAS LONG BEEN the central concept in anthropology. At its most basic, **culture** is understood to refer to learned sets of ideas and behaviors that are acquired by people as members of society. Anthropologists have used the concept of culture in a variety of ways over the years, however, and contemporary anthropologists continue to disagree about how it should be defined. Major debates about the culture concept, however, can be connected to particular intellectual and social struggles in which anthropologists have been involved historically.

2.1 Culture Against Racism: The Early Twentieth Century

Culture gained power as an anthropological concept in the early decades of the discipline, around the turn of the twentieth century, in a social and scholarly context in which the distinctiveness of different social groups of people was widely attributed to **race**. Races were thought to be distinct biological subpopulations, or even subspecies, of humanity. Scholars and physicians usually assigned people to various racial categories on the basis of skin color, hair texture, or other visible physical traits. But these physical traits were thought to be inseparable from a number of other, often less visible traits that were also thought to distinguish one race from another—traits ranging from language and dress and musical ability to morality and intelligence. Many early physical anthropologists hoped that if they could succeed in accurately identifying the "races of Man," they would be able to specify which languages and customs originated with, belonged to, or were otherwise appropriate for which races. Unfortunately, this search for a scientific definition of race took place in a historical context in which ruling groups in the societies from which the anthropologists came were already convinced of the reality of race and so used race-based distinctions to justify their own domination of darker-skinned peoples around the globe.

In this context, the culture concept was a crucial innovation designed to counteract the racism implicit in nineteenth-century physical anthropology and, more broadly, in nineteenth-century social thought. At the turn of the twentieth century, under the influence of Franz Boas (1858–1942), anthropologists were collecting evidence to show that the diverse beliefs and practices that distinguished different groups of human beings from one another were due to differences in *social learning*, not differences in racial biology. This social learning came to be called **socialization**, the process of learning to live as a member of a group, or **enculturation**, the process by which people come to terms with the ways of thinking and feeling that are considered appropriate in the group. For example, immigrants in the United States were assigned by physical anthropologists to a variety of different "races." Yet Boas and his colleagues were able to show that American-born children of immigrants regularly spoke fluent English, wore the clothing, ate the food, and otherwise adopted ways of life common in the United States. Boas even showed that the head shapes of the children of immigrants differed from the head shapes of their parents, apparently under the influence of nutritional changes.

The so-called races of Man were, in actuality, a single *human* race (or as we would say today, populations of a single human species). As a consequence, all were equipped with the same "panhuman rationality" and were equally capable of creating new cultural traits or adopting cultural traits from others. Another way to emphasize the equal humanity of all human groups was to demonstrate that each of them possessed the same kinds of institutions, or **cultural universals**, designed to achieve the same overall goals for the group's members. This was the path taken by Polish-British anthropologist Bronislaw Malinowski (1884–1942), who argued that all human beings everywhere face the same problems of survival or, as he put it, experience the same basic human needs. The members of each society use culture to devise ways of meeting these needs—for food or clothing or shelter or education or reproduction. Different societies meet these needs in different ways, however, and it is the ethnographer's job to catalog the variety.

Boasians chose a different line of attack, arguing that race, language, and culture were independent phenomena. To show this was to show that the concept of biological race corresponded to no material reality and thus explained nothing about variation across human groups. That is, a person's physical attributes—skin color, hair texture, nose shape, stature, or the like—in no way compelled that person to speak or behave in any particular way. Indeed, the rapidity with which people of all "races" could forget old languages and customs and adopt new ones demonstrated the superiority of the culture concept in explaining variation across human groups. Because the capacities to create and learn culture belong to the entire human species, nothing prevents any subgroup from learning languages or beliefs or practices originally developed by some other subgroup.

Work by Boas and his students suggested strongly that the boundaries between various human groups are fuzzy and fluid and that firm distinctions are difficult to identify, let alone enforce. They devoted much effort to documenting an enormous amount of cultural borrowing across social, linguistic, and "racial" boundaries. The culture concept provided an explanation for why different social groups often lived lives that were quite distinct from those of their neighbors, without any need to invoke the notion of race. First, people do, initially at least, learn their native language and the bulk of their cultural practices from those among whom they grow up. Second, social groups often deliberately emphasize unique cultural attributes to set themselves apart from their neighbors. Finally, many of the groups that ethnographers first studied had historically been incorporated into colonial empires (as in Africa) or within the boundaries of a larger nation-state (as in the United States). In such situations, the sorting of peoples into named societies, each associated with its own unique way of life, was strongly encouraged by the ruling elites.

It was not until after World War II, and evidence of the horrors of genocide justified by racial thinking in Nazi biology, that racial thinking in anthropology was officially condemned. The highest-profile critic of racial thinking in physical anthropology was probably Sherwood Washburn of the University of California at Berkeley. Washburn proposed a "new physical anthropology," or biological anthropology, that drew its theoretical inspiration from population biology, a research program that emerged from the evolutionary synthesis between genetics and natural selection that had come about in the 1930s and 1940s. The field of biological anthropology was to focus on the human species as a whole, explaining variation both among and within populations of our species as the outcome of adaptations to particular natural environments that were shaped by natural selection on genes. But it was not until the late 1960s, in the context of collapsing colonial empires and the civil rights movement in the United States, that this orientation became standard in anthropology.

All this work aimed to demolish the concept of biological race for good, and yet at the beginning of the twenty-first century, the concept of "race" has not disappeared. The concept of culture explains why this is so: People can invent *cultural* categories based on superficial physical features of human beings, call these categories "races," and then use these categories as building blocks for their social institutions, *even if such categories correspond to no biological reality*. Thus, when a particular social order depends on racial categorizations of the population in order to function in a particular way, racial categories can persist no matter how powerfully scientists demonstrate that they have no basis in material reality (see Chapter 5). Ironically, racial categories that are condemned for stigmatizing different segments of the human population may be reinforced when, for example, a government asks its citizens to identify themselves by "race" in order to measure the extent to which compensatory government programs have or have not assisted the members of different "racial" groups to overcome past oppression. An ongoing challenge within anthropology has been how to deny the reality of race as a biological concept without ignoring the continuing vigor of race as a cultural construction in societies like that of the United States.

2.2 The Evolution of Culture

Rejecting racial thinking led the Boasians to stress the plasticity of human biology under different environmental circumstances. If human beings could learn any language or culture to which they were exposed, this must mean that they required culture in order to survive and thrive. Along with many founders of the modern synthesis in evolutionary biology, such as Theodosius Dobzhansky and Ernst Mayr, anthropologists came to argue that in the course of human evolution, natural selection on genes produced species (our own and those of our ancestors) whose members adapt and survive as biological organisms by learning the cultural practices of those among whom they live.

Compared even to our nearest primate relatives, we human beings seem to be born remarkably free of specific "survival instincts," or biological programming that would secure food, shelter, and mates for us automatically. Instead, as Malinowski suggested, every human group apparently can invent (and modify) its own particular sets of learned cultural traditions in order to solve those problems. Thus, human beings must learn everything necessary to survive and thrive from older, experienced members of their group.

Put another way, the way that a human group adapts to the environmental challenges of a particular habitat does not depend only on human physiology (or the genes involved in the development of human physiological responses). For example, human beings attempting to survive in cold climates are not obliged to wait until natural selection provides them with thick fur. Instead, they can rely on their cultural capacity to learn to control fire, make warm clothing from skins, invent ways of using cold-adapted plants and animals for food, and so forth. Natural selection on genes still plays a role, but selection would favor those whose genetic endowment allowed them to learn especially easily from those around them and who were curious and creative in devising cultural solutions for new adaptive challenges. Some anthropologists, known as *cultural inheritance theorists*, have used mathematical models borrowed from population biology to demonstrate how the capacity for human culture could have arisen as a result of natural selection on cultural variation. Their work grew out of work by *cultural ecologists* like Julian Steward, active in the mid-twentieth century. Steward connected changes in culture over time in particular societies to the nature of the societies' adaptations to their material environment, adaptations in which their culture and technology played central roles (see Chapter 7).

If people's cultural activities reshape the environments in which they live (and to which they must adapt), then people also alter the selection pressures that they face. This process, called *niche construction*, remodels the environment to which any population must adapt, and is by no means exclusive to the human species: birds building nests and beavers building dams are engaged in the same activity. Niche construction buffers a population from some environmental challenges that they might otherwise face, but it subjects them to new selection pressures shaped by the constructed niche. For example, although good eyesight has long been advantageous to human beings, selection pressures that favor individuals with good eyesight have been relaxed in contemporary affluent constructed niches in the United States where eyeglasses are widely available to correct people's vision. Similarly, most human beings in the contemporary United States live in constructed niches that buffer them from predation by large carnivores but expose them to a different set of dangerous predators: microbes like HIV (human immunodeficiency virus) or the tuberculosis bacillus. When individuals are exposed to such microbes, natural selection will favor those individuals who are more resistant to microbes over those who are less resistant, especially in niches where drug therapy is inadequate or unavailable.

Overall, research into human prehistory strongly supports a view of human beings as a species of "weedy generalists," equipped by our evolutionary history with adaptive traits, including our dependence on culture, that has made it possible for us to construct habitable niches in virtually any environment that the earth has to offer. Some anthropologists have tried to make sense of the patterns of human cultural adaptations revealed by archaeology, history, and ethnography over time and across space during the past 6 to 7 million years that humans and their ancestors have walked the earth. As we saw in Chapter 1, modern anthropology began by rejecting simplistic unilineal schemes of cultural evolution. Today, there is disagreement among anthropologists concerning when or whether it is still appropriate to talk about stages of cultural evolution (see Chapters 5 and 12 for details).

2.3 Culture and Symbolism

Human beings, of course, are not the only animals in the world that learn. Several decades of research, for example, have shown that chimpanzees have invented simple practices of various kinds that other members of their groups acquire through learning, such as fishing for termites with twigs, making leaf sponges to soak up water to drink, cracking nuts open with rocks, and assuming distinctive postures for grooming one another. If culture is defined as practices that are acquired from and shared with other members of one's social group, that mediate one's adaptation to the environment, and that get passed on from generation to generation by means of social learning, then these ape practices certainly can be called culture. At the same time, missing from these forms of ape culture is a key element that is integral to human culture. Unlike the learned behavior of other primates such as chimpanzees, human culture clearly depends on our use of **symbols**.

A symbol is something that stands for something else: "X symbolizes Y." What makes symbols distinct from other forms of representation is that there is *no necessary link* between the symbol (X) and that which it stands for (Y). Put another way, the relationship between a symbol and that which it stands for is conventional and arbitrary. The object that you are reading right now is called a "book" because generations of English speakers have agreed to call it that. It could just as easily be called "libro" or "gludge." Apes such as chimpanzees and bonobos do seem to have some rudimentary symbolic capacities. Just how much remains controversial, however, because the strongest evidence has been produced in the highly constructed niches that are primate research laboratories. In laboratory settings, however, and especially in the wild, these apes do not depend on symbolism to anything like the degree that human beings do. Thus, although learning is not unique to human beings and some learning of shared traditional practices can be found in nonhuman animals, only with human beings do we find a species whose survival depends on its reliance on learned, shared traditions that are *symbolically encoded*.

To depend on symbolic culture is to depend on learning for survival, but it is also much more. Symbols stand for objects, events, and processes in the wider world. But because their link to these phenomena is purely by convention, that which the symbol stands for can never be specified once and for all. The "same" phenomena may be symbolized differently in different societies, or phenomena that are distinguished as "different" in one society may be grouped together as instances of the "same" thing in another. This slippage between symbols and what they stand for makes possible complex human cultural systems, and it enables their remodeling or dismantling under novel conditions. Such slippage also means, however, that effort is constantly required to keep symbolic systems *systemic*—that is, orderly and coherent. Furthermore, nothing guarantees that existing cultural systems will not change over time, due either to internally generated developments or to exposure to new phenomena introduced from outside.

2.4 Ethnocentrism and Cultural Relativism

Still, despite these factors, ethnographers were impressed early on by the high degree of cultural coherence and predictability that they regularly encountered while doing field research in non-Western societies. This was important because it undermined the racist stereotypes about tribal or non-Western peoples widespread in the early decades of the discipline. In particular, such peoples were regularly portrayed as irrational "savages" or "barbarians" leading lives that were, in the words of seventeenth-century philosopher Thomas Hobbes, "nasty, brutish, and short." Such portrayals of tribal peoples by Western observers were based on the universal human tendency to view one's own way of life as natural and as naturally better than other, different ways of life. Anthropologists call this attitude **ethnocentrism**—that is, using the practices of your own "people" as a yardstick to measure how well the customs of other, different peoples measure up. Inevitably, the ways in which "they" differ from "us" (no matter who "they" and "us" happen to be) are understood, ethnocentrically, in terms of *what they lack*.

Ethnocentric Europeans and North Americans believed that to be "civilized" and "cultured" meant to follow an orderly way of life graced by refinement and harmony. But early anthropologists found that they could use the culture concept to counter these ethnocentric beliefs. They could show that *all* peoples were equally "cultured" because every group's social practices were characterized by order, harmony, and refinement. The particular set of customs one followed depended on the group one was born into, from whose members one learned those customs. Another group's customs might differ from our customs, but each group equally had its own orderly, refined sets of customs. Thus, the child of an aristocratic European family, if brought up among people who hunted and gathered for a living, would learn the language and culture of hunters and gatherers just as easily as one of their children, adopted by the aristocrats, would learn the language and culture proper to aristocratic Europeans. To emphasize that every society (not merely western European society) had its own integrated culture was a way of emphasizing that each society was human in its own way—indeed, that all human societies were *equally human.*

The term *culture* came to refer to a coherent set of beliefs and customs belonging to a distinct society. Such a view seemed to entail, at the very least, that those who were outsiders to someone else's culture ought to refrain from assuming that difference automatically meant inferiority. A culture could not be fully appreciated, anthropologists argued, until its various beliefs and practices were seen from the point of view of those who lived their lives according to those beliefs and practices. Ethnographic fieldwork introduced anthropologists to peoples about whom they previously lacked firsthand knowledge. By living side by side with people with an unfamiliar set of beliefs and practices for an extended period of time and learning the local language, anthropologists might hope to get a sense of what the world looked like from their hosts' point of view. This perspective on other cultures developed into the position called **cultural relativism** whereby anthropologists were urged to interpret specific beliefs and practices in the context of the culture to which they belonged. More broadly, anthropologists urged others not to make snap judgments about the value of other peoples' customs but to consider first the role that those customs fulfilled within the culture in which they were found. Cultural relativism gave anthropologists (and the members of the societies they studied) ideological ammunition to use against missionaries or colonialists who felt no compunction whatsoever about moving into "primitive" societies and destroying indigenous customs that were not to their liking.

In this sense, cultural anthropologists in the first half of the twentieth century believed that the ethnographic evidence they collected in societies throughout the world supported their claims of equal capacity and equal dignity for all human beings. Knowledge of the orderly, predictable customs and practices characteristic of tribal peoples became well known in Western circles, largely thanks to the work of anthropologists like Margaret Mead (1901–78) in the United States and Bronislaw Malinowski (1884–1942) in Britain, who communicated anthropological findings through popular media to a wide audience outside university circles.

Still, not everyone was persuaded by their views. Indeed, new stereotypes about "primitive peoples" emerged that took account of anthropological evidence. It no longer seemed plausible to claim that "savages" and "barbarians" were wild, unruly, and irrational. And so ethnocentric Europeans and North Americans began to argue that "they" were different from "us" because of "their" slavish obedience to tradition, their mindless and uncritical repetition of traditions that they'd inherited from their ancestors. People in "modern" Western societies with "scientific" cultures, by contrast, were portrayed as both able and willing to question the validity and rationality of traditional practices and to replace outmoded customs with better-adapted innovations. To view culture as a prison house of custom from which non-Western and tribal peoples were powerless to escape on their own, however, was to take the anthropological concept of culture and apply it in ways that the anthropologists who first developed it had never intended.

2.5 The Boundaries of Culture?

After World War II, European imperial power declined, former colonies were transformed into independent states, and the civil rights movement in the United States began to gather momentum. In the context of so many social, cultural, and political changes and so many challenges to previous authority, the anthropological portrait of a world made up of particular mutually exclusive societies, each with its own, internally consistent culture, increasingly came under scrutiny, both within and outside anthropology.

Some anthropologists had always raised questions about just how sharply bounded, just how internally integrated, any particular culture might be. Boas and his students, as noted previously, had documented much borrowing of cultural objects and practices by one supposedly distinct society from another, suggesting that boundaries between cultural traditions might be rather porous. But if society A borrowed a custom from society B, could that custom ever be made into an "authentic" part of the culture of society A? And if it could be integrated, did that mean that the culture of society A was no longer "authentic"? And who would decide? Furthermore, even if a provisional correspondence could be established between a particular society and a particular set of cultural beliefs and practices, was it plausible to claim that every member of that society shared *every* aspect of its culture—the same beliefs, the same values, the same practices, the same points of view? What if members of the society in question disagreed, say, about how to perform a ritual? Could only one of the parties be correct, and must the others necessarily be wrong? And, again, who would decide?

Ethnographers often sought research settings that seemed to approximate the ideal of cultural uniformity—for example, remote villages or culturally distinct urban neighborhoods. Often they had to acknowledge that this setting was only one part of a larger sociocultural system, even if that larger system was not the focus of their research. This was particularly visible and problematic in the case of ethnographic work carried out during the colonial period: The wider imperial setting would be acknowledged briefly, but little or no reference to that setting would be made in the rest of the ethnography.

In recent years, many anthropologists have begun to question the validity of speaking as if a large and complex society could possess a single, uniform "culture." It has also become obvious that even within relatively small homogeneous societies, members may disagree with one another about what "their culture" actually is. Anthropologists have become increasingly sensitive to the political issues involved in drawing boundaries around a society or a culture or in taking the views of one subgroup of a larger society as representative of "the culture" as a whole. This is why contemporary anthropologists always acknowledge that social and cultural boundaries are not eternally fixed and why they explicitly question, rather than assume they already know, what any particular set of boundaries means.

2.6 The Concept of Culture in a Global World: Problems and Practices

This has led to rethinking of the way ethnography should be pursued in a world in which local conditions are never isolated from global forces. One solution is to undertake *multisited fieldwork*: doing research not only in a particular local setting (a small village, say) but also in a series of other settings (such as political or corporate centers, whether in the same country or abroad). For example, fieldwork might begin in an urban neighborhood in the United States among a group of immigrants from elsewhere. But it might extend into the urban and national bureaucratic settings in which decisions affecting the immigrant group are made, and it might even continue in the communities abroad from which the immigrants originally came. The advantages and disadvantages of multisited ethnography are still being debated, but the fact that such a research strategy exists testifies to anthropologists' awareness of the often wide-ranging network of complex processes in which any particular local community is enmeshed.

Similarly, contemporary ethnographies are often quite explicit about exactly which members of a group have provided cultural information about a particular issue. Thus, anthropologists are careful to distinguish the opinions of, say, older men from those of women or of younger men because they have learned that these subgroups regularly have differential access to social power and different interests to defend and so have different interpretations to offer about the cultural institutions and practices in which they are involved.

With this new awareness has come the realization that a concept of culture that emphasizes uniformity of belief and practice is not only not always liberating but can also be used as a way of enforcing inequality. This is clearest when one subgroup within a larger society insists on its version of the tradition as the only correct version and tries to force other subgroups to profess allegiance to that version or else risk persecution. Such practices are perhaps most obvious in those societies that were once colonies but have since become independent states. A common experience in such new states was the discovery that very little, apart from joint opposition to the colonizing power, united the peoples who were citizens of these new states.

The ruling groups who had inherited the reins of government following the departure of the colonizer all felt very strongly the need to build some kind of national unity based on a shared "national culture." But the elements of such a national culture could be difficult to find when the only historical experience shared by all the new citizens was the tradition of colonial domination. Sometimes appeal could be made to precolonial customs—religious, economic, or political practices, for example—that were distinct from those that had been introduced by the colonial power. If such practices had once been widely shared or at least widely recognized by the bulk of the population, they might become resources on which to build a new national identity. If, however, such practices belonged only to a tiny proportion of the new citizenry—perhaps a powerful tribal group that had come to dominate postcolonial politics, for example—the practices might well be resisted by other groups. Having expelled one colonial power, they would see no advantage in being recolonized by one of their neighbors.

Paradoxically, however, elements of colonial culture often played an important role in the construction of the new national culture. This included not only the bureaucratic apparatus of governmental administration inherited from the colonial past and the new ways of doing business or educating the young introduced during the colonial period but also the language in which all these activities would be carried out. Anthropologists studying the production of national culture have been influenced by the writings of political scientist Benedict Anderson, who argued that nation-states are "imagined communities," most of whose members never see one another face-to-face but who nonetheless experience a sense of fellow feeling for one another. In Anderson's view, much of that fellow feeling in new nation-states develops out of their members' shared experiences of colonial institutions and practices.

Once again, language is a good example. If the peoples who were administered within a single colony came from dozens or hundreds of different ethnic groups, speaking numerous mutually unintelligible languages, any shared sense of belonging to the same nation would likely be very slight. However, once children from all those different groups began to attend colonial schools and learn the colonizer's language, they did have things in common. Moreover, they could then speak with and learn about one another in a way that would not have been possible had they not all learned to speak, say, French in French colonial schools. Again and again, the new nation-states chose the language of their former colonizer as the new national language of government, business, and education. Not only was this "efficient" in that it allowed an important element of continuity in changing circumstances, but it also meant that the official language of the state did not favor any particular indigenous language group over the others.

The culture concept thus can be reformulated to describe an emerging national culture, and attempts can be made to relate that national culture to the local cultures of different groups incorporated within the nation-state. What anthropologists did not expect, however, and what led to their most serious questioning of the traditional culture concept, were cases in which national regimes in various countries did not recognize the existence within their borders of such differentiated and partially overlapping cultures. Thus, if outsiders objected to the way that a particular regime was treating its own citizens, spokespersons for the regime might respond that such treatment was "part of their culture" and, as such, beyond the critique of outsiders whose cultures were different. Most notoriously, under apartheid in South Africa, it was official government policy to endorse the notion that each people had its own unique culture. The apartheid regime assigned indigenous African peoples to "homelands" in rural areas far from mines and farms and factories, on the dubious grounds that Africans properly belonged in rural areas, farming the way their ancestors had done, and were not suited to work in, let alone run, modern commercial or industrial institutions in South Africa because these institutions were part of "European culture."

2.7 Culture: Contemporary Discussion and Debate

What has been the outcome of all this discussion and debate about the culture concept? Some anthropologists assert that the concept of culture has been forever tainted by the older usage that assigned every society its own unique, internally harmonious set of beliefs and practices. Because this use of the concept reflects an outmoded understanding of how societies and cultures relate to one another, they argue, and has permitted culture to be falsely understood as a prison house of custom from which people could never escape, the term should be discarded entirely. They believe that it bears too many traces of the colonial circumstances under which it was developed and to which it proved so useful an intellectual tool in dividing and dominating colonized peoples.

But abandoning the one-society-one-culture model does not mean that the concept of culture needs to be discarded. Many of the anthropologists who reject that model prefer to think of culture as the sum total of all the customs and practices that humans have ever produced. They point out that, with the increasing speed and density of communication and travel, nobody anywhere on the face of the earth is isolated from the major flows of information and activity present in our contemporary world. Fast food, rock music, and computers have a worldwide appeal; there are now more Facebook users outside the United States than inside it. (See Chapter 4 for a discussion of Facebook.) Because we are a species that needs to learn how to survive and are willing to learn new things from others, people everywhere now seem to be involved in stitching together their own patchwork of beliefs and practices from both local traditions and the wide range of global culture locally available. In situations like this, many contemporary anthropologists argue that what counts as anyone's culture is "up for grabs."

And yet those processes that turn culture into something individuals put together on their own are frequently countered by another process in which groups defend a uniform and closed view of their own culture in the face of potential inundation by global culture. Thus, much like some early anthropologists, contemporary activists in movements of ethnic solidarity defend a monolithic, internally harmonious view of their own culture against "outside" forces claiming to know what is best for them. Such a defense, however, is not without its own paradoxes. For example, to present the image of a united front, ethnic activists must downplay the same kinds of internal divisions and disagreements that anthropologists have been criticized for ignoring in traditional ethnographies that emphasize cultural uniformity. Activists may be fully aware of this paradox but still believe that it is justified for political reasons.

At the same time, some individuals defend their right to pick and choose from global culture the customs that they want to follow and resist attempts by other members of groups to which they belong to police their beliefs and behavior. More than that, they may challenge those who criticize them for incorporating borrowed cultural practices alongside those they have inherited, asserting that theirs is a living cultural tradition and all living cultural traditions will sometimes change in this way. Put another way, **cultural hybridization**—the mixing and reconfiguring of elements from different cultural traditions—is acknowledged and even celebrated. Those who creatively recombine local cultural features with features from elsewhere regularly insist that the end result need not be "Westernization" or "Americanization" of their own cultures; rather, they speak of the "Africanization" or "Botswanization" or "Ju/'hoansization"—that is, the **indigenization**—of cultural features that may have originated in the West or in America but have been adopted by local people for local purposes. Because these outside cultural elements are chosen by insiders rather than imposed by outsiders, they are seen to enrich rather than to destroy or replace the cultural traditions into which they are being integrated. Prior to the end of the twentieth century, for example, literacy may not have been part of the cultural heritage of southern African foragers like the Ju/'hoansi. But many contemporary Ju/'hoansi who have learned to read and write and transcribe their own language view these as positive changes that strengthen their ongoing, developing cultural tradition and also allow them to participate more fully in the political and economic life of the country they live in. Picking up on these developments, some anthropologists are paying renewed attention to the kinds of cultural borrowing highlighted by the Boasians a century ago, but with a twist. In the contemporary context, anthropologists take for granted that all living cultural traditions are dynamic and open to change. As a result, they draw attention to the deliberation and choice exercised by members of these societies who selectively adopt elements of other cultures, not as a way of rejecting their own tradition for an alien alternative but in order to reaffirm and strengthen their own evolving cultural identity.

2.8 Culture: A Contemporary Consensus

In recent years, the concept of culture has been taken up by many other disciplines, partly as a result of anthropology's success in demonstrating its value. But these other disciplines often use the culture concept in ways that contemporary anthropologists do not.

If there is a contemporary anthropological consensus about the nature of culture, it would seem to involve at least the four following propositions. First, nobody questions that culture is learned, not genetically programmed. Second, many anthropologists would argue that the kind of culture that is learned (and the way it is learned) is never innocent but is always shaped by power relations of some kind. Third, power relations and cultural forms that are global in scope have penetrated local communities and local cultures; the ultimate consequences for anybody's culture are still to be assessed. But, fourth, it is incorrect to assume that the penetration of local communities by global culture dooms all local cultural traditions to extinction. On the contrary, local societies can and do indigenize cultural elements that arrive from elsewhere, regularly subverting their homogenizing or "Westernizing" potential and putting them to work in ways that preserve and enhance local goals and interests.

For Further Reading

IDEAS OF CULTURE

Bohannan 1995; Fox and King 2002; Gamst and Norbeck 1976; Kuper 1999

CONTEMPORARY CRITIQUES

Anderson 1983; Clifford 1988; Hannerz 1996; Marcus and Fischer 1986; Ortner 2006

THE CONCEPT OF RACE

Baker 1998; Contemporary Issues Forum 1998

APE CULTURE

Campbell et al. 2006; Savage-Rumbaugh et al. 1986

3

Language

The key terms and concepts covered in this chapter, in the order in which they appear:

language
linguistics
anthropological
   linguistics
linguistic
   anthropology

protolanguage
language family

ethnolinguistics

diachronic
synchronic

grammar
paralanguage

code
openness
phonology
morphology

syntax

semantics
communicative
   competence
Sapir–Whorf
   hypothesis
ethnosemantics
ethnoscience
etic
emic

speech community

sociolinguistics
verbal repertoire
code-switching

discourse

pragmatics
ethnopragmatics

pidgin
creole
language ideology
language revitalization

HUMAN BEINGS, ALONE AMONG all living species, rely on spoken language to communicate with one another. This fact has puzzled and intrigued people in all societies, has played an important role in religious and philosophical reflections on the human condition, and has been a central focus of attention in anthropology from the very beginning. Trying to define language in a clear and unambiguous way, however, has proved surprisingly difficult. Today, most anthropologists would probably agree, minimally, that **language** is a system of arbitrary symbols that human beings use to encode their experience of the world and to communicate with one another. While most language is vocal, language need not be spoken. For example, language can be read, transmitted in Morse code, or expressed in sign language. The scholarly discipline that pursues a scientific study of language is called **linguistics**. The terms **anthropological linguistics** and **linguistic anthropology** have been used by anthropologists to refer to the study of language in cultural context.

3.1 Studying Language: A Historical Sketch

The study of language was central to early anthropology because it was a dimension of culture that was easy to observe and study in detail. For example, languages (like the cultures in which they are embedded) show tremendous variation, both over time and across space. The European study of systematic linguistic change over time is usually said to have begun with the work of the British scholar Sir William Jones (1746–94), who studied Sanskrit in India. He pointed out in 1786 that Sanskrit, classical Greek, Latin, and more recent European languages shared numerous similarities, suggesting that they may have all diverged from a common ancestral language, or **protolanguage**, that came to be called *Indo-European*. All languages believed to have descended from a common ancestral language are said to belong to the same **language family**. By 1822, the German scholar Jakob Grimm (of fairy tale fame; 1785–1863) was able to show that regular changes in speech sounds could be traced over succeeding generations of speakers of a single language or among speakers of related languages as they diverged.

In the twentieth century, linguistic anthropologists were interested in the ways that linguistic change often is triggered by unpredictable and unforeseen cultural and historical events, rather than being generated solely within language itself. The longstanding anthropological focus on the relation between language and culture is sometimes referred to as **ethnolinguistics**.

A major shift in the scholarly approach to language study occurred early in the twentieth century when scholars turned their attention from studies of language that were **diachronic** (concerned with change over time) to studies of language that were **synchronic** (concerned with the patterns present in a particular language at a particular point in time). The terms *synchronic* and *diachronic* were invented early in the twentieth century by the Swiss scholar Ferdinand de Saussure (1857–1913), one of the architects of this transformation. And from Saussure's time onward, scholars involved in synchronic language studies became known as *linguists*—distinct from *philologists*, who retained a focus on reconstructing linguistic divergence, primarily from written texts. Interest in language history did not disappear, but, influenced by the orientation and practices of scholars like Saussure, it became known as *historical linguistics*. Finally, followers of Saussure called themselves *descriptive* linguists because their goal was to describe the rules that governed language as people actually spoke it; they contrasted this goal with that of old-fashioned *prescriptive* grammarians, who saw their job as correcting ordinary speech to make it conform to some ideal literary model of proper grammatical usage.

As noted previously, defining language has always been difficult primarily because it has so many dimensions to which attention might be directed. First, people frequently communicate successfully with one another without using language. Second, people can use language to communicate without actually speaking (they can use gestures or exchange written messages, for example). Linguists traditionally have focused on spoken language, showing how human speech sounds can be grouped into recurring sequences, often called *words*, which are combined into longer utterances according to specific rules. The elements of language and rules for combining words are generally referred to as **grammar**. But much besides grammar is associated with spoken language, such as the various qualities with which we utter our words (volume, pitch, emphasis, speed, and so forth), which linguists call **paralanguage**.

Moreover, grammar and paralanguage do not contain all the meaning we convey when we speak; meaning is also carried by such things as our postures, our facial expressions, and our accompanying gestures. These phenomena, which are sometimes called *body language*, have been studied by anthropologists using special systems of notation; the study of body language is called *kinesics*. In addition, we often choose our words carefully, depending on the person whom we are addressing or the setting in which we are speaking, which highlights the important role that context plays in shaping the meaning of our utterances. Finally, as the philologists showed, the language our grandparents (or more distant ancestors) used often differs markedly from the language that we use today. So how much of all this should we take into consideration when we study language?

To answer this question, Saussure made an important distinction between what came out of people's mouths when they spoke (which he called *parole*) and the underlying rules that generated that speech (which he called *langue*). In his view, parole varied from speaker to speaker, reflecting each individual's idiosyncratic interests and stylistic preferences, whereas langue referred to the stable, universal rules that all speakers observed. Saussure wanted to define language in a way that would permit him to study it scientifically. Therefore, he recommended paying attention only to the most systematic and unvarying elements of language—that is, to langue, which corresponds to what other linguists call the linguistic **code** or grammar. Saussure argued that langue (the code or grammar shared by all speakers) was a self-contained system and that the significance of any element in the system (such as sounds or words) depended on its relationship with other elements in the system rather than on some feature of the outside world.

Saussure's approach to language had at least two major consequences. First, it gave linguists a clear-cut object of study, whose intricate details they could probe without distraction; the end result was the birth of the independent discipline of linguistics, which continues this investigation today. Second, it drew attention to the *arbitrariness* of the relationship between the sounds (or words) of language, the meanings they stood for, and the objects in the world to which they referred. Saussure showed convincingly that the sounds of language, by themselves, carried no inherent meaning: a flat-topped piece of furniture with four legs called "table" in English is called "mesa" in Spanish. Subsequent anthropological linguists, like Charles Hockett, would argue that the arbitrariness of the link between sound and meaning in human language was one of a number of related *design features* of language. Furthermore, they would argue that this arbitrariness was a consequence of the design feature Hockett called **openness**, the possibility of using the linguistic code to create totally new combinations of elements in order to articulate meanings never before uttered.

Along with Saussure, Franz Boas often is credited with contributing to the birth of modern linguistics and linguistic anthropology. His focus on language developed as he sought a way of studying culture in a detailed and nuanced way. It seemed clear to him, as it did to other ethnographers of his generation, like Bronislaw Malinowski, that a profound understanding of another culture could not be gained unless the ethnographer knew the language used by members of that culture to articulate their understandings of the world and of themselves. Boas's own observations about language, based on his field experiences, also drew attention to the codelike fashion in which languages were organized.

3.2 The Building Blocks of Language

One tradition of linguistic scholarship that can be traced back to the influence of Boas and Saussure focused on linguistic codes themselves. Early linguists were especially interested in the sound patterns peculiar to particular languages, an area of linguistics that came to be called **phonology**. An important early discovery was that every language has a restricted set of sounds that are recognized by all native speakers and that can be combined according to rules to form all the words of the language. These minimal units of sound recognized by speakers of a particular language, called *phonemes*, are contrasted with the much larger range of speech sounds that human beings are theoretically capable of producing and hearing, the scientific study of which is called *phonetics*.

Many early linguists analyzed the sets of phonemes characteristic of particular languages. They were also interested in minimal units of meaning in languages. Although in languages like English such units often correspond to *words*, comparative work in very different languages, such as those of indigenous Americans, demonstrated that not all languages are put together the way English is. Even in English, not all minimal units occur independently as words. While *walk* is a word and corresponds to one minimal unit of meaning, *walked* is a word with two minimal units, *walk* and *-ed*, the second of which carries the meaning of "past tense." And so linguists adopted a new term, *morpheme*, to refer to the minimal unit of meaning in a language and studied the rules for combining morphemes in a branch of linguistics known as **morphology**.

But phonological and morphological rules alone could not account for the features of all grammatical sentences, a point forcefully made in 1957 by linguist Noam Chomsky. Chomsky argued persuasively that sentences were themselves units of grammatical structure, and he proposed that linguists begin to study **syntax**, the structure of sentences. Chomsky later argued that every grammar ought to contain a component concerned with how that language dealt with meaning. This justified attention to **semantics**, or the study of meaning, a dimension of language that traditionally had been viewed as too vague and variable to serve as an object of linguistic investigation. The fields of formal syntax and semantics have developed in different directions since the 1960s, but all those developments have roots in the initial orientations provided by Chomsky.

Chomsky also observed that people's actual utterances often were full of errors, hesitations, and false starts that might be the result of physical factors such as sleepiness and thus did not truly represent their underlying grammatical knowledge. And so

Chomsky further distinguished between *linguistic competence* (the underlying knowledge of grammatical rules encoded in the brains of all fluent speakers of a language) and *linguistic performance* (the actual things people said, which for the reasons mentioned, might not reflect their actual linguistic competence). Much like Saussure, Chomsky thought linguists should ignore linguistic performance and try to develop theories of linguistic competence.

3.3 Language and Culture

Chomsky's influence in linguistics was nothing short of revolutionary, and it accentuated a split between those linguists who focused on the code alone and other students of language who remained concerned with how speakers used the code in different cultural and social settings. The linguistic anthropologist Dell Hymes summarized the objections of this latter group when he compared Chomsky's notion of linguistic competence to his own concept of **communicative competence**. Chomsky's focus on the linguistic code led him to define linguistic competence in terms of a speaker's knowledge of the difference between grammatical and ungrammatical sentences in a language.

But Hymes pointed out that successful use of language to communicate with other people requires far more than just grammatical knowledge. It requires speakers to choose vocabulary and topics of speech that are suitable to different audiences in different social settings. For example, fluent speakers of a language might show linguistic competence in their use of casual, grammatically correct linguistic forms in their conversations with friends. But they would betray a colossal lack of communicative competence if they used the same forms when introducing a visiting foreign dignitary in a formal public setting. To identify what constitutes communicative competence, researchers must pay attention to parole, to surface structure, and to actual linguistic performance. According to linguistic anthropologists like Hymes, these phenomena are not wholly idiosyncratic but show far more culturally shaped regularity than the followers of Saussure or Chomsky have ever acknowledged.

At midcentury, Hymes represented a second tradition of scholarship on language that could be traced back to Boas. Practitioners in this tradition continued to see the study of a particular linguistic code primarily as a means to a more profound understanding of culture, rather than as an end in itself. After Boas, in the 1920s and 1930s, the best-known proponents of this approach were Edward Sapir and Benjamin Whorf. Both were struck by the ways in which linguistic form and cultural meaning shaped each other, and each in his own way tried to characterize that relationship. Whorf's analyses of the grammatical codes of indigenous North American languages like Hopi attracted attention (and eventual notoriety) both within and outside anthropology. In several controversial articles, he seemed to be claiming that every language had a unique, self-contained grammar that strongly influenced the thought patterns and cultural practices of its speakers.

After World War II, when both Sapir and Whorf were dead, other anthropologists, linguists, and psychologists tried to devise experiments that would test the influence of language on culture and thought. These researchers advanced what they called the **Sapir–Whorf hypothesis**: the claim that the culture and thought patterns of people were strongly influenced by the language they spoke. Immediately, however, the researchers faced a familiar problem: How do you define "language" and "culture" and "thought" with sufficient rigor so that it becomes possible to measure the degree to which one does or does not influence the other(s)? In practice, "language" was equated with "grammatical code," and tests were devised to measure whether speakers whose grammars possessed (or lacked) certain grammatical structures were correspondingly forced to perceive (or prevented from perceiving) those structures when they looked at the world around them. For example, does an absence of grammatical marking on verbs for past, present, and future tense mean that speakers of that language cannot perceive the passage of time? Or, if a language has only three terms for basic colors (for example, *black*, *white*, and *red*), does this mean that speakers of that language cannot tell the difference between the colors an English speaker identifies as *green* and *blue*?

Actual research showed that questions posed in this fashion were far too simplistic, both about grammars and about human perception. Any language is always a part of some culture—that is, it is learned, not innate, and it is intimately interrelated with all cultural practices in which its speakers engage—and thinking cannot easily be distinguished from the linguistic and cultural activity in which it is regularly involved. Thus, it is virtually impossible to tease language, culture, and thought apart, let alone to figure out the direction of the causal arrows that supposedly link them to one another. By the early 1960s, most linguistic anthropologists had concluded that there was no solid evidence that grammatical features of particular languages *determined* thought patterns or cultural practices. The fact that many people throughout the world were bi- or multilingual, successfully communicating with speakers of languages with sometimes very different grammatical codes (for example, Hopi and English), called into question the supposition that people typically were monolingual—that is, they knew or spoke fluently only one language from birth to death.

In the 1950s and 1960s, a number of anthropologists developed a research program known as **ethnosemantics** or **ethnoscience** that aimed for greater accuracy and sophistication. As the labels suggest, their goal was to discover the systems of linguistic meaning and classification developed by people in their own languages and used in their own cultures. Borrowing the linguistic contrast between phonetic and phonemic studies of the sounds of language, ethnoscientists explicitly contrasted **etic** categories devised by outside researchers and **emic** categories devised by native speaker-informants. Their goal was to describe as faithfully as possible the emic categories used by informants in their own language, and so they developed a rigorous set of research practices intended to protect their emic data from etic contamination.

For all their achievements, however, ethnoscientists continued to work with a theoretical model of language and culture in which researchers and informants were understood to belong to mutually exclusive monolingual and monocultural worlds. It was not that anthropologists failed to recognize the inaccuracy of the model. Fieldwork and study had made many of them bi- or multilingual and bi- or multicultural, and a history of colonial conquest followed by linguistic and cultural imperialism had often made many of their informants bi- or multicultural and bi- or multilingual as well.

3.4 Language and Society

The necessity of taking this bi- and multilingualism/culturalism into theoretical account prompted Hymes to urge his colleagues to move beyond the study of individual languages to the study of speech communities. A **speech community** is any concrete community of individuals who regularly interact verbally with one another. It might be a village or a neighborhood or a city; today it might include "virtual communities" created by Facebook, Internet chat rooms, or e-mail. Hymes pointed out that if you delimit a speech community and then do an inventory of all the different kinds of language used by members of that community, you will quickly discover not merely one version of one language in use, but rather a variety of forms of one language (and sometimes more than one language) in use. Some varieties will be *regional dialects*: versions of a particular language associated with particular geographical settings such as the Appalachian versus Texan versus New England dialects of North American English. Some will be *social dialects*: versions of a particular language associated with particular social groups such as the "Cockney" working-class dialect of London as contrasted with the "BBC English" of the educated British upper middle class. Still others will be social *registers*: versions of a particular language associated with particular social settings such as a court of law or an elementary school playground or a house of religious worship. Every member of the speech community may not be able to converse fluently in all the varieties represented in the community, but all members will ordinarily have control of several varieties, each of which will be called for in a different set of circumstances.

This approach developed in linguistic anthropology by Hymes was supported by similar approaches developed in sociolinguistics by sociologists such as John Gumperz. **Sociolinguistics** is usually defined as the study of the relationship between language and society. Traditionally, it has been interested in correlations between social variation (for example, class or ethnic stratification) and linguistic variation (for example, in the form of regional or social dialects), as well as correlations between particular social settings and linguistic registers. Together, Gumperz and Hymes developed analytic concepts that meshed in interesting ways. For example, if every speech community is characterized by a number of different language varieties, then every member of that speech community can be described in terms of her or his **verbal repertoire**: the sum total of verbal varieties a particular individual has mastered.

Gumperz and others were able to show that the number and nature of the varieties within an individual's verbal repertoire not only offer a good set of indicators as to that individual's social identity and status but also are a good predictor of that individual's probable success in interacting verbally with speakers of different identities and statuses. Gumperz described verbal repertoires as sets of weapons that one could deploy in verbal (and social) struggles with others. Like soldiers with a range of weapons, people with more varieties in their repertoires could attain objectives in a range of social situations. They could switch from one variety (or code) to another as the situation demanded, a phenomenon called **code-switching**. Some sociolinguists have described speech communities in which everyone was fluent in two codes (either two dialects of a single language or two different languages), a phenomenon described as *diglossia*. Where diglossia occurs, speakers generally use each code in mutually exclusive settings (for example, one at home and the other at school), switching back and forth between codes as the situation demands. One insight provided by studies of verbal repertoires is that speakers with fewer codes at their command are both socially and verbally limited in their interactions with others.

Hymes's suggestion that linguistic anthropology should focus on how people develop communicative competence in speech communities characterized by multiple codes stimulated research in a number of related areas. One was the comparative study of childhood acquisition of communicative competence, which involved mastering not only grammatical rules but also rules for appropriate use. Another was the study of classifications of forms of talk in specific cultures and examination of the various contexts in which these forms were used. A third was the study of culture-specific verbal performances like storytelling in which the codes known by the storyteller and her or his listeners were resources upon which the storyteller could draw in exercising individual artistic agency.

Studies of verbal performance emphasized all those features of language that formal linguists ignored, such as figurative language, wordplay, deliberate rule-breaking, and code-switching to achieve certain rhetorical effects. Linguistic anthropologists carrying out cross-cultural research on verbal performance were able to show that, however central the rules of grammar remain for effective linguistic communication, in real life, when people struggle to defend their interests using whatever tools are available, rules of grammar and rules of use can be bent or broken to achieve other communicative effects. And if rules can be broken, perhaps they are as much a product of other social and cultural communication as they are shapers of that communication.

The focus on multiple linguistic varieties present in all speech communities and on rules for their appropriate use inevitably drew attention to the fact that not all varieties were accorded equal respect and that most linguists who talk about "the" grammar of language X ordinarily had in mind only one high-prestige variety of language X. If they were, like Chomsky, educated linguists studying their own native language, the grammar in question was likely to be that language's literary standard, such as Standard English. And because native-speaker linguists were told to trust their own intuitions in deciding whether certain usages were "grammatical," it became increasingly clear that in practice "linguistic competence" meant competence in the standard variety. Despite linguists' assertions that their work was descriptive, not prescriptive, nonstandard varieties inevitably appeared ungrammatical with respect to the standard, making those varieties (and, by extension, their speakers) look defective.

3.5 Discourse

Such judgments looked suspiciously like the old-fashioned opinions of prescriptive grammarians. From the point of view of linguistic anthropologists, they reflected sociocultural evaluations of speakers associated with those linguistic varieties, evaluations that inevitably reflected the unequal power relations between evaluators and those being evaluated. Linguistic anthropologists began to focus explicitly on the way linguistic usage and evaluations of linguistic usage were shaped by power struggles between various subgroups within a society. They emphasized that rules of "grammaticality" or "cultural acceptability" often are based on linguistic forms preferred by powerful groups in society. As a result, disadvantaged groups may choose to express resistance against a given power structure by refusing to use the linguistic forms endorsed by the powerful. Some linguistic anthropologists have shown how this takes place in the course of public and private performances of different culturally recognized forms of **discourse** (talk) such as storytelling, oratory, popular theater, and traditional forms of poetic expression (for example, funeral laments). Such work made very clear that those who engage in particular forms of discourse are not forced by rules of grammar or culture to say some things rather than others. Quite the opposite: They struggle to use the rules of grammar and culture as *resources* to convey their own, often subversive, messages to their audiences.

The focus of scholars like Hymes and Gumperz on speech communities whose members each possessed verbal repertoires consisting of multiple language varieties displayed the complexity and coordination of cultural and linguistic variation within a society. It also highlighted the sophistication with which people regularly matched appropriate forms of discourse to appropriate audiences or settings. Following the rise of postmodern critique in anthropology in the 1980s, however, attention began to shift to the prisonlike rules that aimed to constrain people's behavior and censor their speech and to the struggles in which people engaged to resist such limitations. In linguistic anthropology, this reorientation was assisted by the adoption of the concepts and approach of a group of Russian literary and linguistic scholars associated with Mikhail Bakhtin, whose key texts had recently been translated into English. Hymes and Gumperz's image of speech communities whose members made use of multiple language varieties was echoed in Bakhtin's concept of *heteroglossia*, or "many-voicedness," among speakers in a society. The emphasis of Bakhtin's discussion, however, was on how different groups of speakers, each rooted in their own particular (and unequal) positions within society, struggle for control of public discourse.

Linguistic anthropologists influenced by Bakhtin were particularly interested in the discourse of low-status groups whose

vulnerable social position made it unsafe for them to verbally challenge those who dominated them. Such linguistic anthropologists
found Bakhtin's concept of *double-voiced discourse* very useful,
for it emphasized the way the "same" words or expressions can
mean different things to different speakers who use them in different contexts. Bakhtin demonstrated how speakers could maneu-
ver around verbal censorship by the *ironic* use of language—when
speakers and (some) listeners understand that words used in a particular setting mean the opposite of what they ordinarily signify.
Bakhtin also drew attention to the *parodic* use of language—when
officially acceptable language is exaggerated or mimicked with the
intention of poking fun. Double-voiced discourse highlights the
agency of speakers who manage to keep their actual words within
acceptable grammatical and cultural boundaries while the context in which their words are spoken imparts to them meanings
quite different from their formal denotations. Officially, order is
upheld, but unofficially, it is held up to ridicule or critique.

To focus on subversive forms of talk like double-voiced discourse is to emphasize the way in which language in cultural contexts of use twists and manipulates the supposedly unvarying and
stable elements of formal grammar. The demonstration was so
powerful that even formal linguists began to include a **pragmatics**
component in their formal grammars, which purported to catalog
universal rules of use obeyed by all speakers of all languages who
wanted to communicate successfully with others. (Table 3.1 lists
the components of formal linguistic analysis.)

Linguistic anthropologists quickly pointed out that the kinds of
rules proposed by formal pragmatics, however, were based on the
linguists' incorrect assumption that the primary purpose of linguistic
communication is to convey faithfully from speaker to hearer fac-
tual information about the world. This communication, moreover,
is assumed to take place in a conversational setting between disinterested parties of equal social status.

Communication sometimes does involve the transmission of
information between equals. Linguistic anthropologists were able
to show, however, that such communication is only a small and
highly idealized part of what normally goes on when real people
with differential linguistic and cultural knowledge, living in real

TABLE 3.1   Components of Formal Linguistic Analysis

COMPONENT	APPLIES TO
Phonology	Phonemes/sound patterns
Morphology	Morphemes/word formation
Syntax	Sentence structure
Semantics	Meaning
Pragmatics	Language in use

societies characterized by social inequality, try to communicate with one another. As a result, linguistic anthropologists argue that every analysis of language use in cultural context must include information from ethnopragmatics. **Ethnopragmatics** is the study of the culturally and politically inflected rules of use that shape particular acts of speech communication among particular speakers and audiences, in the specific cultural settings in which they regularly occur. Put another way, the "universal" rules of formal pragmatics turn out to be so idealized and culture bound that they are of little help when we try to understand what is going on in most verbal interactions in most cultural settings in most societies.

3.6 Language Contact and Change

Considering linguistic interaction within a context of struggle among speakers with unequal access to valued resources in a society has also refreshed our understanding of languages called pidgins and creoles. A **pidgin** language traditionally has been defined as a reduced language with a simplified grammar and vocabulary that develops when speakers of mutually unintelligible languages come into regular contact and so are forced to communicate with one another. Those who speak pidgins are native speakers of other, fully developed languages and use pidgins only in restricted settings with those who do not speak their native language; for this reason, pidgins are said to have no native speakers. However, when pidgins persist over two or more generations, they often begin to change. Specifically, their grammar sometimes becomes more complex, their vocabularies increase, they are used in a wider variety of social settings, and children learn them as first languages. When this happens, according to the traditional view, the pidgin has developed into a **creole** and functions just like any other natural human language.

For a long time, it was thought that the evolution from pidgin to creole was regular and inevitable, but it has become increasingly clear that pidgins and creoles can persist indefinitely along with other language varieties in the speech communities in which they are found. That is, speakers of pidgins also live in speech communities where different linguistic varieties have specialized uses. Moreover, such communities are regularly shaped by unequal power relations, which means that different varieties enjoy different levels of prestige and that those with more prestigious varieties in their verbal repertoires enjoy decided political and social advantages. Linguistic anthropologists and sociolinguists have pointed out that the most recent wave of pidginization followed European colonization throughout the world. They note further that pidgins and creoles developed under colonial (and postcolonial) political regimes in which mastery of the written language of the colonizer (for example, English, French, or Dutch) has been a prerequisite for economic and social mobility. Thus, groups in the society that have been deprived of the opportunity to become literate in the colonizer's (or nation-state's) official "standard" language variety are also deprived of access to most of the wealth, power, and prestige in society.

Such a situation helps explain the sometimes violent struggles that occur in contemporary nation-states, especially in those that were once European colonies, about which language or languages will be the "official" language of schooling and of government. If people live in a society whose members speak a number of different languages and language varieties and if access to the most highly valued resources in society depends on fluency or literacy in only one official language, then it is easy to see that speakers of each language group will want their own language to be the official language.

Debates over "official" languages illustrate the operation of **language ideology**: the beliefs and practices about language that are linked to struggles between social groups with different interests and that are regularly revealed in what people say and how they say it. The study of language ideology by linguistic anthropologists is central in settings with a history of colonization. Yet even when most members of a society are fluent or literate in the official language, they may be vigilant in policing the "purity" of that language, trying to eliminate linguistic borrowing from other languages. For example, when capitalist business practices and technology, originally developed in European languages, are imported into societies whose members do not speak a European language, the temptation is strong simply to borrow the European vocabulary and expressions for these practices and objects rather than inventing new terms in the local language. The temptation is even stronger if printed instructional materials in the European language are also imported because few poor countries on the periphery of the capitalist global economy have the resources to translate these materials into the languages of the local population. However, the influx of imported vocabulary may well be seen as a form of linguistic colonization. And like political colonization in the past, it is often resisted by *linguistic nationalism*: official, sometimes militant, efforts to proscribe the use of foreign terms and to promote the creation of alternatives in the local language.

Linguistic nationalism is hardly limited to former colonies of European powers. Citizens of European countries like France have periodically displayed linguistic nationalism when they protest the growing popularity among French speakers of expressions borrowed from American English. Like the citizens of former colonies, these French people fear that the influx of American English symbolizes a serious blow to the power and prestige of their own language and the nation to which its speakers belong. Ironically, speakers of regional languages in France, such as Breton in Normandy, have made similar arguments about the way in which the imposition of French by the state has threatened the survival of their own minority tongue!

As it happens, national, regional, and international languages of business and politics have been spreading very rapidly in recent years, often at the expense of minority or local languages with few native speakers. The growth of schooling in languages of global reach, such as English, has drastically reduced the numbers of native speakers fluent in local, indigenous languages in many parts of the world. By creating grammars and dictionaries and archival and educational materials designed to teach and preserve these languages in the future, linguistic anthropologists have been active in collaborating with remaining speakers of such languages to prevent *language death* and to promote **language revitalization.** Ironically, even as native speakers of endangered languages want to prevent them from disappearing, they are often torn about what language they want their own children to learn. Many speakers of endangered languages belong to groups that are economically marginal in the regions or nation-states where they live, and they want their children to have more economic opportunities than they have had. One means to such a goal is for their children to learn national or international languages of commerce that, they hope, will give their children a chance to make a better life for themselves in a world of globalizing capitalism.

For Further Reading

FORMAL LINGUISTICS

Akmajian et al. 2010

LINGUISTIC ANTHROPOLOGY

Agar 1994; Bonvillain 2008; Burling 2005; Duranti 1997; Ottenheimer 2009; Salzmann 2006

READINGS IN ANTHROPOLOGICAL LINGUISTICS/LINGUISTIC ANTHROPOLOGY

Blount 1995; Blum 2009; Brenneis and Macaulay 1996; Duranti 2001, 2006

DISCOURSE

Hill and Irvine 1992; Schultz 1990

LANGUAGE IDEOLOGY

Morgan 2002; Schieffelin, Woolard, and Kroskrity 1998

BILINGUALISM

Zentella 1997

4

Making Meaning: Worldview, Religion, and Art

The key terms and concepts covered in this chapter, in the order in which they appear:

worldview

religion
animism
ancestor religion
gods
polytheistic religions
mana
oracle
dogma
orthodoxy

myths
origin myths
ritual
religious rituals
prayer
sacrifice
congregation
orthopraxy
rite of passage

liminal period
communitas
magic

witchcraft

shamans
priests

conversion
syncretism
revitalization
new religious movements
secularism
fundamentalism

art
aesthetic
art by intention
art by appropriation
art world
ethnomusicology
virtual worlds

Human beings in all cultures try to make sense of their experience in ways that link them meaningfully to the wider world. Anthropologists use the term **worldview** to refer to the result of such interpretive efforts: an encompassing picture of reality based on a set of shared assumptions about how the world works. Anthropologists have long been interested in how worldviews are constructed and how people use them to make sense of their experiences. Worldviews establish symbolic frameworks that highlight certain significant domains of social experience while downplaying others. Multiple worldviews may coexist in a single society, or a single worldview may dominate.

4.1 Religion

As they began to compare cultures, anthropologists repeatedly encountered worldviews that reminded them of the religions they knew from Euro-American societies. Over the years, they have tried with mixed success to craft definitions of religion that took these diverse beliefs and practices into account. A recent definition that tries to take account of the complexities of the beliefs and practices found around the world proposes a two-stage approach. First, **religion** is "ideas and practices that postulate reality beyond that which is immediately available to the senses" (Bowen 2008, 4). The second stage in Bowen's definition is to ask how the specific people whom the anthropologist is studying actually conceive of that reality. Here, the anthropologist tries, through careful ethnographic research, to understand what people think and do; the anthropologist is not imposing the model of "religion" from his or her own society. In some cases, the anthropologist may find people with religious worldviews who conceive of the universe as populated by powerful forces that may understand human language and take an active interest in human affairs. Others, as Bowen observes, may speak about impersonal forces like the East Asian idea of a life force that permeates the natural and social world. Another group of people might not talk about belief at all, concentrating on the correct performance of ritual. They may monitor human behavior and send punishments to those who violate moral rules, but if approached in the proper manner, these forces may use their power to confer benefits on the people. When those beings are personified, they have been variously called gods, goddesses, spirits, ancestors, ghosts, or souls.

Although some anthropologists continue to use the term *supernatural* to refer to invisible beings or the realm they inhabit, most contemporary anthropological writing on religion avoids this term because it imposes on other societies a distinction between "natural" and "supernatural" worlds that those societies often do not recognize. Similar problems affect many other terms that Western observers, anthropologists included, have used to describe and analyze different religions. For this reason, some influential definitions of religion do not mention beings of any kind but focus on symbols and the ways in which people use symbols to bring meaning and coherence to the interpretation of their experiences. This is also why Bowen proposes a two-stage definition of religion; the second stage consists of trying to understand how specific people understand the world, *in their own terms.*

Anthropologists have suggested a variety of reasons why religion seems to be so important in human societies: It is a way for people to deal with uncertainty that they cannot otherwise control, it is a way to provide meaning for people's lives, it explains the otherwise unexplainable (suffering, death, the mysterious in everyday life), and it helps create social solidarity among those who adhere to it.

Confronted with enormous diversity in the religious traditions of the world, anthropologists proceeded to classify them according to type. For example, some religions propose that objects like trees or stones or rivers may have souls or spirits associated with them who may interact with people for good or for ill. The nineteenth-century English anthropologist E. B. Tylor (1832–1917) used the term **animism** to describe religions based on belief in the existence of such souls or spirit beings (*anima* is the Latin word for "soul").

Although most contemporary anthropologists no longer use this term because of the disparaging connotations it has acquired over the years, it may still be found in discussions in the field of comparative religion in which "world religions" like Christianity or Islam are contrasted with "animist religions" in which the only personified forces that are recognized are souls or spirits associated with features of the local landscape. The set of beliefs and practices associated with these souls and spirits are certainly real in some societies in the world today—traditional Inuit and Australian Aboriginal societies, for example—but many scholars prefer to use terms like *traditional religion* to avoid the persisting implication that animism is something that "more advanced" societies have evolved away from.

In societies where the connections of relatedness do not end with physical death, religion may take the form of what is called an **ancestor religion** (for more about relatedness see Chapter 8). In these systems, the ancestors are believed to maintain a strong interest in the lives of their descendents and are believed to act to maintain social order by sending sickness or other misfortune when the rules by which people are supposed to live are violated. In these societies, it is often the most senior people who gain great power from the ancestor religion because they are closest to becoming ancestors.

Other societies recognize the existence of sentient and personified forces that are less local and more powerful. The entities may be called **gods,** and traditions in which there are many such beings are sometimes called **polytheistic religions.** The gods in polytheistic religions may have many of the personal attributes of human beings, including gender, and they may produce children with one another or with human beings as the gods did in the religion of ancient Greece. But in some societies, as we saw earlier, the cosmic force or forces recognized are barely personalized at all. This is true in the case of **mana,** a Melanesian term introduced into anthropology in the nineteenth century to designate a cosmic force whose only humanlike attribute is the ability to respond to human beings who use the correct symbolic formulas when they want to harness or channel this force for their own purposes.

Another minimally personified cosmic force is an **oracle,** an invisible force capable of understanding questions addressed to it in human language and willing to respond truthfully using symbolic means that human beings with the proper cultural knowledge can interpret. Oracles may speak through people, animals or plants, or other objects.

The beliefs that people have regarding the nature of the world and the beings that inhabit it form one part of a religious worldview. But societies differ in how systematically they have organized this knowledge and in how much leeway they allow their members to offer alternative interpretations. In some societies, religious knowledge of this kind is highly detailed, carefully organized, and formally passed on from generation to generation. When the truths it is believed to contain may not be questioned, such knowledge is sometimes called **dogma** or **orthodoxy** (correct belief). In other societies, however, religious beliefs are not systematized, and no great emphasis is placed on orthodoxy, with the result that different adherents to the tradition may offer varied or conflicting interpretations of it.

4.2 Myth

Important components of religious traditions are **myths:** stories that recount how various aspects of the world came to be the way they are. The truth of myths seems self-evident to those who accept them because myths do such a good job of integrating personal experiences with a wider set of assumptions about the way that society or the world in general must operate. Those myths that explain the creation of the world or of particular features of the landscape or of human beings are often called **origin myths.** Other myths may recount the adventures of the gods, the consequences of their interactions with human beings, or what will happen when the world ends. Although enduring religious myths are believed to embody important insights into life's purposes, they are more than morality tales. They are usually a highly developed verbal art form as well, recited for purposes of both entertainment and instruction, and the occasion of their telling offers verbal artists the opportunity to demonstrate their creative, aesthetic skills. Frequently, the "official" myth tellers are the most powerful or respected groups in society, such as the elders, political leaders, or religious specialists. Myths have a social importance because, if they are taken literally, they tell people where they have come from and where they are going and therefore how they should live right now.

The study of myth has always been important in anthropology. Over time, two major approaches to the study of myth have had a lasting impact on the field. The first approach comes from Bronislaw Malinowski, who argued that myths are charters for social action; that is, the beings and places who figure in the myths can be referred to by living people in order to justify present-day social arrangements. For example, an origin myth about a particular kinship group may describe where members of the group first appeared on the land and the places they subsequently visited. This myth can be used by living members of that kinship group to defend their claims to land in the territories that their ancestors visited and to negate claims to the same land made by other members of the society. In short, to understand why myths have the content they do and how that content changes over time, one must understand the social beliefs and practices of the people who tell them.

The second approach to myth comes from the French anthropologist Claude Lévi-Strauss (1908–2009). While not denying Malinowski's observations about the practical uses to which myths could be put, Lévi-Strauss showed that the very structures of mythic narratives are meaningful and worth studying in their own right. In this sense, myths are cognitive tools for resolving logical contradictions in human social experience that cannot otherwise be overcome in the world that human beings know. In particular, myths are attempts to deal with oppositions of continuing concern to members of a particular society, such as the opposition between men and women, nature and culture, or life and death, or opposing styles of postmarital residence (postmarital residence is discussed in Chapter 9). Although these oppositions may be irresolvable in everyday life, myths offer an imaginative realm in which alternative possibilities and their (frequently undesirable) consequences can be explored.

Many scholars, including Malinowski and Lévi-Strauss, have assumed that the people who believe in myths typically are unaware how their myths are structured or how they use myths to defend their interests. Recent anthropological work, however, acknowledges that ordinary members of a society often *are* aware of how their myths structure meaning. And it is precisely this awareness that permits them to manipulate the way myths are told or interpreted in order to gain support for the version or interpretation that furthers their goals.

4.3 Ritual

Anthropologists use the term **ritual** to identify certain repetitive social practices, many of which have nothing to do with religion. A ritual is composed of a sequence of symbolic activities, set off from the social routines of everyday life, recognizable by members of the society as a ritual, and closely connected to a specific set of ideas that are often encoded in myth. What gives rituals their power is that participants assert that the authorization for the ritual comes from outside themselves—from the state, society, God, the ancestors, or "tradition." For example, in a courtroom, when people rise as the judge enters or refer to the judge as "your honor," they are not doing so because they feel like it or because the individual judge insists on it but because of the authority of the state and the Constitution. Thus, by responding in court, "Not guilty, your honor," one is accepting the authority of not only the judge but also the court, the justice system, and the Constitution. (Indeed, this is the difference between a wedding rehearsal and a wedding.) Even when rituals are invented or transformed, those involved with them attempt to connect the innovations to external sources of authority. For example, at our university's graduation ceremony, the graduates are asked to applaud the parents, relatives, and friends who have helped them achieve that moment. Although this part of the ritual was proposed by a former president, his justification for the innovation was that it took account of something profoundly important in the social world that the institution needed to acknowledge and it was in keeping with the other elements of the graduation ceremony.

Much work in recent years in anthropology has explored the relationship between ritual and power, and much of this work has concentrated on rituals that are not religious. But the role of ritual in religious contexts remains an important area of study. If the universe is indeed populated by powerful personified beings that take an interest in human affairs, then it is to the very great benefit of human beings to devise ways of dealing with them. All religious worldviews assume that communication between personified cosmic forces is possible and potentially beneficial, but it can take place only if carried out in the correct way. Most religious traditions have developed specialized social routines for communication with the gods that, if performed correctly, should ensure successful communication. As a consequence, **religious rituals** are distinctive in that they regularly involve attempts to influence or gain the sympathy of a particular personified cosmic being. One kind of religious ritual involves addressing these personified forces in human speech, often out loud, while holding the body in a conventional posture of respect; this is called **prayer**. Another kind of religious ritual involves offering something of value (goods, services, money, or an appropriately slaughtered animal) to the invisible forces or their agents; this is called **sacrifice**. Prayer and sacrifice frequently are performed when members of a religious tradition come together in processions, meetings, or convocations; this is called **congregation**.

Members of some religious traditions insist that correct ritual behavior is essential at times of prayer or sacrifice and that any deviation will nullify the ritual. Indeed, some religious traditions aim to ritualize virtually every waking act that adherents perform, a style of religious practice called **orthopraxy** (correct practice). Not all religious traditions that value ritual are orthoprax, however; many entertain a range of opinion regarding correct practice, and individual people or independent religious practitioners are free to develop their own rituals or variants of more broadly recognized rituals.

One particular kind of ritual has drawn considerable attention from anthropologists: the **rite of passage**, which occurs when one or more members of a society are ritually transformed from one kind of social person into another. Rites of passage often are initiations into adulthood when girls are made women or boys made men, but they may also mark marriages (when single people become a married couple), the birth of children (when a new life enters the world), or funerals (when living relatives become ancestors). These and other so-called life-cycle transitions frequently are marked by rituals that connect participants to ancestors or gods or other cosmic forces. Anthropologists point out that rites of passage regularly follow a three-part sequence. First, the ritual passengers (that is, the persons who are changing their social position) are *separated* from their previous, everyday existence. Next, they pass through a *transitional* state, in which they are neither in the old position nor yet in the new one. Finally, with their new status, they are *reaggregated*, or brought back, into the everyday social world. The second, transitional stage of the ritual was particularly significant for anthropologist Victor Turner (1920–83), who referred to it as the **liminal period** (from the Latin word *limen*, meaning "threshold"). Turner noted that when people are on the threshold, they are "betwixt and between," neither in nor out. In rites of passage, the symbolism associated with the transitional period often expresses that ambiguity: It is described as being in the womb, being invisible, being in the wilderness, or as death. Ritual passengers in the liminal stage tend to develop an intense comradeship with one another; social distinctions that separated them before the ritual and will separate them again afterward become irrelevant. Turner called this liminal social relationship **communitas**, which is best understood as an unstructured or minimally structured community of equal individuals. In rites of passage concerned with initiation, for example, the liminal period is a time in which those being initiated are tutored in knowledge and skills that their elders believe they must master if they are to be successful in the stage of life they are about to enter.

4.4 Magic and Witchcraft

Anthropologists have also paid much attention to another form of ritual called **magic**. The persistence of definitions of magic that include the term *supernatural* is another indication of the difficulty of using one culture's definitions to describe practices in other cultures. Generally, magic refers to ritual practices that do not have technically or scientifically apparent effects but are believed by the actors to have an influence on the outcome of practical matters. People may believe that the correct performance of such rituals can result in healing, the growth of plants, the recovery of lost or stolen objects, getting a hit in baseball, or safely sailing an outrigger canoe in the Pacific Ocean. The classic anthropological explanation of magic comes from the research of Bronislaw Malinowski in the Trobriand Islands early in the twentieth century. Malinowski suggested that all living societies have developed effective knowledge and practical techniques for dealing with the world. At the same time, however, they also realize that their practical control over the world has limits. Where their techniques and knowledge are sufficient for accomplishing their goals, magic is not used. But when the outcome is uncertain, regardless of the skill and insight people may have, they are likely to resort to magical practices. The use of magic in such situations, Malinowski argued, has the practical function of reducing anxiety, thereby allowing people to concentrate on what they can control. He observed, for example, that Trobriand Islanders whom he knew used outrigger canoes to go fishing in both the protected lagoons around the islands and the Pacific Ocean. When they fished in the lagoons, which were safe and secure, they put their canoes into the water and got straight to work. But when they were going past the lagoons into the open ocean, which was unpredictable and dangerous, they recited spells and used other techniques throughout the voyage.

In the late nineteenth century, when unilineal evolutionary schemes were popular in anthropology (see Chapter 12 for details), many anthropologists proposed that magic and religion were separate stages in the progressive evolution of human thought that culminated in science. But subsequent ethnographic research, especially work done in the past few decades, has made it clear that magic, religion, and science may coexist in the same society and may even be used by the same people, who resort to different ways of coping with the world in different social contexts. In some cases, people in search of a solution to a serious problem, such as infertility, may be unwilling to dismiss any beliefs or practices that offer a solution, alternatively consulting medical doctors, praying in church, and consulting practitioners of alternative therapies that some might argue are based on magic. (The topic is also discussed in Chapter 11.)

It is important to stress that interest in identifying and defining the true nature of magic was historically of greatest concern to two categories of Western critics: missionaries eager to demonstrate the superiority of their version of "religion" over what they considered to be the superstitious "magical" practices of "primitive peoples" and defenders of science who wanted to demonstrate its superiority over both magic and religion. The more that science was stressed as the embodiment of rationality, the more necessary it became to stress the "irrational" features of religion and magic.

Anthropologists committed to cultural relativism in the early twentieth century were more interested in stressing the sensible side of seemingly exotic beliefs and practices like magic and witchcraft. Malinowski, as we have seen, focused on the positive practical side effects of belief in the efficacy of magic spells. E. E. Evans-Pritchard (1902–73), in his classic monograph *Witchcraft, Oracles, and Magic Among the Azande* (first published in 1937), demonstrated that the beliefs and practices associated with all three phenomena were perfectly logical if one accepted certain basic assumptions about the world.

Among the Azande, **witchcraft** involves the performance of evil by human beings believed to possess an innate, nonhuman "witchcraft substance" that can be activated without the individual's awareness. (Other anthropologists, using Azande witchcraft as their prototype, have applied the term to similar beliefs and practices found in other societies.*) For the Azande, witchcraft tends to explain misfortune when other possibilities have been discounted. For example, if a good potter carefully prepares his pots and fires them as he always does but they still break, he will attribute his misfortune to witchcraft, and his neighbors will probably

---

*This technical use of the term should not be confused with everyday uses of the word in contemporary Western societies, still less with the practices of followers of movements like Wicca, which are very different.

believe him. But if a careless potter is sloppy when firing his pots and they break, he may claim that witchcraft was the cause, but no one who knows him will believe it.

Evans-Pritchard showed that the entire system of Azande beliefs and practices concerning witchcraft, oracles, and magic was perfectly rational if one assumed that unseen forces exist in the world and that nothing happens to people by accident. For example, when someone falls very ill or dies, the Azande assume that the person has been bewitched. But the Azande are not help-less because they know they can consult oracles who will help them pinpoint the witch responsible. Once the oracle has identi-fied the witch, they can send a ritual message to the accused witch, who can offer a ritual reply that will stop the witchcraft if indeed he (it is usually a man) has been the cause of it. If the bewitched person dies, however, the next step is to obtain vengeance magic, which can be used to seek out the witch responsible and kill him.

The Azande do not collapse in fear in the presence of witch-craft because they know how to deal with it. Moreover, they make an accusation of witchcraft only after cross-checking the ora-cle's pronouncements carefully. Because all the steps in the pro-cess are carried out in great secrecy, who has accused whom and who has killed whom with vengeance magic is not open to pub-lic scrutiny, so contradictions in the system are rarely exposed. This, Evans-Pritchard suggested, is how all complex belief systems operate, even in the so-called scientific West. After all, the "sci-entific method" at its most stringent is hardly followed regularly by ordinary citizens or even scientists once they are outside the laboratory. Evans-Pritchard's work has inspired many subsequent studies that debunk ethnocentric Western notions about the sup-posed irrationality of magic and religion.

Beliefs and practices bearing a resemblance to Azande witchcraft are found in many societies, in Africa and elsewhere. Comparative studies of these phenomena revealed interesting variation in the pat-terns of witchcraft accusations in a given society. According to Mary Douglas (1970), patterns of accusation fall into two basic types: Witches are evil outsiders, or witches are internal enemies, either members of a rival faction or dangerous deviants.

These different patterns of accusation have different effects on the structure of the society in which they are made. If the witch is an evil outsider, witchcraft accusations can strengthen in-group ties as the group unites in opposition to the witch. If the witch is an internal enemy, however, accusations of witchcraft can weaken in-group ties, perhaps to the point at which one or more factions in a community might leave and build a new village; then the entire social structure may have to be rebuilt. This, anthropologists argued, was not really a bad thing because what had prompted the accusations of witchcraft in the first place was a community that had grown too large for the prevailing political organization to maintain order. The witchcraft accusations provided a relatively nondestructive way to restore the community to the proper size for a kinship-based political system. If, on the other hand, the witch is a dangerous internal deviant, to accuse that person of witchcraft might be an attempt to control the deviant in defense of the wider values of the community.

4.5 Religious Practitioners

Anthropologists also have devoted attention to the organization of religion as a social and cultural institution. Virtually without exception, anthropologists have stressed that complex sets of religious beliefs and practices are not merely the by-products of idiosyncratic individual invention. Rather, they are the products of collective cultural construction, performing social and cultural tasks that involve far more than tending to the spiritual needs of supporters.

The contrast between different kinds of religious institutions in different societies can be illustrated with reference to the existence and role of specialized religious practitioners. In many small-scale societies, specialized ritual knowledge or practice may simply belong to elders who perform required rituals for their kin. Other societies, however, do accord a special status to religious specialists, and anthropologists have classified them in two broad categories: shamans and priests. **Shamans** are part-time religious specialists commonly found in small-scale egalitarian societies. The term *shaman* itself comes from Siberia, and Siberian shamans constitute the prototype that anthropologists have used to classify similar religious specialists in many other societies. They are believed to have the power to contact powerful cosmic beings directly on behalf of others, sometimes by traveling to the cosmic realm to communicate with them. They often plead with those beings to help their people—by curing them, for example— and they may also bring back messages for them. In other cases, the shaman enters an altered state of consciousness to seek and remove the cause of an illness that is afflicting a person who has come for healing. In many societies, it is believed that the shaman has no choice in taking on the role—the spirits demand it. The training that a shaman receives is long and demanding and may involve the use of powerful psychotropic substances. The position of shaman may be dangerous. The effects of entering altered states of consciousness can be long lasting. The power to contact cosmic beings or to heal is itself perceived as ambiguous in many societies: The person who can intervene for good can also intervene for ill, and shamans are sometimes feared as well as admired. Once fully recognized as a shaman, a person remains a shaman in service to the society for the rest of his or her life.

Priests, by contrast, are skilled in the practice of religious rituals, which are carried out for the benefit of the group or individuals within the group. Priests frequently are full-time, formally trained specialists. They are found in hierarchical societies in which status differences between rulers and subjects are paralleled in the unequal relationship between priest and laity. Priests do not necessarily have direct contact with cosmic forces; rather, their major role is to mediate that contact successfully for their people by ensuring that the required rituals have been properly performed.

4.6 Change in Religious Systems

Much ethnographic work has sought to describe and explain the details of particular religious systems, but the way that change affects religious belief and practice has also been of great interest. When the members of a society are faced with drastic changes in their experiences—because of conquest, natural disaster, or radical dislocation (for example, by migration)—they frequently seek new interpretations that will help them cope with the changes. In some cases, the individuals or groups in question will adopt an entirely new worldview, frequently a religious system, in the process of **conversion**. But in other cases, the result is a creative synthesis of old religious practices and new ones introduced from the outside, often by force, in a process called **syncretism**. Recently, some anthropologists have pointed out that most studies of religious syncretism have not paid sufficient attention to the unequal relationships between the parties that are syncretizing. Many have assumed that the worldview that changes most is the one belonging to the group with the least power. In some cases, syncretistic practices may indeed be introduced from above by powerful outsiders trying to ease tensions by deliberately making room for local beliefs. In other cases, however, syncretism can be seen as a way of resisting new ideas imposed from outside and above, masking old practices under the labels of the new imported ones.

Sometimes social groups struggling with change defend or refashion their own way of life in a process that anthropologists call **revitalization**: a deliberate, organized attempt by some members of a society to create a more satisfying culture. Revitalization movements arise in times of crisis, most often among groups facing oppression and radical transformation, usually at the hands of outsiders (for example, colonizing powers). Revitalization may take a syncretistic form, but syncretism also may be rejected in favor of *nativism*, a return to the old ways. Some nativistic movements anticipate a messiah or prophet who will bring back a lost golden age of peace, prosperity, and harmony, a process often called *revivalism*, *millenarianism*, or *messianism*.

One of the most important aspects of religious changes in recent years has been the spread of "nonmainstream" religions, called **new religious movements**, into areas of the world that already have established religious systems of their own. These movements are found throughout the world and range widely in their religious positions, political involvements, and tolerance of other religious movements. Much research has been done in Latin America where Protestant denominations and sects have expanded dramatically in recent decades at the expense of the Roman Catholic

Church. These denominations frequently offer a more emotional, dramatic theology as well as altered states of consciousness known as *ecstatic religious experiences*. These include trance, speaking in tongues, exorcisms, and possession. In other cases, they offer a more individualistic theology.

In the United States, anthropologists have studied so-called New Age movements: post-1960s forms of spirituality that explore divinity within the individual. New Age movements have attracted people who seek to break free of the dogmas and restrictions of organized Western religious institutions. Followers of such movements believe that adopting alternative, especially non-Western, religious practices will permit them to develop an individual spirituality free of such restrictions. Among the better known practices are channeling, Harmonic Convergence, and NEOPAGANISM, sometimes known as Wicca.

In recent years, anthropologists have examined not only the power relations involved in syncretism and revitalization but also the way that different worldviews are related to the creation and maintenance of power relations within societies. For example, power differences may be sustained by differential knowledge as when some groups of people within a society have access to important knowledge that is not available to everyone or when a limited number of individuals exercise control over key symbols and ritual practices. In many cases, those with power in the society seem to have successfully made use of the self-evident truths embodied in their worldview to continue to control others.

4.7 Secularism, Fundamentalism, and New Religious Movements

In the context of globalization, it is difficult to talk about religion and not also talk about **secularism**, which can be broadly defined as the separation of religion and state. This separation began in western Europe in the eighteenth century, in response to the brutal religious wars that had characterized Europe since the beginning of the Protestant Reformation in 1517. To maintain the peace, people were allowed to believe what they chose to believe, and the state did not intervene in favor of one religion rather than another (see Asad 2003). Anthropologist John Bowen points out that secularism is used today in three different ways. First, it refers to how modern states define and regulate the place of religious bodies and religious discourse in political processes. That is, in modern states, religious organizations may make their policy positions known, but final, legally binding policy decisions for citizens of the state are made by a civilian political body. Second, it refers to a process called *secularization*, in the course of which social institutions become increasingly differentiated from one another, each with its own rules distinct from others. For instance, the institution of the state is increasingly distinguished from religious institutions and from the family, and each becomes a separate form of organization with its own rules and regulations. To be sure, many people continue to see marriage and divorce, for example, as religious events, but in secular nation-states, it is state institutions that regulate marriage and divorce: Written laws determine, for example, who may and may not be legally married and the procedures that must be followed to obtain a legal divorce. Third, secularization can also refer to the decline of religion, either in the sense that social life is less controlled by religious practices or in the sense that individuals lose their faith in the existence of religious truth or in the existence of religious beings (Bowen 2008, 231). Sometimes secularism is used to refer to a decline in people's allegiance to organized religions. In a contemporary state, the commitment to secularism has the potential to place all religions on an equal footing. The state may protect free exercise of religion to a greater or lesser degree, but it endorses the teachings of no religion in particular.

Despite occasional tensions and frictions, many citizens find that life in a secular state is a successful approach to religious coexistence, but others do not agree. Sometimes this disagreement leads to political–religious tensions, as adherents of one faith (or one version of a faith) reject the premises of secular society. Religious movements of this kind have often been called "fundamentalist," not always accurately. The term **fundamentalism** entered common use in the United States in the late nineteenth and early twentieth centuries. It was applied to a movement in some denominations of Protestant Christianity that promoted a return to what they understood to be the "fundamentals" of their faith. Stressing these fundamentals was intended to serve as a guide for people who had fallen away from the church or who disagreed with more liberal forms of Christian doctrine. Over time, "fundamentalism" has increasingly been used to refer to movements stressing what their followers take to be the "fundamentals" of extremist forms of ideology (Nagata 2001, 483). The world of the secularized state is open and uncertain, and some people respond to the anxieties produced by such openness and uncertainty by becoming uncompromising and antirelativist (see Chapter 2). Today, Judith Nagata suggests, the assumption that fundamentalism is primarily a religious phenomenon is incorrect: "[I]t may be sighted in domains such as ultranationalism, extreme or genocidal ethnic chauvinisms, certain political ideologies, in obsessive quests for linguistic and cultural purity of authenticity" (2001, 493). Thus, Nagata suggests it is more accurate to speak about "fundamentalisms," all of which have in common "a quest for certainty, exclusiveness, and unambiguous boundaries, where the 'Other' is the enemy demonized" (2001, 481).

Another response to the pressures of globalization and to the challenges of life in a secular society has been the creation of a range of new religious movements around the world, as discussed earlier. While contemporary study of these religious movements resembles the studies of revitalization or millenarian movements by earlier generations of anthropologists, the new studies place greater emphasis on both the global political context of these religious movements and their connections to other religions that form the context in which they exist.

4.8 Art

In Western societies, the term **art** includes sculpture, drawing, painting, dance, theater, music, and literature and such similar processes and products such as film, photography, mime, massmedia productions, oral narrative, festivals, and national celebrations. When anthropologists talk about art in non-Western societies, they begin by focusing on activities or products that resemble art in the West. Whether non-Western peoples refer to such activities or products as "art," the activities and products themselves are universal. They seem rooted in playful creativity, a birthright of all human beings, but differ from free play because they are circumscribed by rules. Artistic rules direct particular attention to and provide standards for evaluating the *form* of the activities or objects that artists produce. One anthropological definition of art is that it consists of "culturally significant meaning, skillfully encoded in an affecting, sensuous medium" (Anderson 2004, 277). The term *sensuous* refers to the senses, so a sensuous medium is one that can be perceived by one or more of the human senses. The media through which culturally significant meaning can be encoded are vast and include painting on various surfaces; carving wood, bone, antler, and stone; singing and chanting; creating and playing musical instruments; storytelling; dancing; tattooing; and a theoretically infinite range of other media. These media and the kinds of skills required to work with them are culturally recognized and characterized. For example, the Baule of the Ivory Coast make a number of different kinds of sculptures out of wood, some of which are portrait masks that are supposed to resemble their subjects (Vogel 1997). Others are representations of powerful, dangerous spirits that are not understood as portraits at all.

Art is often said to have an aesthetic element to it. The term **aesthetic** can be used to refer to theories about the nature and value of art but can also be usefully defined as "appreciative of, or responsive to, form in art or nature" (Alland 1977, xii). Something that is aesthetically successful generates a positive or negative response for the artist and perhaps for anyone else who experiences it ("I like this," "I hate this"). Indifference is the sign of something that is aesthetically unsuccessful. It is probably the case that the aesthetic response is a universal feature in all cultures and, as with play, may be part of the human condition. This does not mean that everyone in all places and at all times responds in the same way to a given work of art—quite the contrary, there is ample evidence that aesthetic response varies from place to place. Nevertheless, as part of one of anthropology's projects over the years, anthropologists have been eager to undermine the complacent Western assumption of cultural and social superiority, and emphasizing the presence of "art" in non-Western societies, even when people in a particular society do not recognize a similar term, has contributed to this project.

In recent years, it has become increasingly the case that a very wide range of products of human activity are considered to be art by people in Western societies, and it is equally clear that many of those products were not produced to be "art." Western art museums present furniture, religious or devotional objects, jewelry designed for personal adornment, technology, arms and armor, and much more from Western history as art, and they do the same for objects from non-Western societies as well. Anthropologist Shelly Errington (1998) usefully distinguishes between **art by intention** and **art by appropriation**. Art by intention includes objects that were made to be art, such as Impressionist paintings. Art by appropriation, however, consists of all the other objects that "became art" because at a certain moment certain people (they could be local artists, or museum curators, art dealers, art collectors, interior designers) decided that they belonged to the category of art. Because museums, art dealers, and art collectors are found everywhere in the world today, so too it is now the case that potentially any material object crafted by human hands can be appropriated by these institutions as "art." The set of people and institutions concerned with defining and maintaining art in one form or another make up an **art world**. This includes artists, art historians, art critics, curators, gallery owners, art writers, designers, art collectors, art patrons, museums, galleries, art schools, art magazines, art fairs, paint companies, stone quarries, and so forth. All these people and institutions make it possible for the artist to carry out his or her art but also help define it. Indeed, it is the members of the art world who determine whether a work will be circulated as art or not. This has led anthropologists interested in the arts into studying the ways that non-Western art, tourist art, and "ethnic arts" intersect with or become part of the art worlds of Europe and the United States. Robert Welsch (2006) points out that this is not a new process even if the art worlds that he and his colleagues study are more global than in earlier times.

It is also the case that people whose products have been appropriated as art can also begin to produce art by intention. Australian

Aboriginal peoples began to produce acrylic paintings to be sold in the art market in the 1970s, based on ancient techniques and styles that were originally of profound religious and spiritual significance.

The development of a global art market has been paralleled in popular music where there has been a tremendous amount of cross-fertilization as well as the development of local traditions that meld rock-and-roll styles from several different parts of the world into creative and satisfying musics. The sharing of MP3s via the Internet has led to an extraordinary globalization of musical taste such that heavy metal bands from Finland find eager listeners in Chile.

The study of the musics of the world, particularly the relationship of music to society and cultural ideas and practices, is the field of **ethnomusicology**. Ethnomusicology can include the study of music and social, cultural, or gender identity; the role of music and musicians in a society; the effect of music on social life; and the study of sound as a form of communication. Recent advances in recording technology have made it possible for ethnomusicologists to include CDs of the music they have studied in the books they publish, which has enormously expanded the impact of their work.

As with music, so too with dance. Anthropologists who have studied dance in different human societies have demonstrated how dance is connected with the expression of gender; how it is connected with the expression of emotion; how it is connected with sculpture, masking, and religious practice; and how it is a form of self-expression.

A number of anthropologists have considered how identity becomes connected with art (and vice versa); for example, how indigenous people in Southeast Alaska use commercial and "tourist" art—blankets, pictures, jewelry—to index membership within a cultural group (Bunten 2006). In other cases, anthropologists have traced the influences of Western art markets on the production of figurines or woven goods or have examined how the Aboriginal acrylic paintings have become significant markers of the Australian state. At the same time, an Australian art world has emerged with connections in the remote areas of central Australia, the major cities of Australia, and such art centers as New York City.

4.9 The Anthropology of Media

In recent years, anthropologists have begun to direct their gaze at the ways that the media—television, radio, photography, film, and soap operas—are received, understood, created, and used by people around the world. The media have extraordinary power and exceptional reach, and anthropologists have realized that the effect the media have on people's lives can be very great. Some of this work connects to processes of globalization (see Chapter 10), including the ways that television programming diminishes, if not erases, the boundaries of time and space (somewhere in the world, *Gilligan's Island* is being broadcast). But at the same time, some of the international cable television companies (Sky, for example) have begun regional services that "reterritorialize" the medium by providing programming that is culturally and linguistically appropriate for the different parts of India or China. Some of the most interesting work deals with television and the cultural politics of nation-states—for example, India. Purnima Mankekar (1999) connects television, womanhood, and the nation-state in examining how the television serials (soap operas or mythical or historical serials) on the national television service were created and how they were received by viewers. Mankekar suggests that television broadcasting in India both underlies and undermines the creation of a nationalist consciousness on the part of viewers.

Other anthropologists have been studying computer-facilitated media, including the Internet as an anthropological subject, social media and communication, and the ethnography of virtual worlds. Daniel Miller and Don Slater (2000), for example, were able to show that e-mail and especially chat and instant messaging (IM) were instantly adopted by Trinidadians to facilitate communication among family members on Trinidad and those who had left the island to work. They used these mechanisms to "roll back changes that were dissolving some family relations" (2000, 82). However, Miller and Slater warn readers not to assume that the consequences would be the same in another society, emphasizing that anthropology's focus on the local continues to be one of its key contributions to the study of the contemporary world.

As you might suspect, social media like Facebook and MySpace have also been attracting attention from anthropologists. In 2008,

Ilana Gershon published a study of how U.S. college students used social media to end romantic relationships (2008, 13–15). Most of Gershon's students preferred to use instant messaging rather than e-mail to break up, because IM allowed turn-taking, making the exchange of messages seem like a "conversation." This feature gave the person on the receiving end of the break-up the impression that it was possible to ask "Why?" and get an answer that might provide some closure to the relationship. Gershon cautions current readers not to assume that they share the same media ideologies as her students did in 2008: She was surprised to learn, for example, that her students considered a telephone break-up to be nearly as satisfactory as a face-to-face break-up; this had not been the case with Gershon and her friends when they were in college in the late 1990s.

Some anthropological research concerning Facebook has looked at identity issues. For example, Dhiraj Murthy studied how young Pakistanis living in the United States and elsewhere outside of Pakistan use Facebook sites that specialize in their own popular culture. These young people do not simply listen to and comment about alternative music; they are also attracted by the opportunity of posting on the Facebook walls of their favorite bands in order to express themselves creatively and freely (Murthy 2010, 191). Steffen Dalsgaard studied the way that politicians in the United States and western Europe use Facebook and MySpace to mobilize financial and political support in ways that also allow supporters to make a public acknowledgment of their political identities (Dalsgaard 2008).

Anthropologists have also paid attention to **virtual worlds**, "places of human culture realized by computer programs through the Internet" (Boellstorff 2008, 17). Tom Boellstorff and Bonnie Nardi (2010) have done online fieldwork in Second Life and World of Warcraft, respectively, and both consider ethnography to be an excellent research methodology for the study of virtual worlds. Boellstorff examines ways that Second Life enables certain experiences for its players that are not possible in real life. For example, people interact in Second Life through avatars, which are customized and customizable visual forms that can be shaped to the desire of the individual. In a virtual world, however, nothing prevents a player from creating several different, alternative avatars (known as "alts") to represent different elements of his or her personality or to allow the player to experiment with a completely invented identity. It is possible for a player logged into Second Life to log in a second time as one of his or her alts and to allow the main avatar and the alt to interact in ways that would be impossible in real life.

Nardi studied World of Warcraft in the United States and in China, finding many similarities, including the aesthetic response of the players to the online world, and one big difference: Chinese players tended to play in Internet cafés, often with other people who play the game together (known as a guild). Nardi observed simultaneous online and offline interactions in these settings, both among guild players and among others in the café who were playing the game. She concluded that World of Warcraft is becoming a hybrid, mixed reality in which virtual and physical worlds combine (Nardi 2010, 181). World of Warcraft combines the pleasure of play, competitive performance, and aesthetic enjoyment. Nardi concludes that World of Warcraft is, in fact, an art form.

For Further Reading

GENERAL ANTHROPOLOGICAL WORKS ON RELIGION
Bowen 2008; Bowie 2006; Stein and Stein 2008; Wallace 1966; Winzeler 2008

READINGS ON RELIGION
Hicks 2010; Lambek 2008; Moro and Myers 2010

SECULARISM
Asad 2003

ART
Alland 1977; Errington 1998; Myers 2003; Venbrux, Rosi, and Welsch 2006; Vogel 1997

MEDIA ANTHROPOLOGY
Askew and Wilk 2002; Ginsburg, Abu-Lughod, and Larkin 2002; Mankekar 1999

VIRTUAL WORLDS
Boellstorff 2008; Nardi 2010

5

The Dimensions of Social Organization

The key terms and concepts covered in this chapter, in the order in which they appear:

society
status
role
ascribed status
achieved status
social structure
institutions
social organization
functionalism
mechanical solidarity
organic solidarity

egalitarian societies
stratified societies
rank societies
sodalities
age set
age grades
secret societies
caste

social mobility
class
bourgeoisie
proletariat
clientage
patron–client relationships
compadrazgo
fictive kin
state
bureaucracy
authority

race
ethnic group
ethnocide
genocide

sex
gender
sexuality

ONE OF THE BASIC CLAIMS of anthropology is that human beings are a social species; that is, we have evolved to live with and depend on others of our own species. Biological anthropologists have demonstrated, for example, that human infants are born earlier in the gestational process than are infants of apes and monkeys and that our young are dependent on other members of the group for far longer (15 to 20 years and more) before they are capable of establishing themselves as mature adults. Human interdependence means that we cannot survive as lone individuals but need to live with others; that is, we must live in **society**. When anthropologists speak of human society, at minimum they mean a group of human beings living together whose interactions with one another are patterned in regular ways. Such organized groups might also be identified by the particular geographical territory they inhabit, by the particular language they speak, or by the particular customs they follow—any or all of these features might distinguish them from other, neighboring societies. Such distinctive features are in turn mostly cultural, which is why anthropologists developed the habit of speaking as if each identifiable society came equipped with its own culture, and vice versa. Still, anthropologists recognize that no culture is monolithic, that cultural patterns may be borrowed or shared by people in different societies, and that a single society may contain within it representatives of different cultural traditions.

5.1 What Is Social Organization?

Anthropologists, together with other social scientists, have developed a set of analytic concepts that help describe and explain the orderly interdependence of human life in society. In particular, they have noted that people who interact in society do so not as unique individuals but as incumbents of publicly recognized social positions. Each such social position is called a **status,** and all individuals come to occupy a range of different statuses in the course of their lives as they take part in a variety of social interactions.

People know what to do in such interactions because each status is associated with a corresponding **role:** a bundle of rights and obligations appropriate for occupants of the status in question. Thus, for example, the kinship status of *parent* might include, among other things, the right to discipline one's children and the obligation to feed them and send them to school. Violation of the role requirements associated with a particular social status generally brings about disapproval from other members of society.

Social scientists also distinguish two basic kinds of social statuses found in all societies: ascribed and achieved. An **ascribed status** is a status over which you have little control: You are born into it or grow into it. Anthropologists often use examples from human kinship systems to illustrate ascribed status. When you are born, you are automatically your parent's child, son or daughter; when you have children of your own, you automatically become a parent, mother or father. Such ascribed statuses ordinarily cannot be discarded, and any person who qualifies will be expected to fulfill the role obligations that go with the status. Very different, however, is an **achieved status,** one that you may not assume until or unless you meet certain criteria through your own (or others') efforts. For instance, being a college graduate is an achieved status, and achieving that status ordinarily requires both hard work and financial resources. Each member of a society occupies a mix of ascribed and achieved statuses.

Statuses and their accompanying roles are not isolated but are often linked to one another in complementary pairs or sets. For example, the statuses of parents and children (or mother and daughter, father and son, mother and son, or father and daughter) are reciprocal relationships. Thus, the right of parents to discipline their children matches the obligation of children to obey their parents (in theory, at least). To describe such a cluster of statuses with complementary roles is to begin to identify key enduring social relationships that provide a foundation for regularized, patterned social interaction, or **social structure.** But social structure is not simply a matter of interlinked and complementary statuses and roles attached to individuals. Most societies regularly associate particular sets of statuses with particular social groups defined in such terms as gender, family, lineage, clan, occupation, and political or religious affiliation. The relationships that link members of these various social groups may also be highly structured, often around a common task or cultural focus. The clusters of social statuses and groups that share such a common focus usually are called **institutions**. Thus, we speak of educational institutions that unite individuals and groups whose social statuses focus on educational issues or of political institutions that bring together individuals and groups whose statuses focus on the allocation of power in the society. Sometimes social structure refers only to the arrangement of status positions and groups with respect to each other. By contrast, **social organization** refers to the interlocking role relationships that are activated when statuses have incumbents and groups have members, all of whom are going about the daily business of living.

All this terminology is associated with the school of social scientific thought called **functionalism** (for more about functionalism, see Chapter 12). Functionalism was at its most influential in the early twentieth century and has since been much criticized, but many anthropologists and sociologists continue to find its terminology useful for describing basic social relations, even when they do not accept some of its more elaborate assumptions.

5.2 Dimensions of Social Organization

One issue of great interest in the early years of anthropology and sociology was the contrast between large and powerful European nation-states, with industrial technology and a complex division of labor, and small-scale societies, with little or no social stratification, whose members used simple tools to make a living and who were socially organized almost entirely on the basis of kinship. The contrast was sometimes phrased as an opposition between so-called civilized and so-called primitive societies. Sociologists were supposed to explain how "civilized" societies worked, and anthropologists were supposed to explain how "primitive" societies worked.

One widely influential model was proposed by Emile Durkheim (1858–1917), a French sociologist considered a founder of both modern sociology and modern anthropology. Durkheim was interested in what held a society together, contrasting societies held together by mechanical solidarity with those held together by organic solidarity. **Mechanical solidarity** characterized small-scale, kinship-based societies in which all the tasks necessary for survival were carried out on a family level and families stayed together because they shared the same language and customs.

However, because kin groups were more-or-less self-sufficient in terms of meeting their survival needs, they could split off from one another relatively easily. Thus, mechanical solidarity could not bind together large numbers of people over long periods of time. **Organic solidarity**, by contrast, characterized large-scale societies such as nation-states. In such societies, the tasks necessary for survival became specialties of different subgroups in a complex division of labor. For example, because those who specialized in pot making or metalworking might not have had the time or resources to produce their own food or clothing, they became dependent on other specialists—food producers or tailors—for these goods and services. Such interdependence meant that any single occupational grouping could not easily break away from the larger social whole because it was not self-sufficient. Like the organ systems of a living body, specialized subgroups of complex societies clung together and depended on one another to survive, thereby preserving the overall health and strength of the whole. Thus, organic solidarity could hold much larger societies together far more securely than could mechanical solidarity.

Anthropologists incorporated concepts like these into their own analytic toolkit as they attempted to make sense of the variety of forms that different human societies assumed in different times and places. They also introduced new concepts to highlight further distinctions revealed by ethnographic research. One of the most basic is the fourfold classification of societies on the basis of their form of political organization: band, tribe, chiefdom, and state (discussed at greater length in Chapter 6). Another is the very similar fourfold classification of societies on the basis of their form

of economic organization: foragers, herders, extensive agriculturalists, and intensive agriculturalists (discussed at greater length in
Chapter 7). The correlations between these different classifications
highlight the connections between the ways that people make a
living and the ways that they organize themselves politically.

The correlation is not perfect, however, and this is highlighted
by another pair of concepts that crosscuts the earlier classifications. That is, anthropologists distinguish between **egalitarian societies,** in which all members (or component groups) enjoy roughly
the same degree of wealth, power, and prestige, and **stratified
societies,** in which some members (or component groups) have
greater (and often permanent) access to some or all of these three
valued resources. But the history of the transition from egalitarian societies (bands and tribes, in the current classification) to
stratified societies (chiefdoms and states) is not fully understood.
Some anthropologists pay particular attention to societies known
through ethnography or history or archaeology in which egalitarian relations have begun to erode but in which permanent, inherited patterns of social stratification have not yet been established.
Such societies, like those of the indigenous peoples of the northwest coast of North America or the Trobriand Islanders of Papua
New Guinea, depended on foraging or extensive agriculture for
subsistence, just as many egalitarian societies do. But they also
have social structures that elevate certain individuals and their
families above everyone else, allowing them privileged access to a
limited number of high-status positions. Anthropologist Morton
Fried called these **rank societies,** some of whose members ranked
above others in social honor but did not have disproportionate
access to wealth or power. The consensus is that fully stratified
societies probably developed out of rank societies, but the exact
mechanisms for the transition have been much debated and may
well have been somewhat different in each case.

Ethnographic evidence supported Durkheim's observation that
small-scale societies tend to be organized primarily on the basis of
kinship. As we discuss in Chapter 8, kinship systems must be fairly
elaborate to carry out this task, and anthropology traditionally
has sought to understand and compare the many different kinship

systems that human beings have devised. However, even egalitarian societies whose social organization centered on kinship often invented additional forms of social organization that crosscut kinship groups and bound their members together at a more inclusive level; anthropologists often refer to such groups as **sodalities**.

Sodalities can take many forms. Among the best known ethnographically are the age-set systems from eastern Africa and the secret societies from western Africa. Found in such societies as the Nyakyusa living in present-day Tanzania, an **age set** is made up of a group of young men born within a specific time span such as five years; thus, a new age set is formed regularly every five years. Age sets typically progress through a sequence of statuses, or **age grades**, as their members grow older. There might be three age grades through which every age set must pass—for example, a junior, senior, and elder grade. Promotion from one age grade to the next typically is marked by rituals. Many societies with age-set systems devote particular attention to the *initiation* ritual that transforms boys into adult men, but societies differ in the degree of ritual elaboration with which they surround the passage of different sets from one grade to the next. Age-set systems have played different roles in different societies as well. Those sets belonging to junior age grades frequently have been characterized as *warriors*, but it is important to recognize that their activities as fighters or raiders often were subject to the control of men in senior age grades. Moreover, members of societies with age sets and age grades frequently use the age-grade structure as a way of thinking about time and attempting to regulate its passage by ritual means.

The Mende, Sherbro, Kpelle, and other neighboring peoples who today live in the western African nation-states of Sierra Leone, Ivory Coast, Liberia, and Guinea developed **secret societies** as forms of social organization that crosscut kinship groupings. Some secret societies admit only men as members, others admit only women, and at least one admits both men and women. Only adults may belong to secret societies, and children must undergo initiation rituals to achieve that status and gain admittance; some anthropologists have undergone initiation as part of their research. The "secret" part of secret societies refers to the special knowledge revealed only to initiates, which they are not allowed to share with outsiders. Initiates may also progress to higher positions within the society to which they belong, but they must pay fees and receive special instruction to do so. In addition to these internal activities, secret societies also carry out specific tasks in public. Social relations between men and women tend to be highly egalitarian in cultures with secret societies; for example, the male Poro society and female Sande society of a village might jointly be responsible for supervising public behavior and sanctioning those who violate expected rules of conduct.

Forms of social organization, such as kinship and sodalities, can still be found in societies that are socially stratified, but their scope and importance are modified by new features of social structure that sustain the inequalities on which social stratification is based. That is, stratified societies are internally divided into a number of groups that are arranged in a hierarchy. The two most important such hierarchical structures studied by anthropologists have been caste and class.

5.3 Caste and Class

Anthropologists traditionally describe **caste** societies as stratified societies in which membership in a particular ranked subgroup is ascribed at birth and in which **social mobility**, or movement by individuals out of the subgroup in which they were born, is not allowed. Although the original prototype for caste societies comes from India, anthropologists have used the term to describe similar social arrangements in other societies.

In India and elsewhere in South Asia, each caste traditionally is defined not only as the endogamous group within which members must choose mates (see Chapter 9 for a definition of *endogamy*) but also in terms of a traditional occupation with which the caste is identified (salt maker, farmer, warrior, or priest, for example). Each occupation, and the caste associated with it, is ranked on a scale of purity and pollution, with higher-ranked castes subject to various dietary and other taboos required to maintain caste purity. Highest on the purity scale are the *Brahmins*, the vegetarian priestly caste; lowest are the out-castes, or dalit (formerly called "untouch-ables"), who eat meat and whose occupations (leatherworker, street sweeper) regularly bring them into contact with polluting substances such as dead animals and excrement. Recent studies of caste societies have demonstrated that the high ritual status of the Brahmin caste does not mean that Brahmins dominate the caste system; rather, these studies emphasize the centrality of the king and his warrior caste, the *Ksatriya*. Kings could determine the rela-tive rank of local castes, for example, and from the king's perspec-tive, the function of these other castes, including the Brahmins, was to protect him from pollution. By the end of the twentieth century, caste relations had undergone significant modification in urban India: Castes close in rank sometimes came together in political alliances, and members of the same caste but from different regions of the country (for example, Brahmins) came together to build soli-darity on a national level. Unfortunately, Indian cities have also been the site of caste violence in recent years when members of more favorably situated castes clash with those struggling to escape from a permanent position at the bottom of the caste hierarchy.

Social **class**, by contrast, is the term anthropologists use to describe ranked subgroups in a stratified society whose members are differentiated from one another primarily in economic terms, either on the basis of income level or, as Karl Marx (1818–83) proposed, on the basis of the kind of property owned by members of different classes. In an industrial capitalist society, for example, Marx argued that class divisions had formed between the **bourgeoisie**, or capital-ist class, which owned the means of production (tools, knowledge, raw materials), and the **proletariat**, or working class, which owned only their labor power, which they sold to bourgeois factory owners in exchange for cash wages (see Chapters 7 and 10 for further dis-cussion of these terms). Either way, members of some social classes are seen to have privileged access to material resources, while the access of members of other classes to these resources is more or less severely restricted. Moreover, ruling classes use their privileged situation to dominate less powerful classes.

Traditionally, anthropologists have distinguished class from caste on the grounds that social classes are not closed and social mobility from one class into another is not forbidden. An emphasis on class mobility tends to highlight exceptional, successful individuals who have moved from lower to higher classes while overlooking the enduring rigidity of class boundaries for most people in many societies (Great Britain, for example) as well as cases of downward class mobility. At the same time, emphasizing the inability of individuals in a caste system to move from a lower-ranked to a higher-ranked caste overlooks the ways in which permanent members of different castes sometimes collectively succeed in elevating the relative position of their caste within the overall caste system.

The members of ranked subgroups in stratified societies do not always accept the position they are supposed to occupy in a class or caste hierarchy, and struggles between such groups do occur. Marx, in particular, emphasized the class antagonism between bourgeoisie and proletariat, which he predicted ultimately would produce class warfare in which the workers would overthrow the capitalist order and establish socialism. Anthropologists working in India have challenged the view that people occupying the lowest ranks in the caste system necessarily accept their low status as right and proper. Indeed, the caste violence that has occasionally erupted in Indian cities in recent decades testifies to the unwillingness of those at the bottom of the system to accept such a position. At the same time, interactions between individuals from different levels of a hierarchical social system is not regularly characterized by such violence, and members of different ranked groups find nonviolent ways to establish relationships with one another. If different groups are associated with different occupations, their members may have only impersonal contact with one another when they need one another's services—for example, in the workplace. But many societies have developed institutionalized cross-hierarchy connections that allow individuals belonging to differently ranked groups to create a more personalized relationship. Anthropologists often call such connections **clientage** or **patron–client relationships** because they normally involve a member of a high-ranking group (the patron) and a member of a low-ranking group (the client). A well-documented example of clientage is the Latin American institution of *compadrazgo,* or coparenthood. Such a relationship may be created when a lower-ranking married couple (the clients) asks a higher-ranking individual (the patron) to serve as their child's *compadre* or *comadre* (godfather or godmother) at the child's baptism. If the patron agrees and participates in the baptism ritual, then that individual and the child's parents will have a new relationship. They will call each other by the kin terms *compadre* or *comadre*, and their relationship will become less formal and more friendly. Because they are now *compadres*, the child's parents will feel freer to approach their patron (*compadre/comadre*) when they are in trouble, and he or she will be morally obliged to help them out. Conversely, if their patron needs supporters (for example, in politics), they ordinarily will feel obligated to supply that support. Because clientage institutions like *compadrazgo* frequently remake the relationship of unrelated individuals on the model of formal kinship, anthropologists sometimes describe *compadres* as **fictive kin.**

Stratified societies with large populations and a complex division of labor ordinarily are associated with the political form called the **state** (discussed in more detail in Chapter 6). The organic solidarity of state societies is maintained by a new kind of institution neither present nor needed in small-scale, egalitarian societies: bureaucracy. A **bureaucracy** is a hierarchically organized set of formal statuses, each of which is associated with a highly specific role and all of which are designed to work together to ensure the smooth functioning of complex organizations such as state governments or business corporations. Persons occupying formal statuses in a bureaucracy possess **authority**: the ability to exert specific forms of influence and control by virtue of the fact that they legitimately occupy a formal office. Ideally, bureaucrats defend the avowed purposes of the organizations they serve, and much of their work involves following proper procedures in performing the particular tasks for which they are responsible. Complex organizations could not function without bureaucracies, but the formality and complexity of bureaucratic procedures often frustrates outsiders and may tempt bureaucrats to manipulate their positions for their own personal benefit.

Descriptions in terms of caste or class may be useful in tracing the gross outlines of the structure of complex stratified societies, but they are rarely sufficient to characterize all the significant dimensions of social organization found in such societies. Anthropologists recognize the importance of additional categories used by members of these societies that may be embedded within or may crosscut caste or class structures. With this in mind, they also have long paid attention to the category of race and have grown increasingly interested in distinctions framed in terms of ethnic identity, gender, and sexuality.

5.4 Race

The concept of **race** was deeply intertwined with the very origin of anthropology as a discipline (see discussion in Chapter 2). Although some late-nineteenth-century physical anthropologists hoped to demonstrate a causal connection between the physical attributes of a group and their language and customs, early-twentieth-century anthropologists worked hard to expose the flaws in such attempts. The modern concept of culture was developed to explain how individuals could learn *any* language or culture, regardless of their biological origins, and to argue against schemes that tried to classify the world's peoples into mutually exclusive races and to rank them hierarchically.

At the same time, the absence of any underlying biological basis for racial categories has never prevented people in some societies from inventing *cultural* categories based on a group's supposed origins or physical appearance and then using such categories as building blocks for their social institutions. Precisely because racial categories are culturally constructed on the basis of superficial appearances, however, different societies may draw the boundaries around racially defined social groups in different ways.

For example, as the twenty-first century dawns, people living in the United States tend to classify people into several different racial categories, but the great divide remains between two major racial categories, black and white. The enslavement of Africans by Europeans in the United States and the continued oppression of their descendants even after emancipation in the nineteenth century have created a social reality for residents of the United States in which the divide between black and white appears so obvious as to be beyond question. To be sure, continued world domination by societies whose ruling groups trace their origins to Europe has sustained a global hierarchy in which light skin is valued over dark skin. And yet, outside the United States, in the Caribbean or in Brazil where Africans also suffered under European slavery, race is understood in different ways. Rather than an unchanging identity that people carry around with them everywhere they go, the racial identity one claims, or is accorded by others, may vary from situation to situation, depending on who else is present. That is, in any particular social setting, those with the lightest skin may claim and be accorded the identity of "white," but when they move into a different setting and interact with others whose skin is lighter than theirs, they may have to accept being assigned to one of a variety of lower-status, nonwhite categories. Some anthropologists (for example, Lancaster 1994) use the term *colorism* to describe this pattern of racial classification in contrast to the once-and-for-all pattern of racial classification found in the United States.

Moreover, social mobility and the cultural changes that accompany it—learning the dominant language, getting an education, finding gainful employment, adopting new customs in diet and dress—may be interpreted as movement from one racial group into another. Thus, in some parts of Latin America, indigenous people who cut their hair, speak Spanish, wear European clothing, get an education, and find Western-style occupations may be classified by other members of their society as "white" or "mixed" rather than "indigenous," even though their outward biological features have not altered. Anthropologists sometimes use the term *social race* to describe these cases in which so-called racial labels are used to refer to cultural rather than physical differences between groups.

5.5 Ethnicity

The distinction between classifications based on biology and on culture is thus not clear-cut. This highlights the ways that people can emphasize or downplay any of a wide range of physical and cultural attributes, either to define an identity for themselves or to assign an identity to others. This ambiguity appears when we consider another important social category investigated by anthropologists, that of the **ethnic group**. Ethnic groups usually are distinguished from other kinds of social groups based on attributes defining group membership that are cultural in nature: shared language, shared religion, shared customs, shared history. However, because all this cultural sharing could never have occurred if group members did not regularly interact and even intermarry, ethnic identity is often thought, by both group members and outsiders, to be rooted in some common biological origin. Indeed, some anthropologists think of racial identity as being no different from ethnic identity, except that racial identity supposedly is biological in origin whereas ethnic identity has a cultural origin. And in practice, the concepts of both race and ethnic group often overlap with the concept of nation (discussed in more detail in Chapter 6).

All such cultural identities—whether understood in terms of kinship or race or ethnic identity—develop in opposition to other, similar identities in a complex social setting. Thus, the boundaries that eventually come to be recognized between races or ethnic groups are a product of both internal self-definition and external definition by others. Of course, a sense of group belonging and the ability to distinguish one's own group from neighboring groups stretch far back into the human past. What makes the study of racial or ethnic or national identity so important today, however, is the new role such groups take on within the boundaries of contemporary nation-states.

As discussed in Chapter 6, nation-states are relatively new forms of political organization, first developing in late-eighteenth-century and nineteenth-century Europe and the Americas and later spreading throughout the globe following the dissolution of Western colonial empires. Before the French Revolution, European states were ruled by kings and emperors whose access to the throne was officially believed to have been ordained by God. After the French Revolution, which thoroughly discredited the divine right of kings and proclaimed the "Rights of Man," a new basis for legitimate state authority had to be found. Over the course of the nineteenth century, the notion developed that rulers were legitimate only if they ruled over other members of the nation to which they themselves belonged.

When legitimacy began to depend on the perfect overlap of nation and state, on a recognized bond of cultural or linguistic or religious—that is, national—identity between ruler and ruled, the persistence of groups with different forms of identity within the boundaries of the nation-state became problematic. If such groups successfully resisted assimilation into the nation that the state was supposed to represent, their existence called into question the legitimacy of the state and its rulers. Indeed, if their numbers were sufficient, they might well claim that they were a separate nation, entitled to a state of their own! This situation describes much contemporary political life at the turn of the twenty-first century when ruling regimes in more and more nation-states, fearful of losing stability and legitimacy in the eyes of the world, engaged in violence against all citizens who challenged their right to rule. **Ethnocide** (the destruction of a culture) and **genocide** (the physical extermination of an entire people) have often been the result, generating movements of refugee and immigrant populations whose social and political status is often anomalous and ambiguous in a world of nation-states.

In recent years, anthropologists have paid particular attention to the ways that oppressed racial and ethnic groups, whether resident or immigrant, have struggled to mobilize their members to resist oppression. This has occurred in countries all over the world, including those of Europe and North America. As forces of globalization have weakened nation-states and promoted the flow of large numbers of people of various backgrounds into societies different from their own, new ethnic contacts and ethnic frictions have developed.

5.6 Gender

Some anthropologists would argue that feminism was responsible for one of the most profound transformations of social science scholarship in the late twentieth century. The rise of second-wave feminism in the 1960s and 1970s prompted some anthropologists to rethink many long-held assumptions about the contributions of women to culture. Feminist anthropologists noted that most ethnographies, including those written by women, were based primarily on the views of male informants, even concerning matters pertaining to women. Thus, most discussions of "the culture" of a group in fact portrayed culture from the viewpoint of men (often high-status men). When women were discussed at all, it was usually in the context of marriage and the family, and the assumption seemed to be that women's cultural roles as wives and mothers followed "naturally" from the biological facts of pregnancy and lactation. Margaret Mead's demonstration in the 1930s of the lack of correlation between biological sex and culturally expected behaviors of males and females in society was a well-known exception to this pattern.

By the early 1970s, feminist anthropologists were forcing a serious reexamination of traditional assumptions about the roles of women and men in human society. It became commonplace in cultural anthropology to use the term **sex** to refer to the physical characteristics that distinguish males from females (for example, body shape, distribution of body hair, reproductive organs, sex chromosomes). By contrast, **gender** referred to the culturally constructed roles assigned to males or females, which varied considerably from society to society. At the same time, early feminist anthropologists were concerned that, despite this lack of correlation, male domination of females appeared to be universal. Historical and ethnographic evidence, however, both suggested that women's subordination to men was not inevitable.

By the 1980s, many anthropologists had concluded that women's gender roles could not be studied apart from the gender roles of men. In addition, the growing visibility of lesbian, gay, and transgender individuals in Western societies—and within anthropology—led many anthropologists to reject the assumption that heterosexual males and females were the only "natural" forms in which sex and gender were packaged. Indeed, as ethnographic evidence demonstrating the complexity of women's and men's roles in a variety of cultural settings began to accumulate, anthropologists like Marilyn Strathern (1941–) began to argue that the concept of gender needed to be understood even more broadly because members of many societies regularly drew upon sexual imagery as a resource for categorizing other kinds of people, things, and events. For example, the idea that men are active and powerful and women are passive and weak may be mobilized by members of powerful groups in a society, who imagine themselves as "real men" and who treat members of less powerful, dominated groups (perhaps especially men in such groups) as if they were weak and passive, thereby "emasculating" or "feminizing" them. Complex-gendered social relations of this kind were characteristic of Western colonial settings where a culturally constructed "racial" divide between "white" colonizer and "nonwhite" colonized groups was supplemented by violent opposition to any hint of sexual involvement between indigenous males and "white" women, even as "white" men's sexual relationships with colonized women went unpunished. Colonizers viewed those whom they had colonized (colonized men, in particular) as nonwhite, feminized inferiors incapable of protecting their territories or "their" women from more powerful "masculine," white outsiders (Stoler 2002).

Today, feminist anthropologists continue the struggle to debunk supposed universal "truths" about women, showing that "women" is itself a problematic category that flattened out all the many different ways in which female-bodied human persons might live their lives. Women of different races and classes and ethnic groups, it has been shown, often lead very different lives within the same "culture." The categories of "race" and "class" and "ethnic group" can also be seen as problematic because the experiences of, for example, men and women belonging to the same race, class, or ethnic group are also very different from one another. Moreover, the relevance of one's ethnic identity, as well as one's willingness to acknowledge it, has been shown to differ in different social settings.

5.7 Sexuality

In recent years, one of the most important attempts to pick apart the supposed essence of a cultural category has been made by anthropologists and other social scientists exploring the highly controversial topic of sexuality. Minimally, **sexuality** refers to the ways in which people experience and value physical desire and pleasure in the context of sexual intercourse. But contemporary anthropologists are more likely to refer to sexual*ies*, in the plural, to acknowledge the many ways in which sexual desires and pleasures have always been shaped historically by cultural, social, and political structures of the larger societies in which people live. This approach to sexuality, based on work by the French philosopher and historian Michel Foucault (1926–84), became influential in anthropology in the late twentieth century.

Same-sex sexual practices have become an accepted topic for research in anthropology. One result has been that the traditionally unquestioned "normality" of heterosexual sexual practices has been called into question, and the culturally variable links between biological anatomy, gender identity, and sexuality have been explored in a variety of ethnographic contexts. In a manner parallel to the development of feminist anthropology, legitimation of "homosexuality" as a practice and as a topic of study was followed by critiques highlighting the Western male bias tacitly attached to the term. As a result, the varieties of "homosexual" experience in Western societies have been scrutinized, allowing the recognition of important differences in the experiences of gay, lesbian, bisexual, and transgender individuals. These studies have been supplemented not only by ethnographic research on sexualities in other cultures but also by a reexamination of older ethnographic writings about societies in which nonheterosexual practices have been institutionalized. In this regard, anthropologists have given particular attention to research and writing on the cultural and sexual practices of the so-called berdache.

The term *berdache* traditionally has been used in anthropology to refer to indigenous (especially Native American) social roles in which men (and sometimes women) were allowed to take on the activities and sometimes the dress of members of the opposite sex. Sometimes berdache is defined as "male transvestite," but this definition is inadequate because it ignores the fact that a man who took on other aspects of a woman's role might also, as women did, establish sexual relationships with men. Indeed, the term meant "male prostitute" to the early French explorers in the Americas who first used it to describe the men they observed engaging in such behavior.

Today, many anthropologists refuse to use the term, as do many contemporary members of indigenous societies who view themselves as modern embodiments of these alternative-gender roles. Some have proposed using terms like *third gender* or *two spirit* instead although no consensus has yet been achieved. As ethnographic research on alternative-gender roles and sexual practices in a wide variety of societies accumulates, a more adequate set of analytic concepts is likely to be developed. At present, this research continues to generate controversy, not only in societies whose members condemn nonheterosexual intercourse but also among anthropologists whose theoretical and personal views on sexuality are not easily reconciled.

For Further Reading

GENDER/SEXUALITY (SEE ALSO CHAPTER 8)
Blackwood and Wieringa 1999; Bonvillain 2006; Di Leonardo 1991; Gutmann 1997; Herdt 1994; Miller 1993; Stone 2005; Suggs and Miracle 1993; Weston 1993

SOCIAL ORGANIZATION
Fried 1967; Graburn 1971

ETHNICITY
Williams 1989

COLONIALISM
Pels 1997; Stoler 2002

RACE
Lancaster 1994; Smedley 1999

GENOCIDE AND ETHNOCIDE
Hinton 2002; Messer 1993; Nagengast 1994

6
Political Anthropology

The key terms and concepts covered in this chapter, in the order in which they appear:

state
political anthropologists
politics

coercive power
power
persuasive power

agency

cultural ecology
political ecology
political economy
raiding
feuding
mediator
negotiation
bloodwealth
warfare

egalitarian
band

tribes
chiefdoms

social stratification
caste
class
slaves
sumptuary
wealth
prestige

complex societies
acephalous
consensus

headman
big man

formalization
sanctions
law
substantive law
procedural law

civil law
criminal law
law codes
courts
adjudicate
crime

nationalism
nation
nation-states
imagined
    community
invention of
    tradition

domination
hegemony
biopower
governmentality
ideology
hidden transcripts

WHEN NINETEENTH-CENTURY ethnologists from Europe and North America began to compare societies across space and over time, they noticed not only that members of different societies made a living in different ways but also that daily life in all these varied societies seemed to unfold in an orderly and predictable manner. The presence of apparent social order in societies of different sizes, organized according to a variety of diverse social principles, puzzled some observers because of their own assumptions about what made social order possible. These ethnologists lived in societies whose leaders assumed that individual human beings were naturally selfish and competitive and thus could live peaceably together only if they were compelled to do so by threat of physical force. That is, they believed that social order was not natural but could result only from the external imposition of power.

6.1 Power

Power often has been understood first and foremost in terms of physical coercion, especially by European philosophers and social scientists, who traditionally define power in terms of one individual's ability to compel others to do what he or she wants them to do. This view of power seemed natural in societies like those of Europe and America that were organized into states. Anthropologists agree that states were not invented in Europe but first appeared several thousand years ago in half a dozen different regions of the world. Anthropologists group these states together, ancient and modern, because they appear to share certain prototypical features. That is, for anthropologists, a **state** is an independent political entity that controls a geographical territory with clear boundaries and that defends itself from external threats with an army and from internal disorder with police. States have specialized institutions to raise revenue by collecting taxes and to carry out other public duties such as maintaining roads and markets. All these tasks become possible because the state monopolizes the legitimate use of physical force.

Certainly, European history, following the religious wars of the sixteenth and seventeenth centuries and the revolutions of the late eighteenth and nineteenth centuries, seemed to prove that nothing less than deadly force in the hands of a strong state will keep people in line. Without the state, according to seventeenth-century philosopher Thomas Hobbes, life was supposed to be "nasty, brutish, and short." And yet, historical and ethnographic materials suggested strongly that, elsewhere in the world, many societies not organized into states had long been able to conduct their external and internal affairs in an orderly fashion. Could it be that power was successfully institutionalized in these societies in forms other than the state?

These kinds of questions have traditionally been asked by **political anthropologists**. These scholars share with political philosophers and political scientists an interest in **politics**: the ways in which power relations (particularly unequal power relations) affect human social affairs. Political anthropologists have paid particular attention to how members of different societies go about making public decisions that affect the society as a whole. They also are interested in why people either accept these decisions as right and proper or criticize them as wrong and improper. Political anthropologists compare how leadership is understood and exercised, how competition between rivals is regulated, and how disputes are settled. In all these areas, people's cultural beliefs and practices clearly play a large role. In recent years, increasing attention has been focused on the ways in which larger regional and global power relations shape opportunities for the exercise of power by local groups (see additional discussion of global issues in Chapter 10).

To study all these dimensions of power requires a view of power that does not limit it merely to **coercive power**, or the use of physical force. For many anthropologists, a more useful definition of **power** would be a generalized capacity to transform. From this point of view, coercion is only one kind of power, and attention must be paid to all those other forms of influence that transform people's practical activities or their ideas about the world *without* relying on physical force. Forms of **persuasive power** range from the charisma of a religious prophet, to the formally proscribed but ubiquitous ability of weaker members of society to manipulate social rules to promote their own well-being, to the outright refusal of compliance shown by factory workers who go on strike.

To speak of persuasive power draws attention to the power of individuals. But how much power can individuals exercise? The answer to this question depends on what an "individual" is understood to be. Unlike most other cultures from other places or times, Western capitalist culture exalts individuals and encourages (or forces) them to reject ties to other people, such as relatives, they have not freely chosen. This position, called *individualism*, is based on a view of human nature that sees individuals as the primordial "natural" units in the human world. Individuals are believed to be endowed by nature with the desire to pursue their own personal self-interest above all else. Individualism was well entrenched in the cultures to which the first social scientists belonged, but evidence from their reading and research caused many of them to question its universality. Some anthropologists have used ethnographic evidence showing the ways that individuals are molded by social, cultural, and historical processes in order to criticize extreme defenses of individualism used by Western elites to justify capitalist cultural practices.

At the beginning of the twenty-first century, anthropologists have mostly rejected the old-fashioned, extreme contrasts between "individual free will" and social, cultural, or historical "determinism." Although they remain critical of defenses of individualism that ignore culture and history, they nevertheless now widely agree that individuals are not robots programmed by their cultures to think and behave only in prescribed ways. Contemporary anthropologists use the term **agency** to refer to individuals' abilities to reflect systematically on taken-for-granted cultural practices, to imagine alternatives, and to take independent action to pursue goals of their own choosing. Unlike deterministic accounts, this view recognizes degrees of individual freedom, but, unlike discussions of "free will," it accepts that people's ideas are always embedded in cultural practices of their own time and place, which restrict in some ways both the alternatives they are able to imagine and their abilities to act freely in pursuit of those alternatives.

6.2 Political Ecology and Political Economy

As the above example of factory workers on strike suggests, for anthropologists, political issues do not develop in a vacuum but are intimately related to other dimensions of collective life, especially economic matters. And attention to economic matters, especially how people make a living, has regularly turned some anthropologists' attention to the relationships between particular societies and the wider environments in which they live. *Ecology* may be defined broadly as the study of the relationships among living organisms and their environments; *ecological anthropology* encompasses a number of anthropological approaches to the study of human populations in terms of the wider ecological contexts to which they must adapt to survive (see Chapter 7 for further discussion of ecological anthropology).

In the middle of the twentieth century, Julian Steward and his followers developed the earliest version of ecological anthropology called **cultural ecology**. Cultural ecology focuses on the way specific, often small-scale societies use culture to fashion adaptations to particular, local ecological settings. This approach resonates with the way anthropologists thought about "societies" and "cultures" at the time: as if they were naturally coherent, self-contained, sociocultural units responsible on their own for adapting (or failing to adapt) to particular kinds of natural environments. At the same time, even though human populations can call on culture to invent tools and forms of social organization that mediate their adaptations to local environments, cultural ecology approached human populations as if they faced the same kinds of adaptive challenges as populations of other species living in the same ecological setting. This approach was shared by other scholars who called themselves *human ecologists*.

But other anthropologists who have adopted ecological approaches to the study of human populations have objected to the way in which traditional cultural ecology ignores history, especially the political history that links particular local populations with their neighbors. These anthropologists, who describe their approach as **political ecology**, draw attention to the ways in which human groups struggle with one another for control of (usually local) material resources. Although some political ecologists emphasize the ways in which ecological features of the local environment shape the political struggle for resource control, others emphasize the way in which the outcome of political struggles determines which groups will have access to how much of which resources. For example, in the nineteenth century, eastern African pastoralists such as the Maasai moved their herds of cattle seasonally across large geographical areas in search of water and fresh grass and attempted to control access to permanent sources of water that could sustain herds in times of drought. But in the early twentieth century, after European colonial rule was established in Kenya and Tanganyika, much of the land that Maasai had traditionally relied upon, together with its water sources, was taken away from them by the colonial government and allotted to other farmers—either other Africans or European settlers. Despite the stated goal of the British colonial administration to increase cattle production, Maasai found it increasingly difficult to maintain their herds on such limited resources. But the administration usually refused to acknowledge how their own policies of land and water management had severely altered the ecological conditions with which herders had to contend. They preferred to blame Maasai herders for trying to maintain herds that were too large to be supported on the land they had (Hodgson 2004).

A similar divide has characterized the work of anthropologists who have studied economic institutions in different cultural settings (*economic anthropology* is more fully discussed in Chapter 7). On one hand, the first economic anthropologists, such as Melville Herskovits (1895–1963), tended to assume the existence of distinct, self-contained societies with varied cultural institutions, including economic institutions, the functioning of which it was the job of the anthropologist to describe and explain. Frequently, it was further assumed that these economic institutions had evolved "naturally" to solve the economic needs of those who used them. Other anthropologists interested in economic relations, however, have rejected the view that economic institutions in particular local societies can be understood on their own terms. Instead, they draw attention to the historical and political factors that have shaped a particular set of economic institutions into their current forms. These anthropologists often see their work as falling within the purview of political anthropology rather than economic anthropology; more specifically, they see their work as falling within the purview of what has been called **political economy**; that is, the focus is on the political creation (and consequences) of the division of labor in society. Political anthropologists studying non-Western societies that have been subject to colonial domination often find a focus on political economy useful. This perspective offers a framework for describing and explaining how capitalist colonialism disrupted indigenous precapitalist political and economic arrangements, reorganized relations of production, expropriated local wealth and power, and promoted the formation of new social classes.

6.3 Disputes and Dispute Resolution

One important focus of political anthropology has been on how the members of different societies, living within different kinds of economic and social institutions, handle their relations with their neighbors. Recall that a key task of the state as a political institution was to defend itself from external attack and from internal subversion. Anthropologists were curious about how societies not organized as states handled these matters. The ethnographic record shows that a variety of mechanisms, formal and informal, have been developed in different times and places. As they often have done when confronted with ethnographic variety, anthropologists invented classifications to sort out the patterns of dispute (and dispute resolution) about which they had information.

Scale is always important when considering these various mechanisms. Consider, for example, the issue of warfare. At the turn of the twenty-first century, when those of us who live in industrialized nation-states think about "warfare," we typically think of a conflict like World War I or World War II in which the professional armies of two or more nation-states clash using modern weapons (machine guns, tanks, bombs, and the like). The war ends when one side concedes defeat, lays down its weapons, and agrees to formal, written terms of surrender. But such a model of warfare has almost nothing in common with the kinds of violent clashes more typically found in smaller-scale, nonindustrial societies without states. To make the differences plain, ethnologists worked out a set of categories that could distinguish modern warfare from these other kinds of conflict.

For example, violent conflicts can be distinguished from one another in terms of how long they last and what goals they are expected to achieve. **Raiding,** for instance, is defined as a short-term use of force with a limited goal, such as stealing a few head of cattle or other material goods, usually from a neighboring group. Pastoral peoples commonly resort to raiding to recover animals they believe are owed them or simply to increase the size of their own herds at the expense of a nearby group of herders. Raiding can be contrasted with **feuding,** which describes ongoing, chronic hostilities between groups of neighbors or kin. Feuds are politically destabilizing because they are potentially endless. Often a feud begins when a member of one kin group takes the life of a member of a neighboring kin group. Relatives of the dead person feel obliged to avenge the death of their kinsman or kinswoman and so vow to take the equivalent of "an eye for an eye, and a tooth for a tooth." In this way, feuding can be seen as a form of negative reciprocity (defined in Chapter 7). Feuding groups do not feel obliged to take the life of the specific individual who killed their relative; the death of any member of the group to which the killer belongs will restore the balance. But the group responsible for the first death will then feel obliged to avenge the death visited on them as repayment for the first death, and so on.

Peoples who engage in feuding are quite aware that this form of retaliation can escalate into a bloodbath. Therefore, some groups have invented cultural institutions that feuding groups can call upon to achieve settlement, such as a **mediator:** a formally recognized, neutral third party to whom the disputing parties can appeal to settle their differences. Mediators have no coercive power of their own but instead rely on the persuasive power of **negotiation**— that is, of verbal argument and compromise—to induce the hostile parties to come to a mutually acceptable resolution of their dispute. Mediators play an exceedingly important role when the parties to a feud are close neighbors who must somehow find a way to coexist despite their mutual grievances. Often mediators appeal to traditional practices designed to mollify the aggrieved party, such as an offer by the offending party of a given amount of material wealth (for example, in livestock or other valuables), a payment frequently referred to as **bloodwealth.** Some anthropologists view the invention of bloodwealth as a major cultural achievement that for millennia has managed to short-circuit feuds and restrain their destructive capacity.

Warfare, by contrast, involves violent conflict on a significantly larger scale. Entire societies mobilize against each other, trying to kill as many members of the other society as possible until one side surrenders to the other. Warfare occurs when persuasive means of dispute resolution, such as diplomacy, either do not exist or have failed or are ignored, and physical combat becomes the only avenue open to settle differences. Of course, none of these classificatory labels is airtight; all of them are designed to highlight what appear to be salient similarities and differences from a political point of view. Real-life cases are always more complex and ambiguous than the labels themselves might suggest. For example, feuding carried out on a grand-enough scale begins to look a lot like warfare.

6.4 Forms of Political Organization

The contrast between feuding and warfare draws our attention back to an issue that has preoccupied so many political anthropologists: Societies that engage in warfare typically have some form of centralized political organization, whereas societies that engage in feuding typically do not. Prehistorians and political anthropologists have compared the different political systems known from archaeology, history, and ethnography. Like the nineteenth-century evolutionists, they recognize four broad types of political systems that appear to have developed over the 200,000 or so years our species has existed and that correlate broadly with other cultural attributes such as subsistence strategies and types of kinship organization (for discussion of subsistence strategies see Chapter 7; for kinship organization see Chapter 8). In the mid-twentieth century, anthropologists like Elman Service and Morton Fried offered new interpretations of cultural evolution that incorporated critiques of nineteenth-century schemes. Their work has influenced most subsequent anthropological discussions of comparative political systems.

The earliest political forms appear to have been **egalitarian**; that is, all (adult) members of the society had roughly equal access to valued resources, both material and social. The oldest human societies we know about archaeologically depended on foraging, and the egalitarian political form associated with this mode of subsistence has been called the **band**. Foraging societies are small in scale; historically and prehistorically, they were few in number and widely scattered across the land. Bands of foragers typically number no more than fifty individuals coresident at the same time. Tasks are assigned on the basis of gender and age, but the division is not rigid. Kinship systems are generally bilateral (defined in Chapter 8), and bands create alliances with one another through marriage. Relations of economic exchange are organized on the basis of reciprocity (defined in Chapter 7).

The domestication of plants and animals marked a major shift in the subsistence strategy, supporting somewhat larger egalitarian social groups that anthropologists call **tribes**. The major social change associated with those who took up *horticulture* (extensive agriculture) or those who began to herd animals is seen in the appearance of unilineal kinship groups (defined in Chapter 8) that became the joint owners of property in the form of farmland or herds. New cultural forms such as age grades (defined in Chapter 5) may create social links that crosscut kinship groups. Kin groups may compete with one another for resources, but they are not ranked hierarchically; indeed, within each kin group, the access of adults to communal resources remains broadly equal.

The first evidence of the erosion of egalitarian political forms is found in those societies organized as **chiefdoms**. Chiefdoms

TABLE 6.1   Forms of Political Organization
Band
Tribe
Chiefdom
State

make use of the same forms of subsistence and kinship as tribes, but new social arrangements show the emergence of distinctions among lineages in terms of status or ranking. In particular, one lineage is elevated above the rest, and its leader (the chief) becomes a key political figure whose higher status often derives from his role in redistributive economic exchanges (defined in Chapter 7). The chief's higher rank (and that of the lineage to which he belongs) gives him an increased opportunity to favor his kin and his supporters with material or social benefits, but he has very limited coercive power. Significant power remains in the hands of lineages, who continue to control their own communal wealth in land or herds.

The social differentiation, ranking, and centralization that are incipient in chiefdoms are fully realized with the appearance of states. The state organization described previously (with its territory, army, police, tax collectors, and so forth) did not appear until well after the invention of intensive agriculture approximately 10,000 years ago, which generated surpluses that could be used to support full-time occupational specialists such as potters, weavers, metalworkers, priests, and kings. (Table 6.1 lists the basic forms of political organization.)

6.5 Social Stratification

As well as monopolizing physical force, state organization enforces **social stratification**, a permanent, inherited inequality between the various component groups of which the society is composed. Anthropologists frequently distinguish between **caste** societies, in which the individual members of distinct stratified groups are not allowed to move out of the stratum in which they were born, and **class** societies, in which some individual social mobility up or down the class hierarchy may occur (see Chapter 5 for details). At the very bottom of a class or caste hierarchy may be found a social category whose access to valued resources is so restricted that members do not even control their own labor. Anthropologists often describe these individuals as **slaves**.

Stratification means that some groups have disproportionate access to valued resources. For example, high-ranking groups may have **sumptuary** privileges; that is, they may be the only members of society entitled to wear certain fabrics or eat certain foods. In stratified societies, moreover, valued resources include not just material **wealth** (for example, land or herds) or cultural **prestige** (for example, esteem or respect) but also power itself. That is, those who rule the state are able to use their monopoly on coercive power to keep the lion's share of wealth and prestige and to perpetuate this inequality from one generation to the next. Because of the elaborate division of labor and its hierarchical organization in stratified castes or classes, state societies often are called **complex societies**, especially by archaeologists and prehistorians who contrast them with the less elaborate and more egalitarian bands and tribes that preceded them chronologically.

Those political anthropologists interested in the evolution of the state frequently have speculated on the processes that could have been responsible for transforming egalitarian political relations that had endured for thousands of years into unequal political relations. Many different single, unique causes, or *prime movers*, have been proposed to account for the emergence of political inequality and centralized hierarchy (for example, population pressure, dependency on irrigation, conquest by neighbors, and environmental circumscription, to name but a few). The consensus among contemporary prehistorians seems to be that no single factor can explain all cases in which inequality and centralization emerged from egalitarian political arrangements. For example, archaeologists have uncovered the remains of many early societies organized as chiefdoms that never developed into states. It seems clear that although certain underlying factors must have been present, contingent historical factors also played an important role.

Some anthropologists are further concerned that preoccupation with explaining the "rise of the state" smuggles back into the analysis assumptions of unilineal evolutionism that had supposedly been expunged long ago. Such a preoccupation can make a drive toward social complexity from band, to tribe, to chiefdom, to state seem inevitable and irresistible, even if the paths to complexity are varied and have not always been taken and even though human history is littered with the fall of states and the disintegration of empires. To the extent that states and empires and other encompassing forms of social complexity are seen as powerful generators of inequality and oppression, moreover, the rise of state control will not necessarily be viewed as progressive, and the disintegration of an empire may be viewed as liberating. Overall, the open-ended unpredictability of future sociopolitical changes can then be openly acknowledged, and more attention can be paid to the ways in which societies organized with different degrees of complexity can coexist with and reshape one another.

6.6 Forms of Political Activity

The classification of political systems as bands, tribes, chiefdoms, and states can be useful even if one is not interested in their possible evolutionary relationships. Many political anthropologists have used these categories as prototypes for distinct forms of political life and have been more interested in exploring how these forms actually work. Such anthropologists have been intrigued by the striking contrast between egalitarianism and inequality, between diffuseness of power in egalitarian societies and centralized monopoly of power in stratified societies. As Meyer Fortes and E. E. Evans-Pritchard put it more than 70 years ago, centralized societies like chiefdoms or states have *heads* (chiefs or kings or presidents), whereas uncentralized societies do not; that is, they are **acephalous** (without heads). As Fortes and Evans-Pritchard noted, acephalous societies were not politically chaotic, but political order in such societies clearly seemed to be the result of cultural mechanisms rather different from the mechanisms upon which centralized societies relied. Many anthropologists set about trying to identify just what those mechanisms were. To describe a band or tribe as "stateless" or "acephalous" is to describe it in terms of what it lacks: a state or a head of state. As indicated previously, however, some anthropologists prefer to describe bands and tribes in terms of what they possess, which is a high degree of political equality accorded to all adults (or, sometimes, to all adult males). People in the United States or Europe tend to equate political equality with forms of electoral democracy. But to do so is misleading because our forms of electoral democracy occur within the framework of a state, whereas the political equality found in egalitarian societies exists apart from the state.

To be sure, we find in bands and tribes many characteristics that might be justly described as "democratic"; for example, political decisions that affect the society as a whole must involve the consent of all adults (or adult males) in the society. But members of egalitarian societies typically do not go to the polls to vote formally for or against a particular policy with the understanding that whichever position gains the most votes wins. Instead, informal discussion and negotiation about alternatives take place among all adults who will be affected, a process that is feasible when the group is small as is typical in most band and tribal societies. Eventually, a decision that all adult members of the society accept emerges from this process, a result known as **consensus**. This does not mean that consensus is easy to achieve. Precisely because no adult in an egalitarian society can force any other adult to do anything, negotiations require enormous verbal skill. Successful negotiators often employ a range of techniques, ranging from indirectly suggesting, to cajoling, to shaming, to predicting dire consequences for failure to comply. In all cases, we are referring here to the exercise of persuasive, not coercive, power.

Not surprisingly, some individuals in egalitarian societies are more skilled, imaginative, and successful negotiators than others, and their achievements do not go unrecognized. Indeed, their achievements lead other members of their society to accord them great prestige. Individuals in bands or tribes who enjoy such prestige may be asked for advice or deferred to when decisions must be made because their past achievements—as hunters or ritual specialists, or fighters or diplomats—give their opinions greater weight than those of ordinary folk. Anthropologists have used the term **headman** to identify such individuals who may be the ones chosen by their fellows to deal with outsiders in ambiguous or threatening situations. In fact, outsiders (such as representatives of a colonial power) often have assumed that members of indigenous groups who mediated between their own group and the colonial administration were leaders with coercive power. As we have seen, however, this assumption was incorrect when applied to headmen in bands or tribes, who have no capacity to force others to do their will. When colonial officials tried to incorporate "headmen" into their chain of command, expecting them to enforce compliance on the local level, they regularly discovered that, despite their prestige, headmen had no power to issue orders or force people to obey them. With the passage of time, under continued colonial rule, headmen often found themselves caught in an untenable position: expected by members of their own tribe to defend tribal interests against the colonial administration and expected by the colonial administration to extract compliance with colonial edicts from fellow tribesmen.

Another well-known anthropological example illustrating the exercise of persuasive power in egalitarian societies is that of the **big man**. Big men are "big" because of their ability to use their personal persuasive skills to arrange complex regional public events that involve kin and neighbors. In New Guinea, for example, big men gain personal prestige by organizing elaborate exchanges of valuables between their own and neighboring tribes. Such exchanges often begin as a kind of bloodwealth exchange: An end to hostilities is negotiated when the aggressors promise to present the aggrieved tribe with a quantity of wealth in the form of pigs, shells, money, and other valuables. Big men compete with one another to organize the collection and presentation of these goods, which is a major achievement given that they have no coercive means to compel other members of their tribe to participate. Moreover, the initial exchange that marks the end of hostilities is rarely the last one. If the tribe that has received wealth wants to maintain or enhance its own prestige, it must eventually reciprocate with a return gift. It falls to big men in the receiving tribe to plan and carry out the reciprocal exchange, and they always aim to return more than they received in order to enhance both their personal reputations and the reputation of their group.

6.7 Social Control and Law

State societies function successfully because all the complex activities that take place within them are monitored by a more-or-less complex army of hierarchically organized public functionaries, each occupying a separate formal office with its own proper responsibilities and coercive powers. This form of public administration, or *bureaucracy*, illustrates another distinctive feature of states as forms of political organization: the **formalization** of a wide range of tasks (see also Chapter 5). To formalize a bureaucratic or political office means to specify, explicitly and publicly, the rights and responsibilities of the officeholder. State societies formalize a wide range of tasks that are carried out by informal or barely formalized means in bands, tribes, and chiefdoms. For example, gossip is a very effective way to enforce conformity in small-scale societies without a police force. By contrast, state societies formalize not only leadership positions but also occupational qualifications and the public social rules that members of the society are expected to obey. Perhaps even more significantly, states formalize the **sanctions**, or penalties, to be meted out if social rules are broken.

Most anthropologists agree that in societies without states, including chiefdoms, proper social conduct is enforced largely by local groups using informal means. For example, in the modern nation-state of Indonesia, many local groups have sometimes resisted attempts by the national government to change the way they do things, insisting that compliance is forbidden by their own *adat*, or "custom." When, however, a centralized government publicly sets forth both explicit formal definitions of right conduct and explicit penalties for failure to observe such standards and backs these definitions with its monopoly on coercive power, anthropologists generally agree that it is appropriate to speak of **law**. In particular, they have been interested in comparing the ways in which law has developed or is administered in noncapitalist state societies.

The appearance of formal law in a state does not mean that informal means of social control disappear. Rather, formal law is ordinarily used to sanction only the most serious crimes such as theft, murder, or treason. Formal laws usually aim to be universal in scope, applying to all members of a society who possess certain attributes, and they usually focus on compliance (or lack thereof) with specific obligations (rights and duties) that all such individuals are expected to honor. Such a system of law is known as **substantive law,** and it is often the most interesting ethnographically because it encodes notions of right conduct that show much cross-cultural variation. Substantive law contrasts with **procedural law,** which describes how those accused of breaking the law are to be treated. Anthropologists who compare legal systems cross-culturally also often distinguish between **civil law,** the breaking of which affects only one or a few individuals, and **criminal law,** which regulates attacks against society or the state. Modern states have developed complex **law codes** in which explicit rules covering many areas of social, economic, and political life are articulated, together with the penalties incurred for breaking them.

Of course, members of any society when accused of breaking the law (informal or formal) often deny that they have done so. As we saw, egalitarian societies have developed their own informal ways of resolving such disputes, including mediation, feuding, and wealth exchange. In state societies, by contrast, formal laws and penalties are accompanied by formal legal institutions, such as **courts,** for resolving disputes. Informal dispute resolution remains in the hands of the affected parties: Recall that feuding kin groups, together with a mediator, must work out a resolution of their differences that satisfies the groups. Different disputants, however, might work out their differences in entirely different ways. It is this lack of uniformity in dispute resolution that a state tries to overcome in two ways. First, the state removes resolution of the dispute from the hands of the parties involved and puts it into the hands of a formal institution, the court; second, it evaluates the disputants' claims against the universal rights and responsibilities encoded in laws with uniform penalties. Because the court is supposed to be an impartial forum, care must be taken to ensure that the truth is told. Thus, all court systems develop rituals designed to achieve that end, such as the administration of oaths or ordeals to those who give evidence. In the end, the formal officers who preside in a court of law (that is, judges)

adjudicate the case before them; that is, based on the law code, they decide how a dispute will be settled.

Clearly, this entire apparatus can exist only in complex state societies producing sufficient surplus wealth to support the specialized formal court system with its law code, lawyers, judges, and punishments. In other words, a formal system of laws requires a formal system of punishments, or penal code, without which a full-fledged court system cannot function. Indeed, this system defines, for the society in which it is found, what formally counts as **crime** and what does not. New laws can be promulgated that turn formerly tolerated behavior (for example, public begging) into a crime or that decriminalize formerly illegal behavior (for example, when taxes are abolished, not paying one's taxes is no longer illegal).

Documenting changes in a legal system can offer important insights into the changing values and practices of the society to which the legal system belongs. One of the most powerful recent changes anthropologists have encountered all over the world involves attempts by citizens to petition their national governments or international institutions for legal rulings that will protect their *human rights* or their *cultural rights*. Often the petitioners are members of so-called traditional, or indigenous, groups who have learned how to operate successfully in regional, national, and international courts of law (see Chapter 10 for a fuller discussion of anthropological studies of human rights and cultural rights).

6.8 Nationalism and Hegemony

Much of the ethnographic data on informal dispute resolution were gathered in societies that once enjoyed political autonomy but at some time in the last 500 years came under the economic or political control of Western colonial powers. To be sure, capitalist colonialism did not affect all areas of the world at the same time or to the same degree, and many precolonial political institutions and practices survived, albeit under changed circumstances, well into the twentieth century. But the last two decades of the twentieth century exhibited an intensified push of capitalist practices into those areas of the globe that previously had been buffered from some of their most disruptive effects. And many political anthropologists in recent years have become less interested in local political particularities and more interested in global processes that increasingly shape the opportunities for local political expression.

Such anthropologists pay attention to political processes that began with the spread of European colonial empires. Political conquest and incorporation within one or another European empire destroyed many indigenous political institutions. However, colonial political practices stimulated colonized peoples to rethink and rework their understanding of who they were and how they should do politics. Much current anthropological investigation focuses on the paradoxical consequences of political independence in former European colonies.

The issues are complex and varied, but many anthropologists have been interested in the phenomenon of **nationalism**. Traditionally, anthropologists used the term **nation** as a synonym for ethnic group or tribe—that is, to identify a social group whose members saw themselves as a single people because of shared ancestry, culture, language, or history. Such nations/tribes/ethnic groups did not necessarily have any connection to political systems that we call states until the late eighteenth century, and especially the nineteenth century, in Europe. By the end of the nineteenth century, many Europeans believed that the political boundaries of states should correspond with cultural and linguistic boundaries—that is, that states and nations should coincide and become **nation-states**. In the latter half of the twentieth century, newly independent postcolonial states tried to realize the nation-state ideal by attempting to build a shared sense of national identity among their citizens, most of whom belonged to groups that shared few or no political or cultural ties in precolonial times.

At the same time, many groups that claim a common "national" identity on the basis of culture or history or language find themselves encapsulated within a larger state or, worse, scattered across the territorial boundaries of more than one state. Following the nation-state logic, many of these groups see themselves as legitimate nations entitled to their own states. As the twenty-first century unfolds, the explosive potential built into these situations has created difficult political challenges for millions of people across the globe and seems to cry out for anthropological analysis.

Many anthropologists have borrowed Benedict Anderson's concept of the nation as an **imagined community** (also discussed in Chapter 2), whose members' knowledge of one another does not come from regular face-to-face interactions but instead is based on their shared experiences with national institutions, such as schools or government bureaucracies, and the bonds created from reading the same newspapers and books. Anthropologists have similarly been influenced by the discussion of the **invention of tradition** by historians Terence Ranger and Eric Hobsbawm. For example, many people believe that the kilt is a form of ancient dress that goes back centuries in the Highlands of Scotland. Although Highland plaids are known from at least the sixteenth century, although they belong to a form of dress that originated in what is today Ireland, and the garment known as the kilt is a "tradition" that was in fact invented in the eighteenth century! The notions of imagined communities and invented traditions both highlight the fact that people in all societies exercise creative agency in every generation to fashion their collective identities and histories out of the accumulated cultural resources available to them. When new communities are successfully imagined and suitable traditions are invented for them, moreover, this cultural labor can make a genuine political difference.

The often violent postcolonial histories of aspiring nation-states, involving coups d'état and civil strife, has demonstrated to participants and observers alike that national identity cannot be imposed by coercion alone. Persuasive power must also be used, which is why anthropologists have drawn on the work of Antonio Gramsci (1891–1937). Reflecting on the reasons why the Italian nation-state was so much less successful in becoming unified than its European neighbors, Gramsci emphasized a contrast between the role of authoritarian domination (or coercive power) and hegemony (or persuasive power) that many contemporary social scientists have found useful. **Domination** can put a regime in power, but domination alone will not keep it in power. For one thing, it is expensive to keep soldiers and police on constant alert against resistance; for another, the people come to resent continued military surveillance, which turns them against the regime. This is why long-term stability requires rulers to use persuasive means to win the support of their subjects, thereby making a constant public show of force unnecessary. Gramsci used the term **hegemony** to describe control achieved by such persuasive means.

Anthropologists have also been influenced by another approach to understanding politics in modern states that was developed by French historian Michel Foucault. Foucault and his colleagues identified a new form of state power that began to emerge in Europe after the Middle Ages and was fully developed by the nineteenth century. This form of power, which they called **biopower**, was concerned with managing the behavior of populations of living bodies—the living populations of citizens—in ways intended to promote national policies. Before the 1600s, according to Foucault, political thinkers like Machiavelli were mainly concerned with ways in which a ruler could maintain control of the state. By the seventeenth century, however, political thinkers began to ask new questions about how a ruler might govern a state in ways that preserved and protected its members. They likened governing a state to managing a household, but they realized that to achieve this they would need more detailed information about the people, goods, and wealth of the state that needed to be managed. How many citizens were there—men, women, and children? How healthy were they? What kinds of goods did they produce, and in what quantities? Were there any ways in which the state could intervene to improve their health and increase the quality and quantity of goods they produced? To answer these questions, state bureaucracies invented the discipline of statistics to count and measure people and things subject to state control.

When European states began to govern their populations on the basis of such statistics, they began to engage in what Foucault called *biopolitics* or **governmentality**. For example, statistics on population and production might indicate to bureaucrats that a famine was likely. Bureaucrats might then calculate both potential losses the state might suffer and a set of policies, based on these calculations, that suggested the best way to intervene to prevent or lower those losses. Using statistical information to manage populations in terms of governmentality is widespread today. The outcomes of particular forms of governmentality may be negative or positive for individuals: For example, statistical information can be used to plan mass immunization against communicable diseases, but it can also be used to identify all young people of a certain age in order to draft them into the military. In a globalizing world full of nation-states, anthropologists encounter different forms of governmentality, as well as attempts by citizens to evade or manipulate them. (See the discussion in Chapter 10 on anthropology of the environment.)

A variety of tactics can be used to build hegemony, including neutralizing opposition from powerful groups by granting them special privileges and articulating an explicit **ideology** that explains the rulers' right to rule and justifies inequality. If the ideology is widely promulgated throughout the society (for example, in schools, through media) and if rulers make occasional public gestures that benefit large sections of the population, they may forestall rebellion and even win the loyalty of those whom they dominate. Because hegemony depends on persuasive power, however, it is vulnerable to the critical attention of the powerless, whose reflections on their own experiences may lead them to question the ruling ideology. They may even develop interpretations of their political situation that challenge the official ideology. Sometimes the term **hidden transcripts** is used to describe these alternative (or *counterhegemonic*) understandings because they are frequently too dangerous to be openly proclaimed. Because hidden transcripts offer an alternative, however, they offer openings to more sustained critiques of the status quo that eventually could lead to open rebellion.

Many anthropologists find the concept of hegemony to be useful because it offers a way of showing that oppressed groups that do not rise up in open revolt against their oppressors have *not* necessarily been brainwashed by the hegemonic ideology. Rather, such groups possess sufficient agency to create counterhegemonic interpretations of their own oppression. If they do not take up arms, therefore, this is probably because they have accurately concluded that rebellion would not succeed under current conditions. The concepts of hegemony and hidden transcripts help anthropologists demonstrate that political concepts such as "freedom," "justice," and "democracy" do not have fixed meanings but may be the focus of cultural and political struggle between powerful and powerless groups in a society.

For Further Reading

POWER

Arens and Karp 1989; Wolf 1999

POLITICAL ANTHROPOLOGY

Fried 1967; Lewellen 2003; Service 1962, 1975; Sharma and Gupta 2006; Vincent 2002

LAW

Harris 1997; Nader 1997; Pospisil 1971

NATIONALISM

Anderson 1983; Hughey 1998; Tambiah 1997

HEGEMONY AND HIDDEN TRANSCRIPTS

Hobsbawm and Ranger 1992; Scott 1987, 1992, 1998

POLITICAL ECOLOGY

Biersack and Greenberg 2006; Hodgson 2004

7

Economic Anthropology

The key terms and concepts covered in this chapter, in the order in which they appear:

domestic groups

subsistence strategies
domestication
foragers
food producers
transhumance
slash-and-burn
swidden
shifting cultivation
extensive agriculture
intensive agriculture
mechanized
  industrial
  agriculture
surpluses

capitalism

formalists

economy

scarcity
substantivists
original affluent
  society
modes of exchange
reciprocity
redistribution
potlatch
leveling mechanisms

proletariat
bourgeoisie

labor
means of production
consumers
alienation
mode of production
classes
relations of
  production

peasant
cash crops
production for use
production for
  exchange

use
vs
exchange
value

formal economy
informal economy
global assemblages

consumption
basic human needs

ecological
  anthropology
behavioral ecology
conspicuous
  consumption
anthropology of
  food and nutrition

119

S INCE ITS FORMATIVE YEARS as a discipline, anthropology has been interested in the many and varied ways in which human beings in different societies make a living. In the late nineteenth century, anthropologists devoted much attention to the tools and techniques developed by various peoples to secure their material survival and well-being in a range of climates and habitats. Indeed, the objects people made for these purposes—spears, snares, fish-nets, bows, arrows, hoes, plows, baskets, and the like—formed the collections of early ethnological museums in Europe and North America. Early anthropological theorists paid particular attention to the activities in which these objects figured, called the "arts of subsistence" by Lewis Henry Morgan (1818–81).

7.1 The "Arts of Subsistence"

Morgan focused on large-scale variation in patterns of the arts of sub-sistence in different human societies when he constructed his grand unilineal scheme of cultural evolution (a discussion of this approach is found in Chapter 12). His key criterion for ranking subsistence patterns was technological complexity: the simpler the toolkit, the more "primitive" the society's arts of subsistence. Morgan's final scheme encompassed three great "ethnical periods"—Savagery, Bar-barism, and Civilization—through which, he claimed, every human society either had passed or would pass as it evolved.

Morgan assumed that the society in which he lived had evolved further and faster than others on the globe and that, consequently, the arts of subsistence characteristic of those other societies could accurately be described in terms of not only what they possessed but also what they lacked. Thus, "savages" were all those peoples who had never domesticated plants or animals for their subsistence. Morgan subdivided them into lower, middle, and upper categories based on the complexity of the tools and skills they had devised for living off nature's bounty; "upper savages," for example, not only controlled fire and fished but had mastered the bow and arrow. The invention of pottery signaled for them the beginning of Barbarism. "Barbarians" herded animals and/or cultivated plants, and they also invented new subsistence tools and techniques such as iron implements and irrigated fields. All these advances were incorporated into the next ethnical period, that of "Civilization," which Morgan believed could be identified as soon as writing appeared.

Anthropologists have long since removed terms like *savage* and *barbarian* from their professional analytic vocabulary. They are well aware of how evolutionary schemes like Morgan's can be (and have been) used to rationalize the domination of the world by so-called civilized societies. But one does not have to accept these aspects of Morgan's analysis to recognize the importance of his classification of different arts of subsistence. He had collected information about a wide range of societies. He had hypothesized that variation in their arts of subsistence was systematic, showing up, for example, in correlations between particular technological developments and particular forms of social organization (especially kinship organization) in **domestic groups** (those whose members live in the same household). Karl Marx and Friedrich Engels (1820–95) read Morgan and were persuaded that his ethnical periods documented changes in precapitalist modes of production. But again, one does not have to be a Marxist to be both impressed and puzzled by the patterns of subsistence to which Morgan drew attention.

7.2 Subsistence Strategies

In early-twentieth-century North America, Franz Boas and his students, having roundly rejected unilineal schemes of cultural evolution, were suspicious of grand explanations and unwilling to make far-reaching claims (for more on the Boasians, see Chapter 12). But they were interested in documenting with great care how particular peoples went about making their living. As a result, throughout much of the first half of the twentieth century, anthropologists hesitated to do more than offer a loose categorization of the various subsistence strategies adopted by the peoples of the earth. The

subsistence strategies identified—hunting and gathering (foraging), pastoralism, horticulture, and agriculture—reiterated the distinctions that Morgan had recognized.

The key feature distinguishing these strategies is **domestication:** regular human interference with the reproduction of other species in ways that makes them beneficial to ourselves. Hunter-gatherers— now usually called **foragers** or food collectors—are those who do not rely on domesticated plants or animals but instead subsist on a variety of wild foodstuffs. Their knowledge of their habitats is encyclopedic, and they manage to live quite well by roaming over large tracts of land in search of particular seasonal plant foods, water sources, or game. By contrast, practitioners of the other three subsistence strategies depend on domesticated species and so are sometimes referred to as **food producers** rather than food collectors. Pastoralists rely on herds of domesticated animals, such as cattle, camels, sheep, or goats, and regularly move these herds, sometimes over great distances, as water and forage in one area are used up. In many parts of the world, these movements are patterned in yearly cycles of **transhumance** as herders move from dry-season pastures to wet-season pastures and back again.

Horticulturalists cultivate domesticated plants by using human labor and simple tools and techniques to modify local vegetation or soil texture before planting their crops. In **slash-and-burn** or **swidden** cultivation, for example, hand tools are used to cut down all vegetation except large trees from an area to be planted. The vegetation is then burned, and the ash serves to fertilize the crops. But swidden farmers can use a particular field for only a few growing seasons before the soil is exhausted and must be left fallow for several years to regenerate. As a result, swidden farmers must move on to clear new fields every few years, which is why their practices are sometimes also referred to as **shifting cultivation.** Shifting cultivation is highly productive and energy efficient, but it functions well only when farmers have access to enough land to live on while old fields lie fallow long enough (often from 7–10 years or more) to regenerate. Shifting cultivation is thus sometimes also called **extensive agriculture** because so much land is required to support so few people.

Only with **intensive agriculture** do we find societies exploiting the strength of domestic animals by harnessing them to more complex tools like plows and growing and harvesting crops with the help of irrigation and fertilizers. Intensive agriculturalists first appeared some 10,000 years ago in Southwest Asia. Their farming practices are intensive because the techniques they employ allow them to produce more than shifting cultivators could produce on the same amount of land while keeping their fields in continuous use. Contemporary intensive farming practices, often called **mechanized industrial agriculture**, rely on industrial technology for machinery, fertilizers, pesticides, and herbicides. This form of agriculture uses vastly more energy than does shifting cultivation, but it enables a few farmers to produce enormous amounts of food on vast expanses of land, their "factories in the field." (Table 7.1 lists the major subsistence strategies.)

Intensive agriculture marked an important break from forms of extensive agriculture because it allowed farmers to produce **surpluses** beyond what they required to survive from harvest to harvest and still save enough seed for the next year's crop. Agricultural surpluses supported the first ancient civilizations by making possible new and complex forms of social organization, involving a specialized division of labor that promoted technical developments in all areas of material life. Writing and its analogues (such as the *quipu* in Andean civilizations) did not drive these changes, but they were extremely useful for various kinds of political, economic, and social record-keeping.

TABLE 7.1 Major Subsistence Strategies

Foraging

Herding

Extensive agriculture (also known as horticulture, slash-and-burn, swidden)

Intensive agriculture

Industrialized food production

7.3 Explaining the Material Life Processes of Society

In general, fieldworking cultural anthropologists have left investigation of the origin of subsistence strategies and the rise of ancient civilizations to archaeologists and prehistorians. Given the pernicious use to which extreme and exaggerated unilineal evolutionary claims had been put in the nineteenth century, early-twentieth-century ethnographers preferred to document the enormous amount of diversity still to be found in the material life of living societies. But this pursuit of cultural documentation, apparently for its own sake, struck later generations of anthropologists as unwarranted and pernicious in its own way. They sensed there were patterns to be detected and explained, and this required a professional willingness to develop theories that could generalize across particular cases.

One attempt to reintroduce theory into the anthropological study of material life was made by Melville Herskovits (1895–1963) around the time of World War II. Herskovits urged anthropologists to borrow concepts and theories from neoclassical economics, the scholarly discipline rooted in Adam Smith's efforts in the eighteenth century to make sense of the new Western economic system later known as **capitalism**. Herskovits was persuaded that the concepts and theories of neoclassical economies had been refined to such a degree of scientific objectivity and formal precision that they could be applied to economies very different from the one they originally were invented to explain. Those anthropologists who decided to follow Herskovits's suggestion came to be known as formal economic anthropologists, or **formalists**.

Formalists took concepts like *supply*, *demand*, *price*, and *money*, which had successfully been used to analyze economic activity in capitalist market economies, and searched for their analogues in noncapitalist societies. They realized, of course, that many such societies had no system of coinage performing all the functions Western money performed. But they noted that objects like iron bars or lengths of cloth or shells often seemed to be used much the way people in capitalist societies used money, as a medium of exchange or measure of value. And so formalists tried to use the ideas neoclassical economists had developed about money to make sense of, say, the way people in society X used shells. Or formalists might analyze customs in which a groom's family offered material valuables to the family of a bride to solemnize a marriage. This transaction looked very much like a "purchase" with something other than money being offered in exchange for a highly valued "good," the bride. Formalists thus tried to explain how much it "cost" to "pay for" a bride in the society. Adopting the assumptions of neoclassical theory, formalists assumed that each party to a marriage transaction would try to get as much as possible out of the transaction while giving as little as possible in return. Therefore, the number of cattle actually accepted in exchange for a bride would be subject to the forces of supply and demand, and the parties would agree on a "bride price" whereby supply and demand balanced.

Formalists did not view themselves as ethnocentric when they analyzed noncapitalist economic activities in this way. They thought that any culture-bound features of the concepts and theories they were using had long since been eliminated. But other anthropologists disagreed. These critics believed that, despite its sophistication, neoclassical economic theory still bore many traces of its origins in Western capitalist society. Perhaps the most obvious trace could be seen in the neoclassical understanding of just what **economy** meant: buying cheap and selling dear in order to maximize one's individual utility (or satisfaction).

Critics pointed out that neoclassical economics, like capitalist society itself, subscribes to a particular view of human nature that sees isolated individuals as the only genuine human reality. That is, human beings are viewed as creatures who are by nature self-interested egoists who always act in ways that will increase their own individual well-being. Moreover, human beings all live under conditions of **scarcity**; that is, there will never be enough of all the material goods they desire to go around. As a result, the basic human condition consists of isolated individuals competing with one another, under conditions of scarcity, to obtain as much of what they want for as little as possible. Society might view such behavior negatively as selfish or greedy, but according to the neoclassical view, human society is artificial, secondary, and legitimate only to the extent that social rules do not interfere with each individual's pursuit of his or her own self-interest. That is, in a world of isolated individuals competing for access to scarce goods, looking out for Number One turns out to be a good thing—indeed, the *rational* thing to do—because putting others' needs first might interfere with maximizing one's own happiness.

Still, Adam Smith and others believed that when competition was carried out among individuals of more-or-less equal wealth and power, private vice could lead to public virtue. For instance, if you tried to cheat your customers, word would get around, and they would buy from other producers, causing you to lose money. Thus, you end up happier if you make your customers happy as well. Indeed, the price on which the two of you decide ideally ought to provide the best possible value either party might hope to obtain.

Only if such a view of human nature is accepted does neo-classical economic theory make sense. But anthropological critics were convinced that such a view of universal "human nature" could *not* make sense of the economic practices ethnographers had discovered in the *particular*, noncapitalist societies where they had done fieldwork. They pointed out that many economic systems were built on the assumption that human beings were, first and foremost, social creatures with legitimate obligations to other members of the societies in which they lived. Indeed, economic arrangements in such societies were shaped to the contours of other religious or political or kinship institutions in the society. That is, economic activities were *embedded* in the noneconomic institutions that made the society as a whole function properly. Rather than a measure of how individuals universally allocated scarce resources among alternative (presumably universal) ends, these anthropologists preferred to think of an economy as the concrete (and particular) way in which material goods and services were made available to members of a given society. Capitalism might allow individuals the freedom to pursue their own self-interest apart from the interests of others, but such an economic system was a recent and unusual addition to the ethnographic and historical record. Those anthropologists who defined economic systems in terms of their substantive institutional arrangements for provisioning their members came to be called **substantivists**. Substantivists argued that describing noncapitalist economic systems using neoclassical economic theory could only distort and misrepresent what was actually going on in those economies.

American anthropologist Marshall Sahlins, a leading substantivist, set about debunking what he viewed as formalist misrepresentation of economic life in noncapitalist societies. After surveying a substantial ethnographic literature that described how foragers made a living, for example, Sahlins asked Westerners to reconsider how people might come to obtain more than enough of whatever they wanted—that is, become "affluent." Since the rise of industrial capitalism, many people assumed that the only path to affluence was by producing much, but Sahlins argued that a second "Zen road" to affluence consisted in desiring little. Foragers had very few material desires, and the habitats in which they lived were more than able to satisfy these needs. Thus, Sahlins concluded, the **original affluent society** was not industrial capitalism but foraging.

7.4 Modes of Exchange

Sahlins also drew upon the work of economic historian Karl Polanyi, whose work also showed just how misleading it was to suppose that all human economies, in all times and places, had been based on capitalist principles, given that the key components of market capitalism had come together only within the past few centuries in western Europe. Polanyi distinguished among different **modes of exchange**— the patterns according to which distribution takes place—and argued that the capitalist mode of market exchange followed principles quite different from the principles that governed exchange in pre- or noncapitalist societies. He emphasized two particular noncapitalist modes of exchange: reciprocity and redistribution.

Sahlins borrowed Polanyi's classification of modes of exchange and tested them against a wide range of ethnographic data. He found that **reciprocity** governed exchange in small, face-to-face societies, especially those whose members lived by foraging. He also distinguished different forms of reciprocity. *Generalized* reciprocity involved no record-keeping, and parties assumed that exchanges would balance out in the long run. *Balanced* reciprocity required both that a gift be repaid within a set time limit and that goods exchanged be of roughly the same value. *Negative* reciprocity involved parties who repeatedly tried to get something for nothing from one another in a relationship that might continue over time, each trying to get the better of the other.

Redistribution as a mode of exchange requires the presence in a society of some central person or institution. Goods flow toward this central point and are then redistributed among members of the society according to their cultural norms of what is appropriate. (Table 7.2 lists the basic modes of exchange.) Varieties of redistribution range from such non-Western institutions as the **potlatch** practiced by the indigenous inhabitants of the northwest coast of North America to the income tax and social welfare institutions of modern nation-states. To the degree that they exist, modes of redistribution act as **leveling mechanisms**; that is, they shrink gaps between rich and poor. In noncapitalist societies integrated by redistribution, the person responsible for amassing and then redistributing goods earned great prestige for his generosity, but he was often materially worse off afterward than most other members of the group. Polanyi pointed out that both reciprocity and redistribution may persist in societies organized along capitalist lines. In the United States, for example, exchange relations between parents and children ordinarily are governed by generalized reciprocity, and the collection of income taxes and the dispersal of government subsidies to citizens involves redistribution; but most goods and

---

TABLE 7.2 Modes of Exchange

Reciprocity
   Generalized
   Balanced
   Negative
Redistribution
Market exchange

services are produced and exchanged by means of capitalist market mechanisms.

Similar ideas were developed by French anthropologist Marcel Mauss (1872–1950), one of Emile Durkheim's colleagues, who contrasted *gift* economies of small-scale societies (based on reciprocity and laden with culturally significant noncommercial values) with *commodity* exchanges (in which a good's value is mediated by the capitalist market). A number of contemporary European anthropologists have developed Mauss's ideas to mount their own critique of market-centered analyses of noncapitalist economies.

7.5 Production, Distribution, and Consumption

The debate between the formalists and the substantivists about the proper way to do economic anthropology became quite bitter in the late 1950s and early 1960s, with no resolution. Hindsight reveals that the divide between them was sharpened by the Cold War. In the Cold War years (which stretched from the late 1940s to 1989, when the Soviet Union broke apart), the ideological opposition between the Western "free market" (the First World) and Soviet "communism" (the Second World) was so strong that anyone in the United States who questioned neoclassical economic theory ran the risk of being labeled a "communist sympathizer," which was virtually synonymous with "traitor." Especially after the Cuban Communist Revolution in 1959, views of economic life in other societies that validated the assumptions of neoclassical theory were encouraged by members of the political elite in the United States. They hoped that, by showing a free-market route to economic prosperity, they could keep nations newly freed from colonial control (soon to be known as the Third World) from following Cuba's example. But in the late 1960s and 1970s, citizens in Western countries began to question publicly the official Cold War rhetoric, and some economic anthropologists began to study texts by Marx and his followers, and they tried to use Marxian analysis to make sense of their ethnographic data on non-Western economic life.

Although the debates among economic anthropologists can sometimes still become bitter, dialogue remains viable because all of them, regardless of perspective, largely agree that economic life can be divided into three phases: production, distribution, and consumption. Neoclassical economic theorists, dazzled by the power of modern capitalist markets, saw *distribution* to be key. After all, prices are set in the market when suppliers of goods and buyers of goods reach agreement about how much to offer for what. Historically, capitalist markets developed under circumstances in late-medieval European cities in which certain kinds of people—merchants, artisans—engaged in economic transactions free of the feudal obligations that controlled exchange between lords and peasants in rural areas. This freedom from obligations to others—the freedom to take one's chances buying and selling in the market—seemed to validate a view of human nature that eventually justified neoclassical economic theory in a society in which capitalism had triumphed. And it was a theory written primarily from the point of view of those who had engaged in free-market transactions and prospered.

Marx and his followers, however, paid attention to those whose participation in free capitalist markets kept them mired in poverty. These were the **proletariat**, the workers who toiled for wages in factories owned by the **bourgeoisie**, capitalists who sold for profit the commodities the workers produced. The very different positions of capitalists and workers were due to the fact that capitalists owned or controlled the means of production, whereas the workers owned nothing but their own labor power, which, in order to survive, they were forced to sell to the capitalist at whatever price he was willing to pay. The unequal relationship between workers and owners under capitalism meant that, when both met in the market to buy and sell, some of them (the capitalist owners) had considerably greater economic power than did others (the workers). The origins of that inequality required that attention be paid to the *production* phase of economic life.

Labor is a central concept for a Marxian analysis of economic production, especially social labor in which people work together to transform the material world into forms they can use. In noncapitalist economic systems, people ordinarily work with others to produce goods for their own use, using tools and materials that belong to them. Under industrial capitalism, all this changes. For example, workers might produce shoes in a factory, but shoes, along with the tools, technology, and materials used to make them—what Marx called the **means of production**—belong to the factory owner, not to the workers. Instead, workers receive money wages in exchange for their labor. With these wages, they are supposed to purchase in the market food, clothing, and other goods to meet their subsistence needs; that is, they become **consumers**. Because workers compete with one another for scarce wage work, they must put their individual self-interest first if they are to survive; thus, they come to view their fellows as rivals rather than comrades.

In all these ways, Marx argued, life under capitalism separates workers from the means of production, from the goods they produce, and from other human beings, a situation he called **alienation**. For Marxists, therefore, the isolated individual who is the hero of the capitalist version of "human nature" is actually an alienated social being forced into existence under the historically recent economic conditions of western capitalism. Marx and most of his followers were interested in understanding how these socioeconomic conditions had developed in western European societies. Like Marx, many also found the situation intolerable and believed that the point was not to understand society but to change it.

7.6 Mode of Production

Among those Marxian concepts that have been the most important in economic anthropology, we will emphasize here only one: the mode of production. A **mode of production** refers generally to the way the production of material goods in a society is carried out. Not only does it involve the tools, knowledge, and skills needed for production (the means of production), but it also depends on a particular division of social labor in terms of which different groups, or **classes**, of people are responsible for various productive activities, or the **relations of production**. Marx characterized European capitalism as a mode of production, and he contrasted it with the feudal mode of production that preceded it. In the feudal and capitalist modes of production, the central division of labor was between rulers and ruled: lords and peasants in feudalism and owners and workers in capitalism.

A key element in the Marxian analysis of modes of production concerns the nature of the relationship linking classes to one another in a particular society. Marx's point was that, although both classes had to work together for production to succeed, their economic interests were nevertheless contradictory because of their different relations to the means of production. Eventually, Marx predicted, these class contradictions would undermine the mode of production, leading to a revolution that would bring forth a new and improved mode of production.

Anthropologists studying economic conditions in different societies do not necessarily accept Marx's prophecies about revolution. But they have wondered whether the noncapitalist economic patterns revealed by fieldwork might usefully be understood as different modes of production. Some anthropologists working in Africa, for example, thought that the economic arrangements they observed among people who organized their societies (and their economic activities) on the basis of kinship might be framed as a *lineage mode of production*. That is, the opposed "classes" were elder and younger groups within particular lineages that owned important economic resources like agricultural land and implements (the *means* or *forces of production*). Like owners and workers under capitalism, the economic interests of elders and juniors were opposed and might lead to conflict: Elders wanted to maintain their control over the forces of production, and juniors wanted to take it away.

7.7 Peasants

Other anthropologists have talked about a *peasant mode of production* observable in many contemporary Latin American societies. These societies are seen to be divided into classes, with peasants dominated by a ruling class of landowners and merchants. Anthropologists use the word **peasant** to refer to small-scale farmers in state societies who own their own means of production (simple tools, seed, and so forth) and who produce enough to feed themselves and to pay rent to their landlords and taxes to the government. Anthropologists have wondered how much autonomy peasants might have in particular societies and under what circumstances that autonomy might be undermined by changing political and economic conditions. For example, what happens to peasants who are forced to deal with the increasing penetration of capitalist market relations?

Many of the world's peasants were first introduced to capitalism as a result of European colonization. Colonized peasants continued to grow subsistence crops for their own consumption, but European colonizers regularly encouraged them to grow other crops that they could sell for cash. Sometimes these **cash crops** had been produced traditionally; in northern Cameroon in Africa, for example, peanuts were a traditional crop that local farmers began to sell on the market during the colonial period. Other times, cash crops were introduced from outside; in northern Cameroon, French colonial authorities introduced the variety of cotton now grown by local farmers and sold for cash. In this way, peasant **production for use** was pushed by colonial authorities in the direction of capitalist **production for exchange** in the capitalist market.

This form of agriculture (producing crops to be sold for cash rather than to be consumed at home) has had far-reaching effects on the economic life of peasants. To begin with, peasant farmers could continue to produce much of what they consumed, using the money they received for their cash crops to purchase imported goods or to pay taxes and school fees. Unfortunately, by using some of their land to plant cash crops, less was left to plant subsistence crops. In many cases, this led over time to increasing dependence on the money from cash cropping to buy necessities that could no longer be produced, or produced in sufficient quantity, to keep a peasant household going. Indeed, many ethnographers have documented situations in which members of ostensibly "peasant" households regularly leave the farm to perform wage work on plantations or in factories. Without this additional income, many peasant households would collapse.

And this situation, in which members of the same household are alternately farmers and wage workers, has led anthropologists to wonder exactly how to describe and analyze what they are seeing. Are these peasants no longer truly peasants? Does their increasing reliance on wage work for survival mean that they have been "captured" by an expanding capitalist mode of production? Have they been transformed from peasants into a rural proletariat? Some anthropologists have argued that this is indeed the case, and some ethnographic materials support their arguments. In other cases, however, the situation is more complicated. Although members of peasant households rely on wage work to keep their families going, they continue to farm, producing much of the food needed for household subsistence. Some anthropologists refer to these peasants-who-are-also-wage-workers as members of an emerging *peasantariat.*

From the perspective of neoclassical economic theory, members of this Third World peasantariat were understood to be "in transition" from "traditional" to "modern" (that is, capitalist) economic practices. Neoclassical theory argued that capitalist economic institutions (those that paid taxes, obeyed government regulations, and otherwise adhered to rules set down by the state) belonged to sectors of the modern, national, **formal economy** into which other, so-called backward sectors of the **informal economy** eventually would be absorbed. In former colonies that had recently become independent states, the formal sector was often quite small whereas the informal economy was very important, especially in urban areas. Many migrants supported themselves and their families by engaging in all sorts of unregulated, untaxed, and even illegal economic activities, from smuggling, to peddling, to selling cooked food. They also might move from a period of employment within the formal sector to a period in the informal sector and then back again. Moreover, anthropological fieldwork showed that many people active in the formal or informal economy of a city might also have ties to relatives in rural areas who engaged in agriculture and with whom they pooled economic resources.

Anthropologists working in many so-called Third World societies documented the seeming resilience of precapitalist economic arrangements confronted by more recent capitalist institutions. Such arrangements seemed to be delaying indefinitely the promised transition from "tradition" to capitalist "modernity." Anthropologists of a neoclassical bent might argue that the transition was still inevitable

TABLE 7.3   Modes of Production
Kin-ordered
Tributary
Capitalist
Articulating

but would simply take longer than they originally predicted. Some anthropologists of a Marxian bent, however, argued that the situation was more complex. Rather than precapitalist institutions being replaced by capitalist institutions, they said, what had emerged in these settings was a new kind of social formation composed of two or more *articulating modes of production*. That is, in settings such as former European colonies in Africa, precapitalist modes of production and the capitalist mode of production, each organized according to different relations of production, appeared to have adapted to each other's presence. Under such circumstances, individuals and groups could turn to precolonial relations of production when participation in capitalist relations of production was too costly or did not suit them for other reasons. (Table 7.3 lists some basic modes of production.)

The argument that two or more modes of production might articulate with each other, however, seemed to imply that individual modes of production were not bounded, self-contained sets of economic arrangements. As a result, the concept of mode of production met a fate similar to concepts of society or culture that at one time had also been conceived as bounded and self-contained. After 1989, the end of the Cold War ushered in worldwide changes in economic, political, social, and cultural relations. The boundaries separating societies, nation-states, and cultural traditions from one another turned out to be far more porous than many anthropologists had assumed, and capitalism seemed to engulf the entire world. But as people, wealth, ideas, ideologies, and material goods began to move across these boundaries in unprecedented ways, new possibilities for new ways of life—and new varieties of capitalism—began to take shape. One consequence may be that, as a result of such changes, there will be no room in the post–Cold War world for those people formerly known as peasants.

Perhaps the most striking development in recent years has been the way different kinds of people have come together in new ways and have begun connecting a variety of heterogeneous cultural and material elements to one another, often in places far from their points of origin, to make possible brand-new kinds of economic, political, social, and cultural institutions. Some anthropologists use the term **global assemblages** (Ong and Collier 2005) to identify such newly articulated institutional arrangements, distinctive both for their unprecedented geographical reach and for the diverse nature of the people, objects, and meanings that they link together (see Chapters 10 and 12 for more details).

7.8 Consumption

The final phase of economic activity is **consumption,** when the goods or services produced in a society are distributed to those who use them up, or consume them. Most economists, whether of neoclassical or Marxian persuasion, traditionally have had little to say about why it is that *these* goods and *these* services (as opposed to other goods and services) get produced and distributed. Either consumption preferences are reduced to the idiosyncratic, unpredictable, and inexplicable choices of individuals (as in neoclassical economics) or they are reduced to basic biological needs (as when Marx stated that human beings need first to eat and drink before they can make history). Some anthropologists have made similar arguments. Bronislaw Malinowski, for example, wanted to show that "primitive" peoples were in fact no less human than their "civilized" counterparts. He argued that, although all viable societies must satisfy their members' universal **basic human needs** for food, shelter, companionship, and so forth, each society has invented its own cultural way of meeting those needs. Malinowski's approach, however, failed to address the question of *why*, for example, Trobriand Islanders satisfied their need for food with yams and pork rather than with, say, sorghum and beef.

One way to answer such a question is to point out that yams and pork are locally available for consumption in the ecological setting to which Trobriand Islanders have become adapted. Answers of this form to questions about consumption were developed in the 1950s by *cultural ecologists*, some of the early practitioners of ecological anthropology. **Ecological anthropology** studies the ways in which human populations relate to other populations of living organisms in a particular material environment. As we saw in Chapter 6, the kinds of societies studied by cultural ecologists tended to be small-scale units understood as responsible on their own for adapting (or failing to adapt) to particular kinds of local environments. Although these populations might be connected with other neighboring populations through trade relationships, cultural ecologists generally assumed that the diet and other basic material resources of any population depended largely on what their local environment afforded. Thus, it is not surprising that desert-dwelling herders of camels or cattle do not depend on saltwater shellfish to meet their basic subsistence needs, nor that people who hunt and gather for a living in the rainforest do not depend on fast-food hamburgers. At the same time, research in cultural ecology has revealed the unusual range of local foods on which some populations come to depend, as well as the impressive varieties of food that can be collected and consumed even by people with very simple technologies, such as those who gather and hunt for a living.

Not all ecologically oriented anthropologists agree about the importance of culture in human evolution and ecological adaptation. Some (but not all!) anthropologists who practice what is called **behavioral ecology** have been heavily influenced by the ideas of sociobiology, a school of evolutionary thought that assigns culture little or no role in human adaptation but instead argues that genetically driven and/or environmentally driven necessity keeps culture "on a short leash." Other anthropologists influenced by cultural ecology, such as *culture inheritance theorists*, find sociobiological accounts inadequate. They argue that symbolic culture

TABLE 7.4 Approaches to Consumption

Basic human needs (Malinowski)
Ecological
   Behavioral ecology
   Cultural ecology/cultural inheritance theory
Cultural/historical/contingent

has played a key mediating role in human evolution and that it continues to exert powerful influences on contemporary human ecological adaptations. (Table 7.4 lists some basic approaches to consumption.)

Culture appears to play an important role in consumption patterns for at least two reasons. First, consumption preferences often are more closely linked to membership in particular social groups than to the ecological setting in which one lives. Second, the consumption preferences people share often involve goods and services that are not easily explained with reference to basic human biological needs. A good illustration is the pattern found in capitalist societies that sociologist and economist Thorstein Veblen (1857–1929) labeled conspicuous consumption. **Conspicuous consumption** involves the purchase and public display of goods known to be costly and unnecessary for basic survival. For example, many people who live in the suburban United States find it necessary to own an automobile for transportation. Getting from home to work to the supermarket to the shopping mall in no way requires the extra speed and power of a sports car, but many suburban residents nevertheless spend tens of thousands of dollars for sports cars. Veblen suggested, and cultural anthropologists agree, that people who drive these cars do so more for symbolic than for practical reasons. That is, they want to show other people (especially those whom they want to impress) that they are so prosperous, they are not limited to purchasing goods for purely practical reasons; rather, they can "waste" cash on non-necessities, on luxurious, ostentatious extras.

Even though our continued existence requires a minimal level of food, water, shelter, and human companionship, ethnographic research has powerfully demonstrated that it is virtually impossible to separate people's indispensable *needs* from their discretionary *wants*. This is because all human groups attach cultural meanings to the goods and services they consume. For this reason, Veblen's pattern of conspicuous consumption within the capitalist mode of production constitutes only one end of the continuum of consumption practices documented for different societies with different modes of production. In all cases, what people consume makes a statement about who they are, what they value, and where their loyalties lie.

The anthropological study of consumption has contributed greatly to a critique of approaches to consumption that would reduce it to biological necessity or individual idiosyncrasy. Anthropologists have shown how consumption patterns associated with such seemingly unproblematic foods as meat or sugar have been shaped by cultural beliefs and practices in different times and places. In particular, they have shown what happens when consumption goods are turned into commodities under capitalism. This process has been under way for several centuries and continues to affect the consumption choices of people throughout the world. For example, fast food becomes highly valued when capitalist production draws into the paid workforce those household members who previously had the time, energy, and resources to prepare meals from scratch. And the particular kind of fast food people come to prefer increasingly is shaped by expensive media campaigns designed to persuade consumers using the same tactics Veblen described a century ago.

Many anthropologists have begun to examine the way consumption practices in non-Western societies are changing as a result of these processes, however, and they have been able to show that non-Western consumers of Western-made products are not simply the dupes of advertisers and marketers. Daniel Miller, in particular, has been able to help redirect the focus of studies of commodity consumption by anthropologists. Under conditions of globalization, Miller argues, mass-produced commodities are on offer to people everywhere, and anthropologists should not automatically assume that choosing to consume such commodities signifies the triumph of Western imperialism or the loss of cultural authenticity. Rather, members of many societies in the world have selected some Western material goods and rejected others based on how well they think those goods will enhance or enrich their own traditions. Thus, Otavalan weavers in Ecuador purchase television sets to entertain weavers producing traditional textiles in locally owned shops, with the result that production increases, enabling Otavalan merchants to more successfully compete in an international market for indigenous products. Under such circumstances, the consumption of television strengthens, rather than diminishes, Otavalan tradition. Indeed, the recent successful participation in the institutions of international capitalism by non-Western peoples, from Otavalan textile producers to Japanese, Chinese, and Korean businessmen, suggests that there is perhaps nothing intrinsically "Western" about capitalism or consumption. These cases suggest that consumption of goods sold in capitalist markets need not mean that consumers are being obediently programmed to replace their own traditions with Western consumerism; instead, they are *indigenizing* and *domesticating* capitalist practices and consumer goods as they create their own alternative versions of modernity.

7.9 The Anthropology of Food and Nutrition

Food makes up an important proportion of the commodities that people all over the world are increasingly purchasing in the market, and the way in which foods are produced, distributed, and consumed in global capitalist markets has altered health and dietary practices everywhere. As a result, some anthropologists have turned their attention to the consequences of these changes, especially in societies where people used to grow most of their own food, harvest crops or butcher animals using local methods, and cook and serve meals according to traditional cuisines. (See also Chapter 11.) Anthropologists in this field also study how culturally variable attitudes toward food and eating affect local understandings of fatness and thinness, as well as the connections people make between food and cultural identity. Such work has led to the emergence of a new area of specialization, the **anthropology of food and nutrition.**

One prominent example of the commodification of food consumption involves the expansion of fast foods into communities across the globe. Coca-Cola and McDonald's hamburgers are regularly deplored as prime examples of Western (or U.S.) cultural imperialism, responsible for the destruction of local cuisines and their replacement with commodified foods. Anthropologists have shown, however, that this interpretation is incomplete and misleading. For instance, Daniel Miller (1998) challenged this view with his study of Coca-Cola, which has been sold in Trinidad since the 1930s. Because Coca-Cola spreads through franchises, the bottling plant that originally produced Coke in Trinidad was locally owned; because the plant needed to import only Coca-Cola concentrate from the U.S. corporation, the local owner purchased all other necessary ingredients locally in Trinidad. Eventually, this bottling company was exporting soft drinks throughout the Caribbean, becoming an important local economic force. It bottled other soft drinks in addition to Coca-Cola and competed with other local bottling companies, which shaped company decisions about new flavor lines. The Trinidadians Miller knew did not associate drinking Coke with attempts to copy people in the United States. Not only had the industrial production of Coke and other soft drinks been indigenized, the consumption of Coke was incorporated into a set of local, Trinidadian understandings about beverages that divides them into two basic categories: "red, sweet drinks" and "black, sweet drinks." In this framework, Coke is simply an up-market black, sweet drink used as a mixer with rum, which is also locally produced.

Anthropologists who have studied the multiplication of McDonald's fast-food restaurants all over the world echo Miller's observations. McDonald's, like Coca-Cola, spreads through franchises, which allows every local McDonald's restaurant to be locally managed and to develop a menu customized to local tastes. Like Coca-Cola in Trinidad, McDonald's must also find a place for itself in the food and dining landscape of every community where a restaurant is located. In the early 1990s, for example, when it first arrived in Beijing, China, McDonald's was associated with the United States, and the food was not especially appealing to adult Chinese who ate there. At the same time, the "American-ness" of the restaurant meant that Chinese customers experienced the fantasy of visiting a foreign country every time they walked into McDonald's. In addition, Chinese clients associated America with modernity, and they were positively impressed by the modern industrial efficiency showcased by the restaurant space, including its kitchen, and by its smiling, disciplined workers. Customers were also attracted to the clean, open, egalitarian, family- and woman-friendly ambiance of the dining experience, with clean bathrooms, which contrasted starkly with traditional Chinese institutions and practices associated with meals taken outside the home. The res-taurant space also provided a setting where newly affluent work-ers could celebrate milestones (including birthday parties) in new ways that seemed appropriate in an urban Chinese setting remod-eled by capitalist economic practices (Yan 2005).

During the same period, McDonald's also opened a restaurant in Moscow, Russia, and similarly attempted to accommodate itself to local tastes, securing local sources of beef for the hamburgers and of potatoes for the French fries and emphasizing these local sources in their advertising. As Russian consumers became more familiar with hamburgers and French fries, they began to incor-porate them into their own domestic food practices. As in Bei-jing, however, the restaurant buildings themselves were especially attractive to Russian consumers, who indigenized them by hold-ing private celebrations there, including birthday parties for their children. In both cities, people who visited McDonald's were not interested in eating quickly and leaving, and local employees did not push them to do so. These "slow" dining practices reflect the fact that, outside the United States, fast-food restaurants regularly attract economically better-off customers who linger over their meals; these establishments are not regarded as low-status eateries designed to feed working-class or poor people quickly and cheaply. At the same time, McDonald's employees in Moscow allowed visitors to the city to use the clean restrooms to bathe and wash their clothes and permitted homeless children to finish the food customers left behind on their trays. All these practices permitted Muscovites to indigenize McDonald's so thoroughly that many of them forgot that McDonald's was "foreign" and began to think of McDonald's as just another local restaurant (Caldwell 2005). Surprising ethnographic findings of these kinds inform ongoing work by anthropologists on the complexities of production, marketing, and consumption of food in a global capitalist economy.

For Further Reading

ECONOMIC ANTHROPOLOGY

Carrier 2006; Gudeman 2001; Halperin 1994; Littlefield and Gates 1991; Plattner 1989; Sahlins 1972; Wilk and Cliggett 2007

PEASANTS

Kearney 1996; Netting 1993; Wolf 1962, 1982

CONSUMPTION

Coe and Coe 1996; Colloredo-Mansfeld 1999; Fiddis 1991; Miller 1995, 1998; Mintz 1985, 1996

MONEY

Weatherford 1997

FOOD AND NUTRITION

Caldwell 2005; Counihan 2004; Counihan and Van Esterik 2008; Miller 1998; Mintz 1985; Watson 2006; Watson and Caldwell 2005; Yan 2005

8

Relatedness: Kinship and Descent

The key terms and concepts covered in this chapter, in the order in which they appear:

relatedness
kinship
new reproductive technologies
descent
consanguineal kin
adoption

bilateral descent
cognatic descent
bilateral kindred

unilineal descent
patrilineal
agnatic
matrilineal
uterine

unilineal descent groups
patrilineage
matrilineage
lineage
clan
kinship terminologies
fictive kin
generation
gender
affinity
collaterality
bifurcation
relative age
sex of linking relative
parallel cousins
cross cousins

PEOPLE IN ALL SOCIETIES live in worlds of social ties. They consider themselves to be connected to other people in a variety of different ways and also consider that there are some people to whom they are not connected at all. Some anthropologists refer to these socially recognized connections as **relatedness**. There are many forms of relatedness that may be recognized in a given society, based on such categories as friendship, marriage, adoption, procreation, descent from a common ancestor, common labor, coresidence, sharing food, and sharing some kind of substance (blood, spirit, or nationality, for example). One of the most important forms of relatedness that has interested anthropologists since the birth of the field in the late nineteenth century has been **kinship**: the various systems of social organization that societies have constructed on principles derived from the universal human experiences of mating, birth, and nurturance. Members of Western societies influenced by the sciences of biology and genetics frequently believe that kinship relationships are (or should be) a direct reflection of the biology and genetics of human reproduction. Nevertheless, they are aware that, even in their own societies, kinship is not the same thing as biology.

8.1 Kinship Versus Biology

Europeans and North Americans know that in their societies mating is not the same as marriage although a valid marriage encourages mating between the partners. Similarly, all births do not constitute valid links of descent; in some societies, children whose parents have not been married according to accepted legal or religious specifications do not fit the cultural logic of descent, and many societies offer no positions that they can properly fill. Finally, not all acts of nurturance are recognized as adoption. Consider, for example, the status of foster parents in the United States whose custody of the children they care for is officially temporary and can terminate if someone else clears the hurdles necessary to adopt those children legally.

Thus, mating, birth, and nurturance are ambiguous human experiences, and culturally constructed systems of kinship try to remove some of that ambiguity by paying selective attention to some aspects of these phenomena while downplaying or ignoring others. For example, one society may emphasize the female's role in childbearing and base its kinship system on this, paying little formal attention to the male's role in conception. Another society may trace connections through men, emphasizing the paternal role in conception and reducing the maternal role to that of passive incubator for the male seed. A third society may encourage its members to adopt not only children to rear but adult siblings for themselves, thus blurring the link between biological reproduction and family creation. Even though they contradict one another, all three understandings can be justified with reference to the panhuman experiences of mating, birth, and nurturance.

Every kinship system therefore emphasizes certain aspects of human reproductive experience and culturally constructs its own theory of human nature, defining how people develop from infants into mature social beings. Put another way, kinship is an *idiom*: a selective interpretation of the common human experiences of mating, birth, and nurturance. The result is a set of coherent principles that allow people to assign one another membership in particular groups. These principles normally cover several significant issues: how to carry out the reproduction of legitimate group members (marriage or adoption), where group members should live after marriage (residence rules), how to establish links between generations (descent or adoption), and how to pass on social positions (succession) or material goods (inheritance).

Collectively, kinship principles define social groups, locate people within those groups, and position the people and groups in relation to one another both in space and over time. While this set of principles may be coherent, it is also open to modification, negotiation, and even legal challenge as is shown by the ambiguities and questions raised by the consequences of **new reproductive**

technologies—technologically mediated reproductive practices such as in vitro fertilization, surrogate parenthood, and sperm banks. New types of kin ties are also being created in the United States through the process of organ transplantation from brain-dead individuals to people who need organs to survive. To the surprise of some of the professionals who manage organ transplantation, the recipients and families of the donors not only want to meet one another but also have developed kin relationships (Sharp 2006). A man in his mid-60s who received the heart of a teenager now calls the donor's sister "Sis," and she calls him "Bro." The donor's mother, in her mid-50s, and the recipient call each other "Mom" and "Son." Sharp found that for the people involved the transplanted organ was believed to carry some essence of the donor with it, and this powerfully connected the recipient to the kin of the donor. This was particularly true in the relationship of the donor's mother to the recipient. (See also Chapter 11.)

8.2 Descent

Discussions in anthropology tend to specialize in different aspects of kinship. Culturally defined connections based on mating are usually called *marriage* and are often referred to as *affinal* relationships (the term is based on *affinity*, which means "personal attraction"). These relationships, which link a person to the kin of his or her spouse, will be discussed in the next chapter. In this chapter, we consider culturally defined relationships based on birth and nurturance, which anthropologists traditionally call **descent**. People related to one another by descent are what English speakers often refer to as "blood" relations and are socially relevant connections based on either parent–child relationships or sibling relationships. Anthropologists use the term **consanguineal kin** to refer to all those people who are linked to one another by birth as blood relations (the word comes from the Latin *sanguineus*, meaning "of blood"). In addition, however, a consanguineal kinship group may include individuals whose membership in the group was established not by birth but by means of culturally specific rituals of incorporation that resemble what Euro-Americans call **adoption**. Incorporation via adoption often is seen to function in a way that parallels consanguinity because it makes adopted persons and those who adopt them of the "same flesh." The transformation that incorporates adoptees frequently is explained in terms of *nurturance*: feeding, clothing, sheltering, and otherwise attending to the physical and emotional well-being of an individual for an extended period.

Ethnographers have shown repeatedly that kinship bonds established by adoption can be just as strong as bonds established through birth. An interesting recent example comes from research among groups of gay and lesbian North Americans who established enduring "families by choice" that include individuals who are not sexual partners and who are unrelated by birth or marriage. Given that these chosen family ties are rooted in ongoing material and emotional support over extended periods of time, one might reasonably suggest that the people involved have based their relationships on nurturance and have "adopted" one another.

Because they are based on parent–child links that connect the generations, relations of descent have a time depth. In establishing patterns of descent, the cultures of the world rely on one of two basic strategies: either people are connected to one another through *both* their mothers and fathers or they are connected by links traced *either* through the mother *or* the father but not both.

8.3 Bilateral Descent

When people believe themselves to be just as related to their father's side of the family as to their mother's side, the term that is used is **bilateral descent** (this is sometimes also referred to as **cognatic descent**). Anthropologists have identified two different kinds of kinship groups based on bilateral descent. One is the *bilateral descent group*, an unusual form that consists of a set of people who claim to be related to one another through descent from a common ancestor, some through their mother's side and some through their father's; the other is the *bilateral kindred*, a much more common form that consists of all the relatives, related through males or females, of one person or group of siblings.

The **bilateral kindred** is the kinship group that most Europeans and North Americans know. A bilateral kindred forms around particular individuals and includes all the people linked to that individual through kin of both sexes—people usually called *relatives* in English. These people form a group only because of their connection to the central person, known in the terminology of kinship as *Ego*. In North American society, bilateral kindreds assemble at events associated with Ego: when he or she is baptized, confirmed, bar or bat mitzvahed, married, or buried. Each person within Ego's bilateral kindred has his or her own separate kindred. For example, Ego's father's sister's daughter has a kindred that includes people related to her through her father and her father's siblings—people to whom Ego is not related. This is simultaneously the major strength and major weakness of bilateral kindreds. That is, they have overlapping memberships, and they do not endure beyond the lifetime of an individual Ego. But they are widely extended, and they can form broad networks of people who are somehow related to one another.

Kinship systems create social relationships by defining sets of interlocking statuses and roles (defined in Chapter 5). Thus, a man is to behave in the same way to all his "uncles" and in another way to his "father," and they are to behave to him as "nephew" and "son." (Perhaps he owes labor to anyone he calls "uncle" and is owed protection and support in return.) In anthropology, these are referred to as the *rights and obligations of kinship*. In a bilateral kindred, the "broad networks of people who are somehow related to one another" means that no matter where a person may be, if he or she finds kin there, the person and the kin have a basis for social interaction. This basis for interaction is different from the possible social interactions that the person might have with strangers (in this case, nonkin).

Organization in bilateral kindreds is advantageous when members of social groups need flexible ways of establishing ties to kin who do not live in one place. They are also useful when valued resources, such as farmland, are limited and every generation must be distributed across available plots in an efficient and flexible manner. Bilateral kindreds become problematic, however, in at least four kinds of social circumstances: when clear-cut membership in a particular social group must be determined, when social action requires the formation of groups that are larger than individual families, when conflicting claims to land and labor must be resolved, and when people are concerned with perpetuating a specific social order over time. In societies that face these dilemmas, unilineal descent groups usually are formed.

8.4 Unilineal Descent

The second major descent strategy, **unilineal descent,** is based on the principle that the most significant kin relationships must be traced through *either* the mother *or* the father but not both. Unilineal descent groups are found in more societies today than are any other kind. Those unilineal groups that are based on links traced through a person's father (or male kin) are called **patrilineal** (or **agnatic**); those traced through a mother (or female kin) are called **matrilineal** (or **uterine**). (Note that lineages are institutions—people do not choose whether they'd like to be patrilineal or matrilineal; these are the standardized long-established social forms through which they learn about individuals and groups to whom they are related and how to interact with them.)

Unilineal descent groups are found all over the world. They are all based on the principle that significant relationships are created via links through one parent rather than the other. Membership in a unilineal descent group is based on the membership of the appropriate parent in the group. In a patrilineal system, an individual belongs to a group formed by links through males, the lineage of his or her father. In a matrilineal system, an individual belongs to a group formed by links through females, the lineage of his or her mother. "Patrilineal" and "matrilineal" do not mean that only men belong to one and only women to the other; rather, the terms refer to the principle by which membership is conferred. In a patrilineal society, women and men belong to a **patrilineage** formed by father–child links; similarly, in a matrilineal society, men and women belong to a **matrilineage** formed by mother–child connections. In other words, membership in the group is in principle unambiguous: An individual belongs to only one lineage. This is in contrast to a bilateral kindred in which an individual belongs to overlapping groups.

Talk of patrilineal or matrilineal descent focuses attention on the kind of social group created by this pattern of descent: the lineage. A **lineage** is composed of all those people who believe they can specify the parent–child links that connect them to one another through a common ancestor. Typically, lineages vary in size from 20 or 30 members to several hundred or more.

Many anthropologists have argued that the most important feature of lineages is that they are corporate in organization. That is, a lineage has a single legal identity such that, to outsiders, all members of the lineage are equal in law to all others. In the case of a blood feud, for example, the death of any opposing lineage member avenges the death of the lineage member who began the feud; the death of the actual murderer is not required (feuding is defined in Chapter 6). Lineages are also corporate in that they control property, such as land or herds, as a unit.

Finally, until the modern nation-state extended its reach, lineages were the main political associations in the societies that have them. Individuals had no political or legal status in such societies except through lineage membership. Members of lineages had relatives who were outside the lineage, but their own political and legal status derived from the lineage to which they belong.

Because membership in a lineage is determined through a direct line from father or mother to child, lineages can endure over time and in a sense have an independent existence. As long as people can remember their common ancestor, the group of people descended from that common ancestor can endure. Most lineage-based societies have a time depth that covers about five generations: grandparents, parents, Ego, children, and grandchildren.

When members of a descent group believe that they are in some way connected but cannot specify the precise genealogical links, they compose what anthropologists call a **clan**. Usually, a clan is made up of lineages that the larger society's members believe to be related to one another through links that go back to mythical times. Sometimes the common ancestor is said to be an animal that lived at the beginning of time. The important point to remember in distinguishing lineages and clans is that lineage members can specify the precise genealogical links back to their common ancestor ("Your mother was Eileen, her mother was Miriam, her sister was Rachel, her daughter was Ruth, and I am Ruth's son") whereas clan members ordinarily cannot ("Our foremother was Turtle who came out of the sea when this land was settled. Turtle's children were many and for many generations raised sweet peas on our land. So it was that Violet, mother of Miriam and Rachel, was born of the line of the Turtle . . ."). The clan is thus larger than any lineage and also more diffuse in terms of both membership and the hold it has over individuals.

Historically, anthropologists have shown how lineages might endure over time in societies in which no other form of traditional organization lasted, becoming the foundation of social life in the society. Although lineages might be the foundation of social life, this does not mean that they are immovable and inflexible. People can use lineage and clan membership to pursue their interests. Because lineage depth frequently extends to about five generations, the exact circumstances of lineage origins can be hazy and open to negotiation. Perhaps "Miriam" and "Rachel" from the preceding example have another sister whom everyone "forgot about" until someone appears who claims lineage membership as a descendant of the forgotten sister. If there are good reasons for including this descendant in the lineage, this claim might well be accepted.

By far the most common form of lineage organization is the patrilineage, which consists of all the people (male and female) who believe themselves to be related to one another because they are related to a common male ancestor by links through men. The prototypical kernel of a patrilineage is the father–son pair. Female members of patrilineages normally leave the lineage to marry, but in most patrilineal societies, women do not give up their membership in their own lineages. In a number of societies, women play an active role in the affairs of their own patrilineages for many years—usually until their interest in their own children directs their attention toward the children's lineage (which is, of course, the lineage of their father, the woman's husband).

By contrast, in a matrilineal society, descent is traced through women rather than through men. Superficially, a matrilineage is a mirror image of a patrilineage, but certain features make it distinct. First, the prototypical kernel of a matrilineage is the sister–brother pair—a matrilineage may be thought of as a group of brothers and sisters connected through links made by women. Brothers marry out and often live with the families of their wives, but they maintain an active interest in the affairs of their own lineage. Second, the most important man in a boy's life is not his father (who is not in his lineage) but his mother's brother from whom he will receive his lineage inheritance. Third, the amount of power women exercise in matrilineages is still being debated in anthropology. A matrilineage is not the same thing as a *matriarchy* (a society in which women rule); brothers often retain what appears to be a controlling interest in the lineage. Some anthropologists claim that the male members of a matrilineage are supposed to run the lineage, even though there is more autonomy for women in matrilineal societies than in patrilineal ones; they suggest that the day-to-day exercise of power tends to be carried out by the brothers or sometimes the husbands. A number of studies, however, have questioned the validity of these generalizations. Trying to say something about matrilineal societies in general is difficult because they vary a great deal. The ethnographic evidence suggests that matrilineages must be examined on a case-by-case basis.

For Jews, Jewishness—membership in the Jewish people—has historically been passed matrilineally. A man or a woman whose father was Jewish but whose mother was not would have to go through a ritual that would incorporate them into the Jewish people while such was not the case for people whose mother was Jewish (in the United States, the Reform movement of Judaism has recently moved to accept any person who has at least one parent who is Jewish as Jewish). This has led to interesting consequences in Israel as assisted reproduction has become more common. Israel is a pronatalist state, meaning that having children is encouraged, and the national health system in Israel supports access to reproductive technologies to all women, married or not, who wish to have children. Following the logic of

Jewishness being passed matrilineally, then, means that the children of Jewish women who have conceived through in vitro fertilization are automatically Jewish, and the religious background of the sperm donor is irrelevant. Indeed, due to a particular complication in Jewish family law, it may actually be better in certain instances if the sperm donor is *not* Jewish (Kahn 2000).

8.5 Kinship Terminologies

People everywhere use special terms to address and refer to people they recognize as kin; anthropologists call these **kinship terminologies**. Consider the North American kinship term *aunt*. This term seems to refer to a woman who occupies a unique biological position, but it in fact refers to a woman who may be related to a person in one of four different ways: as father's sister, mother's sister, father's brother's wife, or mother's brother's wife. From the perspective of North American kinship, all those women have something in common, and they are all placed into the same kinship category and called by the same kin term. Prototypically, one's aunts are women one generation older than oneself and are sisters or sisters-in-law of one's parents. However, North Americans may also refer to their mother's best friend as "aunt." By doing so, they recognize the strength of this system of classification by extending it to include **fictive kin** (also discussed in Chapter 5).

Despite the variety of kinship systems in the world, by the middle of the twentieth century, anthropologists had identified six major patterns of kinship terminology based on how people categorized their cousins. The six patterns reflected common solutions to structural problems faced by societies organized in terms of kinship. They provided clues concerning how the vast and undifferentiated world of potential kin may be organized. Kinship terminologies suggest both the external boundaries and the internal divisions of the kinship groups, and they outline the structure of rights and obligations assigned to different members of the society.

The major criteria that are used for building kinship terminologies are listed here, from the most common to the least common:

◆ *Generation.* Kin terms distinguish relatives according to the **generation** to which the relatives belong. In English, the term *cousin* conventionally refers to someone of the same generation as Ego.

- *Gender.* The **gender** of the individual is used to differentiate kin. In Spanish, *primo* refers to a male cousin and *prima* to a female cousin. In English, cousins are not distinguished on the basis of gender, but *uncle* and *aunt* are distinguished on the basis of both generation and gender.

- *Affinity.* A distinction is made on the basis of connection through marriage, or **affinity**. This criterion is used in Spanish when *suegra* (Ego's spouse's mother) is distinguished from *madre* (Ego's mother). In matrilineal societies, Ego's mother's sister and father's sister are distinguished from each other on the basis of affinity. The mother's sister is a direct, lineal relative, and the father's sister is an affine; they are called by different terms.

- *Collaterality.* A distinction is made between kin who are believed to be in a direct line and those who are "off to one side," linked to Ego through a lineal relative. In English, the distinction of **collaterality** can be seen in the distinction between mother and aunt or between father and uncle.

- *Bifurcation.* **Bifurcation** distinguishes the mother's side of the family from the father's side. The Swedish kin terms *morbror* and *farbror* are bifurcating terms, one referring to the mother's brother and the other to the father's brother.

- *Relative age.* Relatives of the same category may be distinguished on the basis of **relative age**—that is, whether they are older or younger than Ego. Among the Ju/'hoansi of southern Africa, for example, speakers must separate "older brother" (*!ko*) from "younger brother" (*tsin*).

- *Sex of linking relative.* This criterion is related to collaterality. The **sex of linking relative** distinguishes cross relatives (usually cousins) from parallel relatives (also usually cousins). Parallel relatives are linked through two brothers or two sisters.

Parallel cousins, for example, are Ego's father's brother's children or Ego's mother's sister's children. Cross relatives are linked through a brother–sister pair. **Cross cousins** are Ego's mother's brother's children or father's sister's children. The sex of either Ego or the cousins does not matter; the important factor is the sex of the linking relatives.

For Further Reading

KINSHIP

Carsten 2000, 2003, 2007; Collier and Yanigasako 1987; Parkin 1997; Parkin and Stone 2004; Peletz 1995; Schneider 1968, 1984; Stone 2001, 2009

ADOPTION

Weismantel 1998

NEW REPRODUCTIVE TECHNOLOGIES

Kahn 2000; Strathern 1992

REPRODUCTION AND POWER

Ginsburg and Rapp 1995

GENDER

Brettell and Sargent 2008; Karkazis 2008; Lancaster and DiLeonardo 1997; Lewin 2006

9

Marriage and Family

The key terms and concepts covered in this chapter, in the order in which they appear:

marriage
exogamy
endogamy

neolocal
bilocal
patrilocal
virilocal
matrilocal
uxorilocal
avunculocal
ambilocal

monogamy
polygamy
plural marriage
polygyny
polyandry
bride service

bridewealth
dowry
hypergamy

sororate
levirate

family
conjugal family
nonconjugal family
nuclear family
polygynous family
extended families
joint families
blended family
family by choice

divorce

Anthropological discussions of marriage and the family complement discussions of descent and round out our study of relatedness. As we saw in Chapter 8, the complexities and ambiguities of descent are many. The study of marriage and the family offers just as many complications, the first of which is how to define these terms.

9.1 What Is Marriage?

If we take what Euro-Americans call *marriage* as a prototype of a particular kind of social relationship, we discover in all societies institutions that resemble what people in the United States would call marriage. At the same time, the range of beliefs and practices associated with these institutions is broad, and the degree of overlap is not great. Nevertheless, we tend to classify all these institutions as *marriage* because of the key elements they do have in common. On these grounds, a prototypical **marriage** involves a man and a woman, transforms the status of the man and the woman, and stipulates the degree of sexual access the married partners may have to each other, ranging from exclusive to preferential. Marriage also establishes the legitimacy of children born to the wife and creates relationships between the kin of the wife and the kin of the husband.

We stress the prototypical nature of our definition because, although some societies are quite strict about allowing females to marry only males, and vice versa, other societies are not. The ethnographic literature contains many examples of marriage or marriagelike relationships that resemble the prototype in every respect except that the partners may be two men or two women (as defined according to biological sex criteria) or a living woman and the ghost of a deceased male. Sometimes these marriages involve a sexual relationship between the partners; sometimes they do not. Apparently, the institution we are calling *marriage* has been viewed by members of many societies as so useful and valuable that they allow it to include partners of many different kinds—even though in all cases the prototype people have in mind seems to be a union between a man and a woman. Thus, the ethnographic evidence demonstrates that claims that human marriage has always been between a man and a women are simply false.

Examining the definition of marriage just offered, we note that marriage is a rite of passage: The parties go from the social status of single to the social status of married. In every society, this transformation of status is accompanied by adoption of new roles, but the rights and obligations associated with these roles vary enormously from culture to culture. Prototypically, among the rights and obligations of spouses are socially sanctioned sexual relations with each other. But, again, the nature and exclusivity of these sexual relations vary from culture to culture: Some cultures insist that the partners may have sex only with each other; some view sexual encounters outside marriage less seriously for one partner (usually the husband) than for the other partner; and at least one culture allowed the husband and wife to have sexual intercourse if they wish, but after spending one night together, they needed never see each other again.

In most cultures, it is assumed that the married partners will have children, and the institution of marriage provides the children with a legitimate ascribed social status, based on who their parents are. In some cases, it is as if the father's and the mother's statuses were plotted on a graph, allowing the status of their child to be placed precisely in the social space where the x- and y-axes intersect; in other cases, the child's status depends solely on the position of one or the other parent. In addition, in most cultures, marriage creates formal relationships between the kin of the husband and the kin of the wife. By contrast, while mating may produce grandparents, it cannot produce in-laws or a formal relationship between the parents of the father and the parents of the mother. This aspect of marriage also has important social consequences.

9.2 Whom to Marry and Where to Live

Societies use kinship systems to exercise control over the marriages contracted by their members. When marriage rules specify that a person is to marry outside a defined social group—extended family, lineage, clan, class, ethnic group, or religious sect, for example—anthropologists say that the society in question practices **exogamy** (or *out-marriage*). The opposite situation—in which a person is expected to marry *within* a defined social group—is called **endogamy**. These patterns may be obligatory (i.e., strictly enforced) or merely preferred.

Once married, the spouses must live somewhere. Anthropologists have identified six patterns of postmarital residence. **Neolocal** residence, in which the new partners set up an independent household at a place of their own choosing, should be familiar to people who have grown up in the United States, Canada, and most of Europe. Neolocal residence tends to be found in societies that are more or less individualistic in their social organization, especially those in which bilateral kindreds also are found. Neolocal residence exists throughout the world but is most common in nation-states and in societies bordering the Mediterranean Sea. Some societies with bilateral kindreds have **bilocal** residence patterns in which married partners live with (or near) either the wife's or the husband's parents. Despite this flexibility in allowing married partners to make decisions regarding where they might live, very few societies with bilocal residence have been described in the anthropological literature.

The most common residence pattern in the world, in terms of the number of societies in which it is practiced, is **patrilocal** residence in which the partners in a marriage live with (or near) the husband's father. (In older anthropological writing, the term **virilocal** is sometimes used to distinguish residing with the husband's kin from residing specifically with the husband's father, for which the term *patrilocal* was reserved.) Patrilocal residence is strongly associated with patrilineal descent systems—about 85 percent of societies in which postmarital residence is patrilocal are also patrilineal. If children are born into a patrilineage and inherit from the father or other patrilineage members, then there are advantages to rearing them among the members of the lineage.

When the partners in a marriage live with (or near) the wife's mother, anthropologists use the term **matrilocal** residence. (Again, in older anthropological writing, the term **uxorilocal** is sometimes used to refer to residence with the wife's kin, as distinct from living with the wife's mother.) Matrilocal residence is found exclusively in matrilineal societies (some matrilineal societies are patrilocal). Anthropologists who study matrilineal societies have observed that sometimes the married partners live with the husband's mother's brother. This is based on the logic of matrilineal descent in which the socially significant older male in a man's life is his mother's brother because he is a member of the man's matrilineage while his own father is not. In these cases, anthropologists use the term **avunculocal** residence, building on the word *avuncular*, meaning "of uncles." As might be expected, avunculocal residence is found only in matrilineal societies, and in contrast to matrilocal residence, it emphasizes the inheritance and labor patterns linking men in a matrilineage. A rare pattern called **ambilocal** residence is associated with ambilineal descent in which the married partners may live with either the husband's or wife's group. This term is sometimes used interchangeably with the term *bilocal* and can be used to distinguish this pattern in unilineal societies from the pattern in bilateral societies.

9.3 How Many Spouses?

You may have noticed that we use the phrase *married partners* rather than the more common *married couple*. This is because the number of people who may be married to one another at the same time also varies across cultures. The major distinction is between societies that permit more than one spouse to a person and those that do not. A marriage pattern that permits a person to be married to only one spouse at a time is called **monogamy**. The term can also be used to refer to any marriage in which one person has only one spouse.

The term **polygamy** is used to refer to marriage patterns in which a person may have more than one spouse, a practice also sometimes called **plural marriage**. Polygamy has two major forms: polygyny and polyandry. **Polygyny** is a marriage pattern in which a man may be married to more than one woman at a time. It is the most common of all marriage patterns in the world in terms of number of societies in which it is permitted. Polygyny enables a lineage, especially one with male children, to establish alliances with many other lineages through marriage.

In polygynous societies, it should be noted, not every man has more than one wife. In Islamic societies, for example, a man is permitted to have as many as four wives, but only on the condition that he can support them all equally well. Today, some Muslim authorities argue that "equal support" must be emotional as well as material. Furthermore, convinced that no man can feel exactly the same toward each of his wives, they have concluded that monogamy must be the rule. Other polygynous societies set no limit on the number of wives a man can marry. However, regardless of any limitations on the number of wives, polygynous societies are faced with a real demographic problem: Because the number of men and women in any society is approximately equal, for every man with two wives, there is one man without a wife. To help solve this problem, men may be obliged to wait until they are older to marry, and women may be pressed to marry at a very young age; but even these practices do not completely eliminate the imbalance. As a result, polygyny is regularly connected with power in societies that practice it. That is, those men who are rich and powerful have multiple wives; those men who are poor and powerless either cannot marry, marry very late, have relationships outside of marriage, or marry women who are equally dispossessed.

Polyandry, a pattern in which a woman is married to more than one man at a time, is the rarest of the three marriage patterns. In some polyandrous societies, a woman may marry several brothers. In others, she may marry men who are not related to one another and who all will live together in a single household. The tendency in polyandrous societies—especially in those in which a woman marries a set of brothers—is to intensify the connections between lineages and to limit the number of potential heirs in the next generation because, no matter how many husbands a woman has, there is a limit to the number of offspring she can bear. (Table 9.1 lists basic marriage patterns.)

TABLE 9.1 Marriage Patterns

MONOGAMY	POLYGAMY
Monogamy	Polygyny
	Polyandry

9.4 Marriage as Alliance

In most societies, a marriage is an alliance between two families or lineages, not merely between two individuals, and it frequently requires traditional exchanges of wealth to legitimize it. These are usually characterized as bride service, bridewealth (or bride "price"), and dowry. In some societies, the prospective groom must work for the family of the bride for a predetermined length of time before they may marry, a practice called **bride service**. Other societies solemnize marriages with an exchange of **bridewealth**: certain symbolically important goods that are transferred from the immediate family of the groom (or his lineage) to the family of the bride (or her lineage) on the occasion of their marriage. *Symbolically important goods* include those things that are considered to be appropriate for exchange at a marriage in a specific society—for example, cattle, cash, shell ornaments, cotton cloth, or bird feathers. Bridewealth exchange is most common in patrilineal societies that combine agriculture, pastoralism, and patrilocal postmarital residence. Through their research in societies that exchange bridewealth, anthropologists have found that it is fundamentally incorrect to think of bridewealth as "buying" a wife. Rather, anthropologists view bridewealth as a way of compensating the bride's relatives for the loss of her labor and childbearing capacities. That is, when the bride goes to live with her husband and his lineage, she will be working and producing children for his people, not her own.

Bridewealth transactions create affinal relations between the relatives of the wife and those of the husband. The wife's relatives in turn use the bridewealth they receive for her to find a bride for her brother in yet another kinship group. In many societies in eastern and southern Africa, a woman gains power and influence over her brother because the cattle that her marriage brings allow him to marry and continue their lineage.

Dowry, by contrast, is typically a transfer of family wealth, usually from parents to their daughter, at the time of her marriage. It is found primarily in the agricultural societies of Europe and Asia, but it has been brought to some parts of Africa with the arrival of religions like Islam that support the practice. In societies in which both men and women are seen as heirs to family wealth, dowry is sometimes regarded as the way women receive their inheritance. Dowries often are considered the wife's contribution to the establishment of a new household to which the husband may bring other forms of wealth or prestige. In stratified societies, the size of a woman's dowry frequently ensures that when she marries, she will continue to enjoy her accustomed style of life. In some stratified societies, an individual of lower status sometimes marries an individual of higher status, a situation in which the children will take on the higher status. This practice is called **hypergamy,** and it is usually one in which the lower-status person is the wife and the dowry is seen (sometimes explicitly) as an exchange for the higher social position that the husband confers.

The ties that link kinship groups through marriage are sometimes so strong that they endure beyond the death of one of the partners. In some matrilineal and some patrilineal societies, if a wife dies young, the husband's line will ask the deceased wife's line for a substitute, often her sister. This practice, called the **sororate** (from the Latin *soror,* "sister"), is connected with both alliance strength and bridewealth. That is, both lines—that of the widower and that of the deceased wife—wish to maintain the alliance formed (and frequently continued) by the marriage. At the same time, if a man marries the sister of his deceased wife, the bridewealth that his line gave to the line of the first wife will not have to be returned, so the disruption caused by the wife's death will be lessened. In many societies, if the husband dies, the wife may (and in rare cases be obligated to) marry one of his brothers.

This practice, called the **levirate** (from the Latin *levir*, "husband's brother"), is intended, like the sororate, to maintain the alliance between descent groups. In some societies, it also functions as a kind of social security system for widows, who might otherwise be destitute after the death of their husbands.

9.5 Family

Marriage frequently is understood, both by scholars and by the people who marry, as creating families. *Family* is another term that seeks to label a practice that is apparently universal but so variable as to make definition difficult. One minimal definition of a **family** would be that it consists of a woman and her dependent children. Some anthropologists prefer to distinguish the **conjugal family**, which is a family based on marriage—at its minimum, a husband and wife (a spousal pair) and their children—from the **nonconjugal family**, which consists of a woman and her children. In a nonconjugal family, the husband/father may be occasionally present or completely absent. Anthropologists note that nonconjugal families are never the only form of family organization in a society and, in fact, are usually rather infrequent. However, in some large-scale industrial societies, including the United States, nonconjugal families have become increasingly common. In most societies, the conjugal family is coresident—that is, spouses live in the same dwelling, along with their children—but in some matrilineal societies, the husband lives with his matrilineage, the wife and children live with theirs, and the husband visits his wife and children.

Families can be characterized according to their structure. The neolocal, monogamous family is called the **nuclear family** and is composed of two generations, the parents and their unmarried children. In the nuclear family, each member has a series of evolving relationships with every other member: husband and wife, parents and children, and children with one another. These are the principal lines along which jealousy, controversy, and affection develop in neolocal monogamous families.

The **polygynous family** is composed of the husband, his cowives, and their children. The polygynous family adds complexity in the older generation not found in the nuclear family—the relationships among the cowives and the relationship of the group of wives with the single husband. Additional complexity arises in the younger generation as children have connections to half-siblings (the same father but a different mother) and full siblings (the same father and same mother), as well as an additional set of adults in their lives— their mother's cowives. These differences make the internal dynamics of polygynous families different from those of nuclear families.

The two family structures discussed so far are similar in that they are two generations in depth and involve one set of spouses (a man and a woman in the nuclear family, a man and his wives in a polygynous one). When families include a third generation—parents, married children, and grandchildren—anthropologists speak about **extended families**. When families maintain a two-generation depth but expand outward so that a set of siblings and their spouses and children lives together, anthropologists talk about **joint families**. Simply put, a joint family is composed of several brothers and their wives and children or several sisters and their husbands and children. In societies in which they are found, extended and joint families are ideal patterns, which means that although people might want to live that way, not everyone is able to.

In recent years in the United States, anthropologists have observed the emergence of new family types. The **blended family** occurs when previously divorced people marry, bringing with them children from their previous marriages. The internal dynamics of the new family—which can come to include his children, her children, and their children—may sometimes have some similarities to the dynamics of polygynous families. Specifically, the relations among the children and their relations to each parent may be complex and negotiated over time. (Table 9.2 summarizes the basic family types.)

A second new form is the **family by choice**, a term used by some LGBT (lesbian, gay, bisexual, transgender) people to refer to families that are not the product of heterosexual marriage. Derived from a model that resembles kinship based on nurturance (defined in Chapter 8), some North American LGBT people argue that "whatever endures is real." As a result, the group of people that endures—which may include some or all of the kin of each member of the couple, their close friends, and children of either member or

TABLE 9.2   Types of Families

NONCONJUGAL FAMILIES	CONJUGAL FAMILIES	FAMILIES BY CHOICE
Mother and children	Nuclear	Enduring ties that are
	Polygynous	not the product of
	Extended	heterosexual marriage
	Joint	
	Blended	

children who may be adopted—forms a family. LGBT activists have used this model as a resource in their struggle to obtain for long-standing families of choice some of the same legal rights enjoyed by traditional heterosexual families, such as hospital visiting privileges, partner insurance coverage, joint adoption, and property rights.

Marriages do not always last forever, and almost all societies make it possible for married couples to **divorce**—that is, to dissolve the marriage in a socially recognized way, regulating the status of those who were involved with the marriage and any offspring of the marriage. In some societies, it is not merely the people who were married who are involved in the divorce; it may also include other family or lineage members of the divorcing parties whose relationships are also changed by the divorce. In societies in which bridewealth is part of the marriage ceremony, for example, divorce may cause difficulties if the bridewealth must be returned. In such societies, a man who divorces a wife or whose wife leaves him expects her family to return to him some of the bridewealth he offered in exchange for her. But the wife's family may well have exchanged the bridewealth they received when she married to obtain wives for her brothers. As a result, her brothers' marriages may have to be broken up in order to recoup enough bridewealth from their in-laws to repay their sister's ex-husband or his line. Sometimes a new husband will repay the bridewealth to the former husband's line, thus letting the bride's relatives off the hook.

Grounds for divorce vary from society to society as does which party may initiate divorce. Common grounds for divorce often include nagging, quarreling, cruelty, violence, stinginess, and adultery. Cross-culturally, a frequent ground for divorce is childlessness.

Families break apart and new households form in other ways besides divorce. In joint families, for example, the pressures that build up among coresident brothers or sisters often increase dramatically on the death of the father. In theory, the eldest son inherits the position of head of household from his father, but his younger brothers may not accept his authority as readily as they did the father's. Some younger brothers may decide to establish their own households, and so the joint family gradually splits. Each brother whose household splits off from the joint stem usually hopes to start his own joint family; eventually, his sons will bring their wives into the household, and a new joint family emerges out of the ashes of an old one.

For Further Reading

Many of the readings for Chapter 8 also deal with marriage and family. Here are some readings specific to these topics:

MARRIAGE

Goody and Tambiah 1973; Hirsch and Wardlow 2006; Levine 1988; Padilla et al. 2007; Sacks 1979; Schuler 1987

FAMILY

Netting, Wilk, and Arnould 1984; Ottenheimer 2006; Weston 1991

10

Globalization and the Culture of Capitalism

The key terms and concepts covered in this chapter, in the order in which they appear:

colonialism
neocolonialism

corvee

cultural imperialism
westernization
internal colonialism

subaltern
nationalism

modernization
   theory
revolutionary
   movements
proletarianization

dependency theory

neoliberalism
international political
   economy
world system theory
core
periphery
semiperiphery
deterritorialization
reterritorialization
diaspora

globalization
tourism

identity politics
cultural pluralism
multiculturalism
acculturation
cargo cults

cultural
   hybridization
long-distance
   nationalism
transborder state
transborder
   citizenship

human rights
cultural rights

cosmopolitanism
global assemblages
development
anthropology of
   the environment
nongovernmental
   organizations
   (NGOs)

ANTHROPOLOGISTS HAVE SPECIALIZED in taking seriously the ways of life of people in "remote" parts of the world—remote, that is, from the activities and concerns of most people in the Western capitalist nations from which the anthropologists traditionally came. Until very recently, limitations rooted in the technologies of transportation and communication meant that, even when political or economic ties linked territories at some distance from one another, the movement of people or goods or ideas from one place to another was slow and cumbersome. By 5,000 years ago, the growth of states and their expansion into empires drew peoples in several regions of the world into intensified contact with one another. At the beginning of the twenty-first century, however, economic or political events whose consequences used to be felt only within restricted geographical regions regularly affected people living in regions of the world that used to be considered distant from one another. It was only a little over five centuries ago that European explorers began to make contact and then to conquer indigenous groups on all continents, eventually establishing far-flung colonial empires that lasted until the middle of the twentieth century. The relationships established by European colonial domination created the conditions for the emergence, by the end of the twentieth century, of a fully integrated global economy.

10.1 The Cultural Legacy of Colonialism

Europeans did not invent **colonialism**, which can be defined as political conquest of one society by another, followed by social domination and forced cultural change. Since the rise of the first states in antiquity, regions of varying sizes have been brought together in different parts of the world as a result of imperial expansion, and what is today western Europe was marginal to most of them. None of those earlier empires, however, ever attained the scope of the European colonial empires, especially during their period of greatest expansion, which stretched roughly from the end of the nineteenth century until shortly after World War II when European colonies began to gain their independence. At that time, many observers hoped that the relationships of subjugation between colonizer and colonized would dissolve. They hoped that different geographical regions of former empires would regain the kind of autonomy that had so often followed the breakup of empires in the past. Such hopes were dashed, however, when the ties between former colonies and their former imperial rulers not only did not disappear after independence but instead often reappeared in the form of "consultancies" to the new governments. These persisting relationships in the absence of imperial political domination have often been called **neocolonialism**, and social scientists have struggled to explain why they are so resilient.

Many scholars, anthropologists included, decided that neocolonial ties were basically economic in nature and that their strength came from an international division of labor, which colonialism itself had established. Once certain geographical regions within an empire became specialized in specific economic tasks within the imperial economy, the argument went, those relationships became very difficult, if not impossible, to dislodge, even when the empire itself no longer existed. Much evidence was collected to document the forced social and cultural change wrought on the economic, social, and cultural lives of colonized peoples in order to create this international division of labor during the period of European colonial rule.

The European empires of the last two centuries were, by and large, not made up of settler colonies. Except for select areas like southern or eastern Africa for the British or Morocco and Algeria for the French, European soldiers and administrators were always relatively limited in number; the colonizers relied on superior military technology, rather than sheer numbers, to impose their will. They were neither able nor, in most cases, interested in remaking colonized societies from top to bottom, but they did institute certain changes that would make it easier for them to achieve the economic goals that were their primary motivation. Thus, large tracts of land were regularly appropriated from colonized peoples for the purpose of resource extraction (mining, for example) or for growing cash crops valued in Europe (see Chapter 7 for further discussion of cash crops), displacing indigenous farmers and herders from their lands and turning them into wage workers forced to seek employment on plantations, in mines, or in the growing cities. Economic efficiency further required the building of infrastructure (roads, ports, and so on) by which cash crops or minerals could be transported out of colonies and back to Europe. Colonists regularly relied on the labor of colonized peoples to build such infrastructure, sometimes resorting to the use of **corvee**, or forced labor, in which laborers were required to work a given number of days on a given project or risk fines or imprisonment.

As colonial economic control increased, colonized peoples became familiar with European economic practices such as the use of money to purchase commodities or the production of goods for exchange. Adopting wage work and purchasing goods to meet subsistence needs increasingly became a necessity as people were deprived of the land on which they formerly had grown subsistence crops or as their traditional artisanal production of pots or cloth or farm implements was supplanted by manufactured items produced in and imported from Europe. Over time, indigenous peoples had to come to terms with these cultural practices, and the way they did so has varied from time to time and place to place. They were coping with what many scholars have called **cultural imperialism,** a situation in which the ideas and practices of one culture are imposed upon other cultures, which may be modified or eliminated as a result. Western colonialism appeared to produce a distinctive kind of cultural imperialism, frequently called **westernization,** in which the ideas and practices of western European (or North American) culture eventually displaced many of the ideas and practices of the indigenous cultures of the colonies. In places where European settler colonies eventually broke from Europe, as in North, Central, and South America, anthropologists often speak of **internal colonialism** imposed on indigenous peoples within the borders of independent states.

10.2 Analyzing Sociocultural Change in the Postcolonial World

The contradiction inherent in most colonial policies urging cultural assimilation, however, was that even the most highly "assimilated" members of colonized societies could never hope to be treated as equals by their colonial masters. This realization by growing numbers of educated members of **subaltern** (lower-ranked) groups helped fuel the movement for independence from colonial control, which gained momentum after World War II. By virtue of their shared colonial history and their shared rejection of domination, independence leaders argued that they and their followers had developed a distinct sense of themselves as "a people" or "nation," an orientation that came to be called **nationalism**. Nationalist leaders in colonies claimed that colonized peoples, like other "nations" of the world, had a right to political self-determination; that is, they were entitled to become independent nation-states.

In the postcolonial world of the 1950s and early 1960s, the leaders of many newly independent nation-states were hopeful that their countries could escape the impoverished status they had occupied under colonial rule. Although such leaders rejected the notion that their citizens needed to become "civilized," they were committed to the idea that their societies needed "development" and "modernization." Many economists in Western nations agreed with them. In a manner reminiscent of Lewis Henry Morgan, these economists subscribed to a unilineal theory of economic development, often referred to as **modernization theory**. They studied the economic histories of the first nations in the world to "develop" or to "modernize"—that is, to create economies based on industrial production and capitalist business practices. Some economists believed that they had discovered a universal recipe for modernization, "a technological fix" that would guarantee economic development in any new nation that followed their advice. (For more on modernism, see Chapter 1.)

Modernization theory did not view industrial capitalism as a distinctive cultural system but rather as the most highly developed economic system yet produced on the face of the earth. It assumed that "nations" were units that passed naturally through stages of economic growth at different rates and that the more "mature" nations ought to assist the "young" nations to attain maturity. However, economists from Western industrial nations insisted that the leaders of new nations carefully follow their recipe for development. Like parents dealing with sometimes unruly adolescent children, they worried that young nations eager to modernize might resist disciplined evolution through the stages of economic growth and look for a shortcut to economic prosperity.

During the Cold War years when modernization theory developed, the tempting shortcut was seen as socialist revolution. The twentieth century has been marked by a series of revolutions all over the globe, the best known being those in Mexico, Russia, China, Vietnam, Algeria, Cuba, and Nicaragua. In 1969 anthropologist Eric Wolf characterized all but the Nicaraguan revolution (which would take place 10 years later) as wars waged by peasants to defend themselves from the disruptions caused in their societies by capitalist market penetration. Following the Russian Revolution, opponents of the capitalist system elsewhere in the world also formed **revolutionary movements** whose explicit aim was to throw capitalists out of the country by force. Although many rank-and-file members of the revolutionary movements had modest dreams of return to a more prosperous status quo ante, their leaders often hoped to replace capitalism with some locally appropriate form of socialist society. After the successful Cuban Revolution in 1959 when Fidel Castro and his supporters openly committed themselves to socialism and allied with the Soviet Union, modernization theory became the foreign-policy option of choice in the United States, a potentially powerful approach to economic development that might woo potential revolutionaries elsewhere away from the Marxist threat (see Chapter 7).

The Marxist threat was real because Marxists argued that the factor responsible for the impoverished economies of postcolonial states was precisely what the modernization theorists were offering as a cure, namely, capitalism (see Chapter 7 for a detailed discussion). A key feature of capitalism is the way it creates separation, or *alienation*, of workers from the tools, raw materials, and technical knowledge required to produce goods. When, for example, peasants are pushed off the land and forced to work for wages in mines or on commercial farms, they are caught up in a process sometimes called **proletarianization**: a process of class formation that transforms people deprived of subsistence resources into workers at the bottom of the capitalist political economy.

Once these transformed relations of production are well entrenched, political independence alone will not make them go away. For example, successful commercial plantations will not automatically be dismantled so that peasants can reclaim lands to farm because the landlords (whether outsiders or locals) will be unwilling to give up the wealth that can be accumulated by using wage laborers to produce cash crops for the international capitalist market. This, it is argued, is why political independence brought neocolonialism rather than economic independence to so many parts of the world. The economies and cultures of colonized peoples had been so thoroughly remade under capitalist colonialism that cutting off all ties to former masters would have resulted in economic catastrophe.

In the 1960s, Latin American economists and sociologists were trying to understand why their nations, free of official colonial domination for over a century, were no better off than the newly independent states of Africa. Articulating an analytic framework that came to be called **dependency theory**, they argued that poverty and "underdevelopment" were a *consequence* of capitalist colonial intervention in otherwise thriving independent societies, and not some original lowly state in which colonized territories had been languishing until the colonizers arrived. Capitalist colonialism *reduced* colonies to a state of underdevelopment in which their economies came to depend on decisions made outside their borders by colonial rulers who were promoting their own interests, not the interests of the colonies. Indeed, they argued, the "development" of rich countries depended on the deliberate impoverishment of other parts of the world. From this perspective, capitalist recipes for economic "development" could hardly be the solution to "underdevelopment" because capitalism had created the underdevelopment in the first place.

Modernization theory and dependency theory both see "development" as a process that is a natural part of all social life, but they differ in their understanding of the forces that encourage it or block it. Modernization theory not only views capitalist entrepreneurship as the key to self-sustaining economic growth but also personifies nation-states as primordial sociocultural units, each of which is individually responsible for its own successful modernization. In recent years, the individualism at the center of modernization theory has reappeared in the guise of **neoliberalism** in which international institutions like the World Bank and the International Monetary Fund urge individual nation-states to pursue their own economic self-interest in competition with one another. Neoliberalism replaces the goal of achieving prosperous national self-sufficiency with the goal of finding a niche in the global capitalist market. State bureaucrats have had to divert funds away from state institutions that subsidized poor citizens in order to invest in economic enterprises that would earn income in the market.

Dependency theory, by contrast, rejects the individualistic analysis along with its conclusions. Nation-states are *not* primordial entities but are historical creations; and some nations of the world were able to become powerful and rich only because they forced other societies into weakness and poverty. The fates of a rich country and its poor colonies (or neocolonies) are thus intimately interrelated. Social–scientific perspectives that take this observation as their starting point usually are said to pay attention to an **international political economy** (see Chapter 6). In recent years, many anthropologists interested in the international political economy have become sharp critics of neoliberalism.

An ongoing struggle between anthropologists favorable to modernization theory and those critical of it was a feature of the Cold War years of the 1950s and 1960s. By the 1970s, critics of modernization theory were active in anthropology, many of them influenced by dependency theory. By the 1980s, however, many anthropologists agreed that dependency theory was too simplistic to account for the complexities of the postcolonial world. Many anthropologists thus adopted the broader perspective of **world system theory**, an analytical framework first suggested in the 1970s by sociologist Immanuel Wallerstein.

World system theory expanded upon and strengthened the Marxist critique of capitalist colonialism inherent in dependency theory. Wallerstein's most original idea was to apply a functionalist analytic framework (see Chapter 12) to the capitalist world system, which was, in his opinion, the only social system that came close to being self-contained and self-regulating in the structural–functionalist manner. Wallerstein stressed that capitalism was a *world* system, not because it included the entire world, but because the system incorporated territories scattered across the globe in order to maintain itself and to grow. Unlike empires, which in the past had united far-flung territories under a single political authority, the capitalist world system united far-flung territories *by economic means alone* through the capitalist market.

Modernization theorists, as we noted, conceive of nation-states as autonomous actors ranked in various positions along a continuum from "backward"/"underdeveloped"/"less-developed" and so on to "developed" industrial economies. By contrast, analysts who adopted a world system perspective use a different terminology, classifying nation-states and other political entities in terms of the role they play within the world system's international division of labor. Thus, those countries that are fully industrialized, monopolize technological expertise and innovation, control financial decision making for the system as a whole, and pay relatively high wages to skilled workers are said to belong to the **core** of the world system. Core nations today include the former European colonial powers, the United States, and Japan. By contrast, those countries whose main contributions to capitalism are raw materials for industries in the core and expanding markets for manufactured goods are said to belong to the **periphery** of the world system. The ranks of peripheral nations are dominated by former colonies. Finally, some countries are said to belong in the **semiperiphery;** these nations either were once part of the core or look as though they might someday be able to move into the core. In recent years, China, India, Brazil, and Indonesia often have been considered semiperipheral by world system theorists.

World system theory has established itself within anthropology as a powerful analytic framework for making sense of recent historical developments in the global political economy and their effects on the local communities in which anthropologists have traditionally carried out fieldwork. Thinking in terms of world systems, rather than empires, has also changed the way historians and social scientists approach world history outside Europe prior to the rise of capitalism. Geographer Janet Abu-Lughod, for example, has made a persuasive case for the existence of a thirteenth-century world system centered in India that organized trade by land and sea from Southeast Asia to western Europe and from China to East Africa. Some anthropologists have been inspired by Abu-Lughod's work because it not only provides a fuller historical context for understanding the development of cultures they study in the lands that formerly belonged to this world system but also shows that the capitalist world system is not the only world system ever to exist and that Western cultural hegemony is not inevitable.

Following the end of the Cold War in 1989, cultural anthropologists were among the social scientists who observed a series of far-reaching and intensifying global changes. From one point of view, it looked as though the fall of socialism in the former Soviet Union and the adoption of capitalist economic practices in China was making it possible for the capitalist world system to swallow up the entire world. From another point of view, however, the forces that were responsible for these new interconnections appeared to be so powerful that they were undermining key features of the world system.

For example, world system theory rests on the assumption of an international division of labor in which people in different geographical regions specialize in different economic tasks. This makes it both possible and meaningful to distinguish core from semiperipheral from peripheral nations. However, the vast improvements in transportation and communication technologies in recent decades has permitted a breakdown in the link between economic role and territory. Anthropologists have described a massive **deterritorialization** of both peoples and activities from their former exclusive locations in one or another region of the world system, together with complex processes of **reterritorialization** of those migrants and those activities elsewhere in the world. Anthropologists often face the challenge of carrying out fieldwork among people whose ancestors may have been rooted in a single territory but who themselves may be living in a **diaspora** of migrant populations located in many different places.

In the past, such movements of peoples encountered many barriers, but today demand for certain kinds of workers in core countries has promoted migration, both legal and illegal, of people from periphery, to core. At the same time, technology-dependent manufacturing activities that used to take place exclusively in the core have been relocated in peripheral nations to take advantage of low wage rates. Wage work in manufacturing formerly enabled citizens of core nations with little formal education to earn middle-class incomes; the cost and inconvenience of moving factories out of the core meant that workers could bargain for higher wages and greater benefits with some success. Today's cutting-edge manufacturing plants, however, can be shipped to peripheral countries and quickly set up. They can also be quickly dismantled in order to move them elsewhere in the periphery where labor costs are lower. Increasingly, jobs that require knowledge of computerized technology are also reterritorializing to peripheral or semiperipheral locations: Workers' salaries can be lowered with no decrease in work efficiency, thanks to modes of high-tech electronic communication such as the Internet. Although the manufacturing jobs that have been deterritorialized out of the core are welcome in poor peripheral countries, the loss of such jobs in core countries has caused severe hardship and dislocation for the newly unemployed.

10.3 Globalization

The intensifying flow of capital, goods, people (tourists as well as immigrants and refugees), images, and ideas around the world has come to be called **globalization**. For example, over the past 20 years or so, tourism has become an important target of anthropological interest. This is not surprising since it is one of the largest industries in the world, moving nearly a billion people annually. **Tourism** is any activity that involves the self-conscious experience of another place (Chambers 2010, 6). As might be expected, anthropologists focus on how tourism is experienced, not just by tourists, but by the local communities that receive tourists. Here, there is a great deal of variation, and generalizations are difficult.

For some communities, tourism is an excellent source of income, local identity, and pride, while for others tourism has brought pollution, inequality, and unemployment. Some anthropologists have been concerned with the issue of authenticity as something tourists seek; intermediaries like tour operators, travel writers, and travel agents promise; and local hosts may provide. There seems to be a popular view of authenticity as connected with traditions that have been maintained from an autonomous, premodern past. While there have been sharp arguments within anthropology about whether authenticity is possible, Chambers reasonably argues that "the authentic occurs under conditions in which people have significant control over their affairs, to the extent that they are able to play an active role in determining how changes occur in their social settings" (2010, 101). Under that definition, the tapestries based on graphics by Dutch artist M. C. Escher that Lavenda and Schultz observed for sale in the indigenous textile market in Otavalo, Ecuador, in 1978 were authentic because the weavers themselves had chosen to weave those designs, despite the objections of the Ecuadorian textile experts who were trying to convince them to weave ancient designs from Otavalo itself.

People need not ever leave their homes, however, to be buffeted by the forces of globalization. The explosive development of computer technology, e-mail communication, and the Internet has not been confined to the kind of economic restructuring described above. It has also enabled many other kinds of links among people who have never seen one another, creating global networks, or *virtual communities*, that reach beyond the boundaries of nation-states. Many anthropologists have become interested in the growth of *cyberculture*: the distinct beliefs and practices developing in connection with the growth of computer-mediated communication. The cultural possibilities that might be produced by unbridled cyber-exchanges on a global level remain limited, however, because access to computer-mediated communication is still largely the preserve of middle-class users with mastery of computer technology and literacy in English. In addition, various national governments continue to try to restrict their citizens' access to cybercommunication, with varying degrees of success. (See Chapter 4 for more on virtual worlds.)

The forces of globalization have little respect for the kinds of social, cultural, religious, political, and geographical boundaries that are used to discipline and routinize contacts between vastly different categories of ideas, images, practices, and peoples. Thus, globalization and its consequences—especially the way it appears to have overcome traditional limits of time and space—are an excellent illustration of what many anthropologists and other scholars describe as the *postmodern condition*. This term refers to the situation in which human beings find themselves at the dawn of the twenty-first century: Time is compressed; distances are annihilated. Under these conditions, the supposed benefits of "rational scientific modernity"—prosperity, equality, peace—appear more elusive today than ever and have increasingly been called into question (see Chapter 1).

After 1989, for example, the certainties of the Cold War years gave way to bewilderment for many citizens of the United States: Who were our enemies? Who were our friends? Indeed, who are "we" and who are "they"?

Since a terrorist attack destroyed the World Trade Center in New York City on September 11, 2001, many Americans have been persuaded that "terrorists" have stepped into the slot that used to be occupied by "communists." But this has hardly led to unanimity in the United States regarding how "terrorists" are to be identified or how they should be fought. Some terrorist groups might be international, but both the United States and Europe have experienced attacks by terrorist groups that were home-grown.

The struggle to manage situations of uncertainty and insecurity of this kind has given rise to a phenomenon sometimes called **identity politics**: struggles by groups to create and sustain exclusionary political alliances defined more narrowly than and often in opposition to a common identity as citizens of a nation-state. Although neither the nation-state nor citizenship has disappeared, many groups and individuals clearly refuse to accept them as overriding standards beneath which all other communities and identities should be subordinated or eliminated. Put another way, the hegemony of the nation-state and citizenship has been challenged.

The postmodern challenge of identity politics exposes the fact that societies and cultures that have been portrayed, either by their members or by outsiders, as homogeneous and harmonious are more often characterized by **cultural pluralism**. That is, they are made up of a multiplicity of heterogeneous subgroups whose ways of thinking and living vary, whose interests may be opposed, and whose cooperation is not automatic. Coercion by ruling elites may give the appearance of cultural uniformity. It may seem that members of heterogeneous subordinate groups have willingly adopted the dominant majority culture, a process called *assimilation*. When coercion weakens, however, pluralism often reemerges. It becomes apparent that some members of a society have serious reservations about the values and practices they have been pressured to accept. Rather than assimilating, therefore, they have simply refrained from challenging openly the cultural practices of the majority, a process called *accommodation*.

Cultural heterogeneity becomes even more complex in societies that have experienced recent immigration, producing a situation that is often called **multiculturalism**. The nation-states of western Europe, for example, have all received large numbers of new immigrants from all over the world in recent decades. Citizens who already have differences with one another are challenged to make room for various groups of new arrivals while each set of migrants is faced with constructing a place for itself among a variety of other contending groups with different cultural backgrounds. Living permanently surrounded by cultural heterogeneity regularly produces struggles over pressures to assimilate and disputes about how much the members of each group ought to accommodate each other or the norms of the wider society.

10.4 The Cultural Effects of Contact

Anthropologists probably have always been aware that the non-Western societies in which they were doing fieldwork had been heavily affected by imperialist forces of one kind or another. This awareness was surely responsible at least in part for the relativistic defense of bounded, internally harmonious "cultures" so important in the early twentieth century. Anthropologists like Margaret Mead (1901–1978) and Bronislaw Malinowski (1884–1942), for example, regularly drew attention to what they saw as the misguided and pernicious effects of colonizers and missionaries on indigenous cultures. Shortly before his death, Malinowski wrote about the enormous changes taking place in indigenous cultures as a result of colonialism, and American anthropologists like Melville Herskovits (1895–1963) were drawing attention to the processes of cultural change that colonial encounters (external and internal) had set in motion. It was only after World War II, however, and especially after the achievement of political independence by former European colonies that the colonial situation itself became an explicit focus of ethnographic study.

When anthropologists began to address the consequences of cultural contact, they invented a new vocabulary to try to describe the processes that seemed to be at work. In the United States, Herskovits and his colleagues spoke of **acculturation**: a process by which cultures in contact borrow ideas and practices from one another, thereby modifying or replacing traditional ideas and practices. The study of cultural borrowing had always been important in North American anthropology, and anthropologists pointed out that the process often involved reshaping the borrowed item to make it fit into preexisting cultural arrangements. When viewed by an outside observer, the result often was described as *syncretism*: a mixing of elements from two or more traditions. For example, a syncretistic religion emerges when missionary Christianity and a traditional indigenous religious system both contribute to new shared spiritual practices that are neither wholly "Christian" nor wholly "traditional" (see Chapter 4).

Frequently cited examples of religious syncretism are the so-called **cargo cults** that developed in Melanesia and New Guinea in the decades after colonial conquest, many of them stimulated by contact with the U.S. military during World War II. The *cargo* refers, in general, to the abundant manufactured goods brought to the islands by Western missionaries, traders, and soldiers. Although cargo cults differed in many specifics of belief and practice, they had in common the mixture of Christian religious doctrine and traditional indigenous beliefs about ancestors. A key feature was the belief that the ancestors would return on ships or planes, bringing for their kin the cargo that Europeans possessed in such abundance. In some places, members of the cargo cult even constructed models of airplanes or control towers that had the ritual function of enticing the ancestors and their cargo. (See the discussion about religious change in Chapter 4.)

Acculturation theorists realized that processes of cultural borrowing and modification might be mutual—with the partners involved taking from and giving to one another on an equal, unconstrained basis—or that they could be skewed in one direction only as a result of unequal power relations. The latter situation could often be found under colonial rule. For example, children in colonies frequently were taken from their home villages and taught the colonizer's language and culture in boarding schools deliberately designed to cut off children from the influence of their families' traditional way of life. In such cases, the goal was often explicitly to "civilize" the children, which in the circumstances meant to replace the children's culture with that of the colonizer. That is, the colonizers wanted these children to assimilate to colonial society and culture, to cut off identification with their culture of origin and become totally absorbed in the ways of Europeans. Pressure to assimilate is not unique to colonial situations; it is commonly encountered by refugee or immigrant groups moving into societies dominated by cultural traditions very different from their own. In both cases, however, the goal of assimilation is the same: the disappearance of distinctive cultural features that set the lower-ranking and less influential subaltern groups apart from those privileged and powerful groups who dominate them.

Struggles over multiculturalism at home and charges of cultural imperialism abroad forced anthropologists to reexamine the processes that ensue when people of different cultural backgrounds come into contact. Their field research showed that the realities of cultural exchange were much more complex than the struggles of identity politics or the worries about cultural imperialism would lead one to imagine. Their efforts were complemented by the actions of individual members of different subaltern groups who refused to assimilate to a hegemonic culture, asserted their right to pick and choose from global culture the customs they wanted to follow, and resisted attempts by other members of the groups to which they belonged to police their beliefs and behavior (see Chapter 2).

The charge of Western cultural imperialism—that Western cultures were dominating and destroying other cultures, producing global cultural homogenization—did not hold up to scrutiny. The notion of cultural imperialism denies agency to non-Western people who make use of Western cultural forms. It also ignores the fact that many non-Western cultural forms have been adopted by members of Western societies (sushi, for example). Finally, it ignores the fact that cultural forms sometimes bypass the West entirely as they move from one part of the world to another (movies from India, for example, have been popular in Africa for decades). These are all examples of the active reconciliation of cultural practices from elsewhere with local practices in order to serve local purposes: That is, they are examples of indigenization—sometimes also called *domestication* or *customization* (see Inda and Rosaldo 2007; see also Chapter 2).

The rate of cultural borrowing followed by indigenization has speeded up enormously under conditions of globalization. This has led many social scientists to describe the process as **cultural hybridization**. The emphasis in discussions of cultural hybridization is on forms of cultural borrowing that produce something completely new from the fusing of elements of donor and recipient cultures. Rather than speaking of dependency and cultural loss, this discourse emphasizes creativity and cultural gain. It acknowledges the agency of those who borrow and helps discredit the notion that "authentic" cultural traditions never change. This approach offers a new angle from which to consider such phenomena as cargo cults. Rather than being viewed simply as curious products of culture contact, cargo cults began to look like creative attempts by colonized groups deprived of the promised benefits of capitalist colonialism to make sense of their deprivation and to overcome it by innovative religious means.

But the concept of cultural hybridization is not without problems. Cultural hybridity implies the mixture of two or more non-hybridized, "pure" cultures, which are not supposed to exist. Furthermore, hybrid identities are not always liberating if they are not freely adopted. In fact, anthropologists have been able to show that cultural hybridization is experienced differently by those with power and those without power. Those with power are the ones more able to pick and choose as they please from the offerings of global culture. Indeed, cultural hybridity has been commodified, on display and for sale at international music festivals and ethnic art markets. Those who can consume these multicultural offerings on their own terms experience cultural hybridity very differently from those who have hybridity thrust upon them. These latter are often members of poor and marginal migrant groups who feel unable to protect themselves from forms of cultural hybridization they have not chosen and that threaten their own fragile survival structures. When cultural hybridity becomes fashionable, the experience of hybridized elites is highlighted, and the class exploitation and racial oppression that hybridized nonelites continue to experience often disappears from view. To ignore these alternative ways of experiencing hybridity is misleading and dangerous.

10.5 Globalization, Citizenship, and Human Rights

Identity politics practiced in a context of globalization has led to the development of a variety of new understandings about the nature of the nation-state and citizenship that anthropologists have begun to study. For example, in the contemporary world migrants from one part of the world to another regularly keep in touch with those they left behind, and this can lead to their continuing support of nationalist struggles in their homeland, a phenomenon called **long-distance nationalism**. Sometimes, those left behind in the homeland try to create a **transborder state**, by reaching out to those who have migrated elsewhere, claiming them as citizens of their nation of origin even if they are also citizens of the state to which they have migrated. Such **transborder citizenship** may be written into laws granting dual nationality or extending voting rights in the country of origin to migrants who are citizens elsewhere (Schiller and Fouron 2002).

The emergence of transborder states exposes the fact that some formally recognized nation-states in fact cannot meet the needs of all their citizens, some of whom they must send abroad as migrants. The emergence of transborder citizens calls into question traditional beliefs about citizenship in a nation-state. It becomes clear that *legal citizenship*, granted by the state, is often at odds with the *substantive citizenship* in which migrants engage in their new homelands as they take action to build better lives for themselves and their families. Indeed, given the unparalleled opportunities for mobility that globalization offers those with the right connections and resources, the very idea of citizenship in a single nation-state is undermined. For example, elite overseas Chinese families with business interests all over the world have created a kind of *flexible citizenship* that allows them, with multiple passports and ample funds, to move from one nation-state to the next or to settle family members in different nation-states, depending on which regime serves their family interests best. Cultivating the ability to reap the advantages or to circumvent the obligations connected with citizenship in any particular nation-state, these elite Chinese have developed a *postnational ethos* in which the very concept of nationalism has lost meaning (Ong 1999).

In a globalized world, people in many peripheral countries have become familiar with the ideology of individual **human rights** developed in powerful core cultures, and local groups may claim that they have been deprived of their natural rights to life, liberty, or property. They often find allies in core nations who support their demands that their human rights as individuals be respected. Such claims frequently have been made by citizens of nations whose leaders signed the United Nations Declaration on Human Rights but who find their own rights being violated by those same leaders.

When minority groups are subject to coercive attempts at cultural assimilation, they may resist and demand that the wider society respect not only their individual human rights but also the shared **cultural rights** of the group to which they belong. The argument has been made in recent years, in national and international legal forums, that cultural groups have rights of their own, distinct from the rights of their individual members. Such cultural rights usually include whatever is seen as necessary to keep the group's culture viable, such as adequate economic and political resources to preserve their values and practices, including their language, and pass them on to future generations. Indeed, international debates over human rights—individual versus group rights, political and civil rights versus socioeconomic rights, rights as defined by nation-states versus the right of self-determination by indigenous and other minority groups within their borders—show that defining human rights is an ongoing multicultural project of global proportions.

This has led some anthropologists to suggest that a culture of human rights has emerged under globalization in which individuals and groups of many different kinds, in many different parts of the world, resort to courts of law to receive redress when they believe their human rights have been violated. (See Chapter 6 for discussion of law.) One of the most striking consequences of this development has been the ways in which *filing* a human rights claim itself shapes the kind of claim plaintiffs can make. That is, plaintiffs must craft their cases using the categories that human rights law recognizes. If these legal categories are at odds with categories that are meaningful to the plaintiffs, plaintiffs often have no choice but to tailor their case to match the categories that the law recognizes. Plaintiffs may be forced to portray themselves or their culture in ways that contradict their own self-understandings or else give up the opportunity to have their day in court. Even if they win their case—perhaps especially if they win—these experiences are bound to affect their views of themselves and their culture in ways they may not have intended but cannot easily reverse. At the beginning of the twenty-first century, there is probably no place on earth where the discourse of human rights has not penetrated, and global networks established by human rights treaties and courts of law make it possible for a local case to gain international attention with great rapidity.

That claims for cultural rights, as well as individual rights, are taken seriously at the beginning of the twenty-first century often is seen as evidence for the postmodern circumstances in which we live. Sociopolitical entities like nation-states, however, depend for their legitimacy on their being run by representatives of the "nation." The pressures to assimilate recalcitrant minorities may range from *ethnocide,* or the deliberate destruction of a cultural tradition, to *genocide,* or the mass murder of an entire social or cultural group whose presence is seen as threatening to those who run a state as has been documented in Nazi Germany, Cambodia, the former Yugoslavia, Rwanda, and elsewhere. (See discussion of ethnocide and genocide in Chapter 5.) In the face of such intergroup violence, anthropologists and other social scientists have struggled to define ways of dealing with the differences that divide cultural and political groups that cannot avoid having to deal with one another. Is it possible to imagine a way of managing cultural or political differences in ways that do not lead to violent conflicts, that do not require complete assimilation, but that allow people of different backgrounds to live comfortably with the differences of others?

One recent suggestion has been that the contemporary multicultural challenges may be met if we find a way to promote among all the value of cosmopolitanism. **Cosmopolitanism** refers to being at ease in more than one cultural setting. It was promoted by the Stoic philosophers of ancient Rome and revived by the philosopher Emmanuel Kant during the Enlightenment. For Kant, to be a cosmopolitan meant to be experienced in the ways of western Europe, and it was applied to elites only. Those who would promote cosmopolitanism today, however, want to extend the concept to include the alternative "cosmopolitanisms" of nonelites such as poor migrants who manage to deal gracefully with the culturally hybrid experiences they encounter and the multiple perspectives they must juggle whenever they find themselves answerable to different groups of people with different values and practices.

To cultivate this kind of cosmopolitan awareness is often difficult. For one thing, it requires more than simply being open to or inclusive of other cultures. Many anthropologists would argue that it also requires acknowledging the legacy of inequality bequeathed on many of the world's people by colonialism. In addition, it requires recognition that the cosmopolitanism of the future must involve active input from individuals and groups whose views have not been acknowledged in the past. For example, it may well be that a Western concept like "human rights" will become widely accepted, but a cosmopolitan understanding of human rights will need to pay attention to the understandings of human rights that grow out of struggles by non-Western peoples who have indigenized the concept to make it better reflect their own experiences. In the best of circumstances, both Western and non-Western contributors to cosmopolitan projects may be able to offer each other the tools they need to achieve less polarized ways of living simultaneously in multiple worlds. This is a form of cultural hybridization that many anthropologists, and those among whom they work, would very much endorse.

10.6 Global Assemblages

Not all global connections, however, involve cultural hybridization of this kind. Some anthropologists are drawing attention to the emergence of new and sometimes surprising social arrangements that articulate people, objects, meanings, and institutions into networks called **global assemblages** (see discussion in Chapter 7; Ong and Collier 2005). Global assemblages come in many varieties. One kind is the *commodity chain*, the series of linked moves that take commodities, such as garden vegetables, from farms where they are produced to sites where they are purchased by consumers. In the early twenty-first century, commodity chains that supply North American supermarkets with year-round fresh vegetables, for instance, stretch beyond the borders of the United States to growers in other parts of the world.

For example, the commodity chain that ensures the regular delivery of fresh broccoli grown in rural Guatemala to supermarkets in various parts of the United States has many links. The producers and consumers of broccoli (as well as other participants in the chain) usually know only about those with whom they must deal in order to receive the commodity from the previous node and pass it successfully on to the next one. Different people and institutions that form links in the chain (farmers, buyers, truckers, airlines, distributors, supermarket consumers) often choose to participate in the commodity chain for local reasons that are unrelated to the reasons why others involved at different links have decided to participate. Some Guatemalan broccoli farmers, for example, are persuaded that growing a nontraditional export crop that they do not eat will earn them sufficient cash to build a better future for their families in the aftermath of a genocidal civil war. Some health-conscious North American consumers, by contrast, may know nothing about recent Guatemalan history but choose to purchase broccoli because they view it as part of a healthy diet (Fischer and Benson 2006).

The emergence of heterogeneous assemblages of this kind in many different domains of life, across sometimes vast geographical distances, is a prominent feature of contemporary processes of globalization. Some global assemblages come into existence for the purpose of economic "development" in one or another part of the world that has traditionally been considered "underdeveloped" from the perspective of Western societies. In the context of a neoliberal capitalist world economy, **development** ordinarily involves investment by governments and/or by outside donors in projects designed to change institutions and individual behaviors in impoverished local communities, such that poverty will be diminished. Development projects can aim to improve local health, education, and welfare in many ways, but overall, the goal is to enable people in targeted communities to escape poverty by adopting practices that allow them to make money in the formal capitalist market. Anthropologists have studied development interventions for a long time, but under conditions of globalization, development projects have taken on new configurations.

One important area of research into globalized development is in a field that some call the **anthropology of the environment,** which draws together insights from political ecology, science studies (see Chapter 11), development studies, and studies of environmental social movements. Over the past several decades, environmental movements have emerged in different parts of the world in efforts to protect the so-called natural environment from forms of industrial, capitalist "development" that are seen to destroy resources, engender pollution, and fail to relieve poverty. As forms of global interconnectedness have increased, environmental movements in different nation-states and on different continents have connected with local environmental activists and lent one another support. One of the more prominent forms of environmental movement has been directed at protecting rainforests from destruction.

In understanding the successes and failures of environmental developmental projects, many anthropologists draw on Foucault's concept of governmentality (see discussion in Chapter 6). For example, anthropologist Arun Agrawal has shown how the British imported European forms of governmentality into India during the colonial period, using statistics to manage not only human populations, but also populations of trees in Indian forests. In Kumaon, India, these attempts were initially resisted violently by the people who lived in the forests, so in the early twentieth century, colonial officials and forest communities worked out a new set of arrangements that allowed local communities to devise their own ways of undertaking the statistics-based management of their local forests. Participation of community members in these new institutions of forest management fostered a new local awareness of forests and the ways in which their resources were threatened. This new environmental awareness, acquired through practical involvement in forest management, led to the development of new forms of individual subjectivity in many local residents, who became supporters rather than opponents of governmental forest management and conservation. This entire process (the governmentalization of localities, the local development of regulatory communities to manage forests, and the subsequent development of environmentally sensitive subjectivities in the managers) is what Agrawal calls *environmentality* (2005).

With the end of colonial empires, attempts to promote development did not end. Governments of newly independent states have been actively involved in such efforts, often with the assistance of other governments. In recent decades, however, a large number of new institutions have become involved in development work. Members of these **nongovernmental organizations (NGOs)** provide different forms of expertise that apparently qualify them to advise state officials and members of local communities on how best to solve particular development problems. Many NGOs began as institutions designed to bypass national or local governments, which were seen to be corrupt or ineffectual. Today, NGOs have become major players in all sorts of development projects—and a focus of much ethnographic fieldwork. Sometimes NGOs are

donors who fund development projects; sometimes NGOs propose projects of their own in a competition for donor funding.
Ultimately, local and national government representatives, target
populations, NGOs, and donors become stakeholders invested in
the successful outcome of the development projects in which they
are involved. But additional groups and institutions may assert
their own stakeholder status and be drawn into the development
project as it unfolds.

In the context of neoliberal globalization, development projects
that focus on forests ordinarily regard them as storehouses of natural resources, which, if properly developed, can provide income
for local communities and revenue for the state. In keeping with
dualistic notions that separate "nature" from "culture," development experts often ignore preexisting involvements of local populations with the forest that do not fit into capitalist models of natural
resource management or extraction. Before the 1970s, experts usually insisted that proper forest management involved the conservation of resources, and forest dwellers were often seen as threats to
conservation. Since the 1970s, the need to take into account the
effects of forest management on the people who were living there
has become more prominent. One development model that combines conservation with poverty reduction has been attempted in a
number of forests in recent years, with mixed results. For example,
local people may earn money as forest rangers or from tourists who
pay to visit the forest; unfortunately, this income is often insufficient
to reduce poverty in any substantial way. Even when such projects
look promising, they may not be sustainable, due to a variety of
complications, including the funding cycles of donors.

But local people are not passive, and they have often been able
to find allies to support their efforts to defend their interests. For
example, anthropologists have documented cases in which local and
international environmental activists have worked with indigenous
social movements and NGOs to defend ownership of their traditional resources, sometimes by nontraditional means. For example,
they may create maps of their traditional territories and use these
in lawsuits that are sometimes decided in their favor. Such alliances
are examples of contemporary cosmopolitanism and are often an

encouraging contrast to other kinds of global alliances that have dispossessed indigenous peoples and appropriated their lands and resources (Brosius, Tsing, and Zerner 2005). In the twenty-first century, global assemblages that manage to stabilize their newly articulated parts into established institutions are likely to play important roles in the social, cultural, political, and economic lives of people in many parts of the world.

For Further Reading

OVERVIEW

Inda and Rosaldo 2007; Kearney 1995; Robbins 2004

COLONIALISM

Dirks 2008; Pels 1997; Stoler 2002

REFUGEES, GENOCIDE, AND HUMAN RIGHTS

Daniel and Knudsen 1995; Goodale 2009; Malkki 1995; Merry 2006; Messer 1993; Nagengast 1994

GLOBALIZATION

Abu-Lughod 1989; Appadurai 1996; Featherstone 1990; Fischer and Benson 2006; Hannerz 1996; Lewellen 2002

TOURISM

Chambers 2010; Gmelch 2010; Smith, 1989

DEPENDENCY AND DEVELOPMENT

Edelman and Haugerud 2005; Lewellen 1995

MIGRATION AND LONG-DISTANCE NATIONALISM

Schiller and Fouron 2002

CITIZENSIP

Ong 1999

COSMOPOLITANISM

Breckenridge, Pollock, Bhabha, and Chakrabarty 2002

GLOBAL ASSEMBLAGES

Brosius, Tsing, and Zerner 2005; Li 2007; Ong and Collier, 2005

11

THE ANTHROPOLOGY

OF SCIENCE, TECHNOLOGY,

AND MEDICINE

The key terms and concepts covered in this chapter, in the order in which they appear:

normal science
paradigms
anomaly
revolutionary science
paradigm shift

science studies
technology
science and
   technology studies
cyborgs

health
medical anthropology
biomedicine
disease
suffering

sickness
culture-bound
   syndromes
illness

cosmopolitan medicine
ethnomedical systems
medical hegemony

demography
epidemiology
epidemic
endemic
paleodemography
paleopathology
adaptation

maladaptation
nutrition
malnutrition

critical medical
   anthropology
biology of poverty
subjectivity
trauma
structural violence
biologization
medicalization

biosociality
health activism
biological citizenship

W E OBSERVED IN CHAPTER I that the discipline of anthropology was founded as a scientific study of human beings. Science is still central to the work of many contemporary anthropologists. By the beginning of the twenty-first century, however, it has become clear that not all anthropologists understand science in the same way. In the course of the past 50 years, historians, philosophers, and other scholars (including scientists themselves) have reconsidered traditional assumptions about what science is and how it works. This body of work, often called "science studies," has led to widespread agreement across many disciplines that "science" in practice often does not conform to the idealized images of science often presented to nonscientists. But the conclusions of science studies scholars do not amount to a rejection of science or a denial of scientific achievements; on the contrary, it would be more accurate to say that the result has been a richer understanding of how science is done. For example, greater insight into scientific practice has been brought to light by anthropologists and others who have undertaken ethnographic research in scientific laboratories.

11.1 Science and Anthropology

Science studies research from the 1970s and 1980s became controversial among some scientists, who felt that their work was being unfairly criticized by outsiders who had no understanding of science. In the years since the 1990s, however, it has become clear that much of this controversy was misplaced. Even in those early years, science studies scholars from disciplines like sociology and anthropology regularly collaborated with working scientists in fields like physics and biology, and this kind of cross-disciplinary cooperation has increased over time. By the end of the first decade of the twenty-first century, science studies had taken deep root within anthropology, and research in the anthropology of science, technology, and medicine was well established.

A watershed moment in science studies scholarship is often associated with the publication of Thomas Kuhn's *Structure of Scientific Revolutions* in 1962. Kuhn challenged the common assumption that scientific advances build on older achievements in a linear fashion and that scientific knowledge accumulates and expands in a smooth, progressive manner. Kuhn argued instead that historical evidence concerning scientific change called this view into question. Kuhn coined a number of new terms that have become part of the standard vocabulary in science studies. The traditional view of science as unbroken progression was most plausible during periods of what Kuhn called **normal science,** when groups of scientists, working within specific disciplines, systematically carried out research, guided by exemplary forms of disciplinary achievement that Kuhn called **paradigms.** Paradigms provided models of successful work in specific scientific fields that scientists trained in that field could use to direct and shape their own work. Common examples of such paradigms included, for example, Newton's work in physics or Darwin's work in biology. Working under the guidance of innovative and successful paradigms, scientific researchers engaging in normal science attempted to explore and push the possibilities of their paradigm. Success in solving a wide range of puzzles using a particular paradigm was what gave scientific research the appearance of linear progress.

But every so often, Kuhn argued, normal science would be interrupted by the appearance of an **anomaly,** often in the form of new data that could not easily be explained within the current paradigm. Scientists would then attempt to tinker with the paradigm, or to reinterpret the anomalous data, in an effort to reconcile paradigm and anomaly with one another. But if these efforts failed, and the anomaly persisted, scientists might be forced to question the validity of their current paradigm and to look for alternative paradigms that might do a better job of dealing with the anomaly. At this point, Kuhn argued, normal science gives way to **revolutionary science.** New paradigms may gain followers if they promise to explain the anomaly, even if they are less successful in accounting for other phenomena that were easily explained in terms of the old paradigm. It may happen that alternative paradigms become rivals, vying for the allegiance of scientists. In many cases, a new paradigm might eventually supplant the old paradigm, ushering in a new period of normal science under its guidance. One of Kuhn's main examples of this kind of **paradigm shift** was the "Copernican Revolution" in the sixteenth and seventeenth centuries, in the course of which European astronomers replaced the earth-centered view of the cosmos prominent since the time of the ancient Greeks and Romans with the sun-centered view first proposed by Polish astronomer Nicolaus Copernicus.

Kuhn's concept of paradigm became very popular, but he defined it in different ways that scholars found confusing or contradictory. A fuller understanding of paradigms and paradigm shifts meant that research needed to include the social, political, economical, and historical conditions that made particular paradigms both possible and successful. **Science studies** is the overall umbrella term under which scholarly research exploring these issues has come to be known, and anthropologists have become active contributors to science studies.

One science studies innovation important for anthropology was *laboratory ethnography*. Ethnographers followed scientists as they went about their everyday laboratory practices, discovering (among other things) the range of embodied skills that scientists in certain fields must master if they are to effectively operate the often-elaborate technical apparatuses that makes successful research possible. Ethnographers like Bruno Latour also revealed the significance of a range of "nonscientific" institutions and individuals *outside* the laboratory, whose support was essential if "strictly scientific" research projects *inside* the laboratory were to continue. Successful directors of laboratories, for example, had to wear many hats: Not only did they need to be able to secure proper working conditions for their scientific staff, they also had to cultivate good relationships with university administrators, laboratory instrument makers, and government funding agencies. Scientists themselves, of course, had long been aware of the nonscientific factors that were essential to scientific success. Wider public awareness of these factors, however, called into question popular images of scientists as individual geniuses isolated in their laboratories, exclusively concerned with pushing back the frontiers of knowledge. Frank acknowledgment that research priorities and funding could be shaped by sociocultural, economic, and political interests challenged idealized views of science as a pure, disinterested search for universal, objective truth. While some science studies critics still object that science studies research has tarnished the image of science, other observers (including many scientists) disagree. Together with many anthropologists, they value science studies for having provided a more accurate, if less exalted, view of the complex alliances and entanglements that produce scientific outcomes. Historian of science Steven Shapin encapsulates the science studies perspective in the title of a recent collection of his essays: *Never Pure: Historical Studies of Science as If It Was Produced by People with Bodies, Situated in Time, Space, Culture, and Society, and Struggling for Credibility and Authority* (2010).

11.2 Anthropology, Science, and Technology

As we noted earlier, Kuhn saw paradigms as exemplary pieces of research, and part of what made them exemplary might be the technical apparatuses they involved. The power of Western science has been furthered for several centuries by innovations in technical apparatuses used in laboratories. The Industrial Revolution owed a great deal to the technological innovations to which scientific research contributed, and contemporary industries rely on scientists and engineers to continue to innovate in ways that allow them to compete more successfully in the capitalist marketplace. But what is technology? At the most general level, **technology** is usually thought to refer to material objects shaped by human beings in order to increase their ability to act on the world and reshape it for their own purposes. Stone tools made some 2.5 million years ago in Africa by our ancestors are the oldest examples of human technology, which long predate the emergence of our own species, *Homo sapiens,* some 200,000 years ago. Technologies became much more elaborate and diverse a few thousand years ago, when humans began to settle down, domesticate animals and plants, and create the first complex societies. It has been only within the past 300 years or so that the Industrial Revolution in Europe marked a new burst of technological creativity with far-reaching consequences for all human societies everywhere.

At times, the power of technology has seemed so enormous that humans have seen it as almost a living entity, pushing human beings and their concerns aside, bending us to its will, and determining the direction our societies will develop. There is no question that some technologies are indeed powerful: From steam engines to atomic weapons to computers, the profound consequences that followed their incorporation into human societies are undeniable, and often frightening. But technology is not an autonomous force. **Science and technology studies** (sometimes called STS) is an offshoot of science studies that has been able to demonstrate that technologies, like science itself, require support of various kinds if they are to be effective. Technologies, from electrical power grids to cell phones, help stabilize new forms of human sociocultural arrangements, but they must in turn be supported by other forms of technology, as well as sociocultural institutions and practices, if they are to be successfully adopted and maintained. Controversial technologies may be denied funding, and controversial forms of scientific research may be stifled because of social or political or ethical opposition.

In common with other scholars who study science and technology, anthropologists have come to think of many features of culture and social organization as being, themselves, technologies. Anthropologists influenced by the work of French theorist Michel Foucault may have been the first to think and speak about technology in this way. In his historical studies, Foucault highlighted the ways in which practices characteristically associated with social institutions (clinics, madhouses, hospitals, and prisons) act on their inmates in ways very similar to the way a material artifact (such as a whip) might act on them, directing their movements and enforcing discipline. Indeed, those who think about technology this way may agree with feminist science studies scholar Donna Haraway, who argued some years ago that human beings are **cyborgs,** hybrid entities that are part living organism, part machine, living in worlds that are simultaneously material and symbolic, living and nonliving, human and nonhuman. It is not necessary to think of science fiction when thinking about cyborgs—a cataract operation that inserts a plastic lens into a human eye turns that human into a cyborg.

Many contemporary anthropologists have been attracted to science and technology studies. Some anthropologists who study processes of globalization explore the way technology intervenes in a variety of ways to reorganize social ties across the globe. (see Chapter 10 on anthropology and globalization.) Anthropologists who study computer technology analyze not only the economic and business sides of this phenomenon but also the transformations of individual identities and social ties that accompany individuals' increasing involvement with various forms of online social networking (Kelty 2008). Other anthropologists explore the way that online platforms open up possibilities for the creation of new art forms, such as massively multiplayer online role-playing games like World of Warcraft. (see Chapter 4 on media anthropology.) A recurring feature in many anthropological studies of technology is recognition of the uneven way in which different human communities are (and are not) incorporated into computer-mediated forms of social interaction. Access to this technology is highly skewed in favor of wealthy, educated members of powerful states with strong economies, although Internet cafés have reduced some of that disparity. Success in the cyber world depends not only on literacy in a written language (usually English), but also on mastery of the machines themselves and the software that runs on them. At the same time, some forms of cybertechnology (such as cell phones and now smart phones) have spread quickly throughout the world and are rapidly being customized to meet the needs of users of many kinds, at all income levels.

In recent decades, programs of science studies and STS have become widely institutionalized in university departments throughout North America, Europe, and elsewhere. Anthropologists are often members of these departments, working alongside scholars trained in a range of other scientific and social scientific disciplines. Science studies is now well entrenched within anthropology, and its findings are increasingly being incorporated into a number of anthropological specialties, including the anthropology of the environment (see Chapter 7) and medical anthropology.

11.3 The Anthropology of Medicine

Members of the same society who share understandings of what it means to be healthy are also likely to agree about what symptoms indicate an absence of health. Many people in the United States are likely to understand **health** as a state of physical, emotional, and mental well-being, together with an absence of disease or disability that would interfere with such well-being. But anthropologists recognize that what counts as wellness or its opposite is very much shaped by people's cultural, social, and political experiences and expectations. This means that measuring health (or its reverse) in a straightforward way can sometimes be challenging. Increasing numbers of anthropologists now apply insights and practices of the various subfields of anthropology (including science studies) in efforts to understand and find solutions to health challenges faced by members of the many communities where they work. This area of specialization is generally called **medical anthropology.**

Medical anthropologists have been deeply influenced by (as well as critical of) findings by Western physicians and medical scientists that claim to describe normal human biological functioning, the causes for impairment of such functioning, and the scientifically developed therapies available to cure or manage such impairment. These traditional scientific forms of knowledge and practice are often called **biomedicine,** and forms of biological impairment identified and explained within the discourse of biomedicine are those to which medical anthropologists often apply the term **disease.** However, medical anthropologists regularly deal with systems of belief and practice in relation to human health that developed outside the influence of biomedicine. This is why they have developed a technical vocabulary that does not presume the universality of biomedical understandings of health and disease. For example, many medical anthropologists prefer to use the term **suffering** to describe the forms of physical, mental, or emotional distress experienced by individuals who may or may not subscribe to biomedical understandings of disease or that do not fall under the categories of suffering recognized in biomedicine. One of the earliest discoveries made by Western anthropologists was that people with different cultural traditions often had particular ideas of their own about the sources of human suffering and how it might be healed. As a result, medical anthropologists have often used the term **sickness** to refer to classifications of physical, mental, and emotional distress recognized by members of a particular cultural community. Sometimes, such sicknesses may bear a close resemblance to diseases recognized by scientific biomedicine, but other times, the sickness (and therapy to relieve it) may be unique to a particular cultural group: Such sicknesses have been called **culture-bound syndromes.** Finally, some medical anthropologists contrast both the biomedical understanding of disease and local cultural categories of sickness with a suffering person's own understanding of her or his distress, which is called **illness.**

Anthropologists have long been intrigued by the range of explanations people in different cultures offer to explain why people get sick and how they may be cured. While knowledge of medicinal plants and other treatments resembling biomedicine often plays a role, many ethnographers have been impressed by explanations that attribute sickness to the breaking of taboos, punishment by ancestors, witchcraft, or sorcery. Evans-Pritchard's celebrated study of witchcraft, oracles, and magic among the Azande, for example, demonstrated how sickness and death (but also healing) could be explained in mystical terms, even while the Azande accepted that the material causes recognized by Western biomedicine also were implicated. For example, Evans-Pritchard found that the Azande understood the material causation involved when a person trips over a root and cuts his foot in the same way as a Western scientific observer understands it; nevertheless, the Azande might also invoke witchcraft to explain why the cut fails to heal. (see discussion of the Azande in Chapter 4.)

By the 1960s, the anthropology of medicine had expanded. Inspired by the work of Clifford Geertz, whose contemporary work in interpretive cultural anthropology focused on the systemic features of cultural domains like religion and common sense, Charles Leslie and his associates urged that non-Western medical beliefs and practices be understood as cultural systems (Leslie 1976). Leslie was particularly interested in "great tradition" medical systems that developed over centuries in the civilizations of South Asia and China. Recognizing the sophistication of fully fledged alternative medical systems (like Ayurvedic medicine in India) helped relativize Western biomedicine. Leslie also pointed out that Western exploration, colonial expansion, and industrialization had fostered the spread and adoption of

Western biomedical practices around the world. Because scientific biomedicine has become incorporated into medical systems throughout the world, and is no longer the exclusive property of "the West," Leslie argued that it was more accurately characterized as **cosmopolitan medicine.** Around the world, cosmopolitan medicine enjoys high status, but it coexists with a range of alternative **ethnomedical systems** based on the practices of local social groups—a state of affairs known as *medical pluralism.* Under conditions of medical pluralism, people seeking medical care develop *hierarchies of resort:* First, they consult local practitioners whom they know and trust, and who treat them with respect; if they fail to receive satisfaction, they will seek out practitioners associated with other ethnomedical systems. In the United States, biomedicine enjoys **medical hegemony:** It is the most highly valued medical system and the standard against which others are regularly compared. But medical pluralism means that residents of the United States who are dissatisfied with biomedical treatments, or who cannot afford to pay for them, are able to choose from a range of alternative ethnomedical systems such as acupuncture, herbal medicine, or visits to a shaman.

11.4 Human Health in Evolutionary Context

Medical anthropologists who study patterns of sickness and health in different human populations may have training in evolutionary biology or medicine and may regularly become skilled in disciplines like **demography,** the statistical study of human populations, or **epidemiology,** which collects information on the distribution of disease in human populations and seeks explanations for such distributions. They learn to distinguish **epidemic** diseases that spread quickly over a short period of time from **endemic** diseases that are always present in the population. Demography and epidemiology were originally developed to collect information in large settled populations in nation-states, which means that medical anthropologists who carry out fieldwork in other kinds of human populations need to adapt demographic and epidemiological techniques accordingly. Research by ethnographers working in small isolated communities requires such modification, for example, as does research by archaeologists and biological anthropologists who attempt to calculate demographic patterns characteristic of past human populations, a field called **paleodemography.** Some archaeologists use evidence from the biological remains of human populations to reconstruct patterns of sickness and health in past societies, a field called **paleopathology.** However, contemporary medical anthropologists work in complex societies all over the world, regularly collaborating with biomedical scientists to solve health problems in particular communities. The ethnographic insights cultural anthropologists can bring to such collaborations is increasingly recognized and valued.

The anthropological perspective has always emphasized that human biological adaptations to physical environments are mediated by cultural practices. How this relationship is understood, however, varies among medical anthropologists, depending on the subfields within which they were trained and the particular theoretical orientations that prevail within those subfields at particular points in time. Some anthropologists (including some medical anthropologists) are comfortable speaking of both biological and cultural evolution, and they focus on the biological and cultural evolutionary contexts of human sickness and health. This approach tends to accept the traditional Western modernist distinction between "biology" and "culture" and conceives of both biological and cultural evolution as processes shaped by natural selection on units of "information." (see Chapter 2 on cultural inheritance theorists.) Units of biological information are associated with "genes," and biological evolution is measured by changes in gene frequencies over time (in conformity with the modern synthesis that is the foundation of contemporary evolutionary biology). Cultural evolution is measured by changes in the frequencies of particular units of cultural information across space and time, as these are acquired and passed on by means of social learning (Boyd and Richerson 1985; Durham 1991).

For medical anthropologists who seek to understand human sickness and health in an evolutionary context, a key concept is that of **adaptation:** an adjustment by an organism (or group of organisms) that helps them cope with environmental challenges of various kinds. Most evolutionary biologists tend to restrict their attention to *biological adaptations:* modifications of anatomical or physiological attributes of organisms, produced by natural selection, that better adjust organisms to the environmental settings in which they live. Examples would include the wings of birds, the heightened sense of smell in mammals active at night, and the fact that humans walk upright on their hind limbs. Anthropologists, however, are also committed to the view that human adaptation to any environment is always mediated by culture. As a result, medical anthropologists who adopt an evolutionary perspective are also on the lookout for *cultural adaptations* that help human individuals or groups adjust to the demands of their environmental settings. Human populations began to rely on cultural adaptations long ago. Major cultural adaptations included not only the manufacture of tools out of stone, bone, and other materials; they also included the domestication of plants and animals and the modification of landscapes to create farms and pastures and dwellings of various kinds. It is important to recognize that such cultural adaptations do not free humans from the pressures of natural selection; rather, they *change* the nature of the selective pressures human populations face. For example, populations that shift from hunting and gathering food to tending domesticated crops may be able to produce more food for more people on less land, which can be viewed as an adaptation. At the same time, living together in a settlement means that infectious diseases pass easily from person to person and become endemic in the population, which can be viewed as a **maladaptation.** Medical anthropologists, as we saw earlier, are very sensitive to the kinds of social arrangements that may appear adaptive for some individuals or groups, but highly maladaptive for others.

11.5 Human Health and Nutrition

The concerns of medical anthropology were not always central to traditional ethnographies, but many ethnographies nevertheless contributed to medical anthropology by showing connections between particular subsistence strategies (for example, hunting and gathering or farming) and particular forms of social organization (that is, a particular division of labor), explaining how these shaped human diets and were related to local patterns of sickness and health. In fact, many medical anthropologists are concerned with **nutrition** (the content and quality of the diet regularly consumed by members of particular human communities) and the relationship between human cultural practices and nutritional adequacy. Anthropologists have long known that foraging groups who gathered or hunted in their traditional territories regularly enjoyed adequate caloric intake and a varied and balanced diet, despite occasional periods of food scarcity, even in challenging environments. They also protected their health by regularly moving away from their own waste, and they could walk away from diseases that people in settled communities could not escape. Traditional hunters and gatherers also did not suffer from high blood pressure and other chronic complaints endemic among their settled neighbors. Unfortunately, this state of affairs began to change when hunters and gatherers adopted sedentary lifestyles themselves, together with diets that relied on a narrow range of domesticated species, processed foods, and alcohol (Lee 2003). These changed diets were less varied and often lacking in key nutrients, creating the conditions for **malnutrition.** Often, the amount of food was also inadequate, creating a situation of *undernutrition.*

The health profiles of communities all over the world have been affected in recent centuries by changes in nutrition that resulted when large-scale socioeconomic and political changes affected the traditional subsistence practices (and hence the diets) of local communities. These changes were associated with global processes such as the expansion of Western colonial empires, the eventual dismantling of those empires, and the integration (often on unequal terms) of newly independent nation-states into a global capitalist economy. (see Chapter 10.) In the 1930s, British social anthropologist Audrey Richards was already drawing attention to problems of hunger and work among indigenous groups in Africa whose traditional forms of subsistence had been disrupted by British colonial economies. In the 1940s, American anthropologists like Margaret Mead were concerned about problems of diet and nutrition both in the United States and abroad and stressed the importance of understanding culturally shaped food practices of the groups whose nutrition the government was trying to improve. Access to adequate, nourishing food has regularly been a challenge for many cultural groups that have been marginalized by social, political, or economic changes that undermine their traditional livelihoods. Matters have gotten worse in recent decades, when more recent political, economic, and social changes have created large populations of displaced persons and refugees who struggle to survive in a context of violence, often living in camps that are poorly supplied with food, water, and basic shelter. (see also Chapter 7 on the anthropology of food and nutrition.)

11.6 Health and Human Reproduction

Good nutrition is not only essential for individual survival; it also is a requirement for healthy biological reproduction. Women have always been expected to integrate their reproductive labor with productive economic labor in their households and communities. Ethnographic work that recorded information connecting the level of women's reproductive health with particular subsistence strategies—and particular gendered divisions of labor—provided a useful comparative framework for later medical anthropological research. Medical anthropologists have drawn attention to a range of factors that affect women's health and fertility and their ability to care for their children. Many formal studies of *fertility* by government agencies or biomedical authorities have exclusively been concerned with the challenges of population growth in many poorer societies and have pressured families to reduce the number of offspring they produce. Medical anthropologists have been instrumental in drawing attention to the challenges that *infertility* poses for individual women living in societies with particular gender and family structures. In societies like China, where descent is traditionally traced through males and property and status move through lineages of related men, women who fail to produce sons for their husbands may be regarded as extra mouths to feed and may find themselves isolated when their husbands die and they have no son to take care of them in old age. In addition, the spread of global capitalism may undermine traditional sources of livelihood and social organization, which in turn erode traditional supports for reproductive health. In many countries, landless peasants who are forced out of the countryside into cities in search of work often live under extraordinarily difficult circumstances that have a serious negative impact on pregnant and nursing women and their children (Scheper-Hughes 1992).

11.7 Sickness and Health in the Global Capitalist Economy

As these examples suggest, susceptibility to health risks often has less to do with genetics, or biology, or even with culture, than with the unequal social and political circumstances under which people must live. **Critical medical anthropology** draws attention to the ways in which many forms of physical, mental, and emotional suffering correlate with forms of socioeconomic and political inequality. For example, people who live in low-income neighborhoods in large cities, with inadequate housing, high unemployment, and a lack of nourishing food, may also be exposed to a high level of violence, drug and alcohol dependence, and other environmental assaults on their health. Diseases such as AIDS (acquired immune deficiency syndrome) or tuberculosis thrive among poor people whose health is compromised by poor housing, poor nutrition, inadequate clothing or shelter, and insufficient or nonexistent access to regular medical attention. Critical medical anthropologists often refer to this set of health conditions as the **biology of poverty.**

In recent years, anthropologists have examined how individual psychological functioning is affected by the biology of poverty. Suspicious of concepts like "self" or "personality" that are closely associated with Western notions of individualism (see Chapter 6), many anthropologists prefer to speak of individual **subjectivity:** interior experiences of persons that are shaped by their locations in a particular field of power relations. To focus on subjectivity in an anthropological analysis is to acknowledge the way in which individuals are to some extent initiating subjects, or *agents*, of their own actions. However, subjects are never absolutely free to act as they choose. Our action is circumscribed by various forms of social, economic, and political inequality that we encounter in the societies in which we live. That is, we occupy various *subject positions* in society and are subject to the institutional forms of power in which those *subject* positions are embedded.

Predictable institutional relationships enculturate, or socialize, individuals into forms of subjectivity that reflect established forms of political power. But social and cultural patterns are sometimes overturned by unpredictable experiences that leave enduring marks on the subjectivities of individuals who live through them. Unfortunately, such experiences are increasingly common in the early twenty-first century as societies in many parts of the world experience violent conflicts. Armed conflict and war regularly produce **trauma,** severe suffering caused by forces and agents beyond the control of the individual. Large-scale violence aims to destroy not only individuals but also the social order. Both individual and cultural factors contribute to the trauma and are equally implicated in recovery from trauma. Anthropologists have also drawn attention to less dramatic forms of violence that cause considerable human suffering. Medical anthropologist Paul Farmer, for example, speaks of **structural violence,** which is the outcome of the way that political and economic processes structure risk differently for different subgroups within a population, such that some groups are more vulnerable to infectious disease or domestic violence than are other groups (Farmer 2003).

Biomedicine has difficulty coping with notions like the biology of poverty. For biomedicine, diseases are located exclusively within the physical bodies of individuals, and attempts by scientists to locate more and more forms of suffering within the body are sometimes called **biologization.** Once suffering is biologized, it is *reduced* to just those attributes of an individual physical body that are accessible to biomedical science. Biologized conditions are turned into diseases and become candidates for **medicalization:** that is, the development of biomedical therapies designed to cure individuals diagnosed with the disease. Medicalization can certainly lead to positive outcomes, when the medical therapy relieves symptoms, perhaps indefinitely. At the same time, critical medical anthropologists highlight the fact that biomedicine leaves untouched the socioeconomic and political factors responsible for ill health and suffering in the first place—factors that may well contribute to the recurrence of the disease when treated individuals return to their old environments.

At the same time, critical medical anthropologists are sometimes able to show how people's health improves when their socioeconomic circumstances improve. For example, biomedical treatment in the form of antiretroviral medications can turn AIDS into a manageable condition. However, if people who live with AIDS must struggle to survive in conditions of poverty—homeless, jobless, under- or malnourished, and without a family, friends, or neighbors to look out for them—the support system that enables them to continue taking their medicine as prescribed is undermined, sometimes fatally. Many critical medical anthropologists are concerned that in the contemporary world, more and more forms of human suffering are being medicalized, despite widespread agreement by many observers that relief is likely to come only from social, economic, or political solutions, not from medication alone. At the same time, some prominent critical medical anthropologists, like Paul Farmer and Didier Fassin, are also medical doctors. By combining biomedical practices with sociocultural and political innovations, they, their allies, and the people they serve have worked to improve access to high-quality health care in a number of poor and marginalized communities.

Research by some critical medical anthropologists has begun to focus on public policies that influence practices of health care—work that relies on insights from science studies. One area of interest concerns biomedical technologies that make possible health care interventions such as organ transplantation and assisted reproduction. Such biotechnologies hold great promise, and access to them is desired by people all over the world. But access to them is skewed by inequality, and the outcomes they promise are often oversold. Their availability and desirability also can generate new complications and ethical dilemmas: In some parts of the world, a poor person will sell organ traffickers a kidney that will then be transplanted into a rich person's body. The organ sellers hope the cash they receive will get them out of debt, but often it does not. The transplant recipients sometimes prefer to purchase organs from strangers to protect the well-being of close kin who might be a closer tissue match. Is this exploitation of the poor by the rich? Or do poor people own their own bodies and, therefore, have a right to sell their organs if they wish? But the very idea that a person's body is separate, self-contained, and autonomous is deeply rooted in Western philosophy. Does export of such an understanding of the body along with the biomedical technology ride roughshod over alternative views of bodies as well as turn a blind eye to exploitation?

Critical medical anthropologists have also become interested in the global spread of other biomedical commodities such as pharmaceuticals, whose impact they study from several perspectives. For example, pharmaceutical manufacturing is a big business that makes enormous profits, and the search for profit in new markets has been promoted by the spread of neoliberal economic practices as a result of globalization. The way pharmaceuticals and the companies producing them find a place for themselves in the medical institutions of different societies is complex and often problematic, and ethnographic research is often able to tease apart the many factors involved. Some critical medical anthropologists have studied the way in which pharmaceutical companies are now looking for fresh populations to test the effectiveness of new drugs in poor countries where health care is often meager. They expose the contradiction of testing pharmaceuticals on people who will never be able to afford to buy the successful drug once it is manufactured. They expose the paradox of governments that will supply drugs for free to people suffering from diseases like AIDS, but that simultaneously allow the public health care infrastructure of their societies to crumble. They have also explored the consequences that follow when people with a shared biomedical diagnosis find one another and develop a shared identity based on this diagnosis, a form of biological identity that anthropologist Paul

Rabinow has called **biosociality.** People who share a biosocial identity may become involved in **health activism,** banding together and organizing politically to demand that the state acknowledge the existence of the disease and provide funding for research to seek a cure, actions generating a phenomenon sometimes called **biological citizenship.**

All these forms of research are increasing the prominence of contemporary medical anthropology as an applied anthropological subfield with a rich and diverse history. Some of the more recent directions in medical anthropology, moreover, rely heavily on research in science and technology studies that grew out of the critique of traditional understandings of science prompted by the work of Thomas Kuhn; indeed, medical anthropology actively contributes to the ongoing development of science and technology studies. In many ways, the anthropology of science, technology, and medicine offers a promising model of new and valuable ways in which the subfields of North American anthropology may support one another in the twenty-first century.

For Further Reading

THOMAS KUHN AND POST-KUHNIAN STUDIES OF SCIENCE
AND TECHNOLOGY

Galison 1987, 1997; Hackett et al. 2008; Haraway 1991, 1997; Kelty 2008; Kuhn 1996; Labinger and Collins 2001; Latour 1987; Latour and Woolgar 1986; Pickering 1985; Shapin 2010

COLLECTED ESSAYS IN MEDICAL ANTHROPOLOGY

Good et al. 2010

MEDICAL ANTHROPOLOGY AND HUMAN ADAPTATION

Boyd and Richerson 1985; Durham 1991; Lee 2003; McElroy and Townsend 2008; Wiley and Allen 2009

CRITICAL MEDICAL ANTHROPOLOGY

Baer et al. 2004; Biehl 2007; Farmer 2003; Fassin and Pandolfi 2010; Kiefer 2007; Lock and Nguyen 2010; Scheper-Hughes 1992; Singer and Baer 2007

12

Theory in Cultural Anthropology

The key terms and concepts covered in this chapter, in the order in which they appear:

theory
empirical
fact

unilineal cultural
  evolutionism

biological
  determinism
races

diffusion
culture traits
historical
  particularism
culture areas

functionalism

structural
  functionalism
social determinism
cultural determinism
superorganic

configurations of
  entire cultures
culture-and-
  personality school

ethnoscience
emic
etic

structuralism
French structuralism
bricolage

agency
symbolic
  anthropology
ecological
  anthropology
cultural ecology
multilineal
  evolutionism
behavioral ecology

cultural materialism
utilitarian

historical materialism
political ecology

ORIGINALLY, ANTHROPOLOGY AIMED to be a science of culture. Its early practitioners modeled themselves on the most successful scientists of their day—the physicists, chemists, and especially the biologists. As much as possible, they aimed to adopt the methodology of science and described their activities using scientific terminology. Thus, important late-nineteenth-century scholars like Lewis Henry Morgan and Herbert Spencer were most explicit about the fact that their work involved a search for the laws of society and culture and that discovering such laws would permit them to describe the relationships of material cause and effect that underlay social and cultural phenomena.

Since their day, the applicability of the scientific method to the study of human social and cultural life has been questioned. Although some cultural anthropologists maintain that the scientific method is appropriate to anthropology, many of their colleagues have concluded either that human cultural life is not an appropriate subject matter for "scientific" analysis or that, if it is, science itself must be reconfigured and its methodology revised to provide accounts of human cultural life that are not distorted beyond all recognition (also discussed in Chapters 1 and 11).

12.1 Anthropology as Science

Why did early anthropologists think that culture could be studied scientifically? If we believe E. B. Tylor, it was because culture was patterned, orderly, *lawlike*. As Tylor famously said, if law is anywhere it is everywhere. Like physical scientists and social scientists such as Herbert Spencer (1820–1903) and Emile Durkheim (1858–1917), Tylor and other early anthropologists believed that the phenomena of culture—languages, customs, techniques, rituals, and so forth—were *material phenomena*, phenomena that existed in the world and were tangible and measurable and could be registered by the senses. The current shape of these phenomena was the effect of other material causes at work in human society, not of metaphysical or spiritual causes. Durkheim echoed this when he later argued that social facts could be explained only by other social facts. Much of culture seemed resistant to rapid change, but when it did change, it did so in a patterned and lawlike manner. Thus, Tylor, Spencer, and Lewis Henry Morgan described culture as evolving rather than changing unpredictably or randomly with the passage of time.

In anthropology, as in science, a **theory** is a formal description of some part of the world that explains how, in terms of cause and effect, that part of the world works. Anthropology followed the lead of scientific theorizing in other fields in which the aim was to explain a complex phenomenon by *reducing* it to a set of simpler elements whose interactions were both necessary and sufficient to produce the phenomenon in question. Because human culture in general and individual cultural traditions in particular are enormously complex phenomena, anthropologists hoped that they might discover those simpler elements and laws that *determined* the direction of cultural evolution.

Early scientists, and anthropologists who wanted to imitate their method, argued that the plausibility of any theory depended on the evidence used to defend it, and they were universal in urging that only solid empirical evidence be allowed. To be **empirical** means that the evidence used to support a theory is the product of hands-on experience and can be inspected and evaluated by observers other than the original researcher. Only evidence that could meet this standard could be considered scientific **fact**. Scientific investigation has always stressed the importance of empirical research, arguing that the evidence of one's senses is a surer foundation for reliable knowledge than speculation unsupported by direct experience and that the objectivity of one's evidence must be tested against the critical observations of others before it is granted.

12.2 Nineteenth-Century Approaches

Nineteenth-century **unilineal cultural evolutionism** is generally regarded as the first theoretical perspective to take root in the discipline of anthropology. Evolutionary thought in nineteenth-century biology is ordinarily associated with Charles Darwin (1809–82), but cultural evolutionary thought actually predated Darwin's 1859 publication of *On the Origin of Species* and was already well developed in the work of Darwin's contemporary Herbert Spencer. Spencer thought that human societies could usefully be compared to living organisms and stressed that, over time, like living organisms, societies increased in both size and internal complexity. Spencer's ideas had parallels with the work of his contemporary, Lewis Henry Morgan. Morgan is best remembered for two key contributions to the development of anthropological theory: his emphasis on patterned variation in kinship terminologies, which led him to speculate about the different forms human families might assume in different societies, and his attempt to connect these patterns of family organization to patterns of subsistence in a universal evolutionary sequence. The sequence he proposed drew together many contemporary ideas about the evolution of culture, including the idea that all cultures everywhere either had evolved or would evolve through the same sequence of stages: Savagery, Barbarism, and Civilization (also discussed in Chapter 7).

Morgan recognized that his scheme was tentative in places and required more evidence to sustain certain claims. Nevertheless, like other cultural evolutionists in this period, he was convinced that he had discovered underlying laws of cultural change and that better empirical evidence collected by future researchers would refine the patterns he had exposed.

In a scientific world where researchers hope to reduce complex effects to simple causes, theories of cultural evolution were challenged by other theories that claimed to explain the diversity of human social life in different ways. One of the strongest competitors in the late nineteenth century was the argument that biological differences between different human populations explained their different ways of life or, put another way, that a group's way of life was determined by its distinct, innate biological makeup. This approach, called **biological determinism**, is also known as *scientific racism*, for it claimed to have empirical evidence that supported both the existence of biologically distinct human populations, or **races**, and the relative rankings of these races on a scale of superiority and inferiority. Not surprisingly, this Eurocentric framework assumed that light-skinned European races were superior to darker-skinned African or Asian or Native American races because the latter had been conquered and dominated by the former.

Late-nineteenth-century evolutionary anthropologists never fully separated themselves from the biological determinists. Even though their defense of a universal set of cultural evolutionary stages presupposed a common humanity and common destiny shared by all the peoples of the world (which they sometimes described as the *psychic unity of mankind*), they believed that this common potentiality had not been equally developed in all living human populations and that its actual degree of realization was indicated by the stage of cultural evolution a particular society had achieved. Thus, although the descendants of people whose way of life was classified as "savage" might one day achieve the same level of sophistication as a contemporary people classified as "barbarian," there was no question of considering them equal at the present time. People living at a more highly evolved level of culture were simply viewed as more highly evolved *people* than those living at lower levels. Not until the twentieth century and the work of North American anthropologists like Franz Boas and his students would scientific racism be rejected as an explanation of human cultural diversity (also discussed in Chapter 2).

12.3 Early-Twentieth-Century Approaches

Although unilineal evolutionary schemes were built on valid observations about changes in human subsistence strategies and incorporated empirical evidence about kinship that has proved reliable over time, these schemes also included (as all scientific theories do) considerable speculation. As the twentieth century began, German anthropologists were offering a very different universal theory of culture change, based on the supposedly regular spread of various cultural items from group to group by **diffusion,** or borrowing. Some proponents of both views were becoming increasingly extreme in their claims. In the face of this extremism, Boas in the

United States denounced both theories. In the best scientific fashion, he used empirical ethnographic and historical evidence to expose the inadequacies of both forms of reductionism. Boas agreed that cultures changed over time, but such change could not be confined to passage through a single sequence of progressive evolutionary stages. Rather, historical evidence showed that cultures sometimes simplified over time, instead of becoming more complex, and in any case could easily skip stages by borrowing advanced cultural inventions from their neighbors. Similarly, although cultures are full of cultural items or activities, called **culture traits**, borrowed from neighboring societies, anthropologists go too far if they assume that most human groups are incapable of inventing anything on their own and must await the innovations that spread from a few favored sites of cultural creativity. Boas pointed out that some social problems—how to organize kinship, for example—have only a few possible solutions and are likely to be independently discovered again and again by widely separated peoples.

Boas and his students rejected both extreme evolutionary schemes and extreme diffusion schemes, preferring to focus on the distinct histories of change in particular human societies, an approach that came to be called **historical particularism**. By comparing the culture histories of neighboring peoples, they were able to trace the limits of diffusion of many cultural traits, eventually producing maps of **culture areas** far smaller and more complex than the vast maps of the German diffusionists.

The theoretical extremism that Boas rejected was also rejected in England and France at about the same time. Although not ruling out the possibility of one day being able to construct a theory of cultural evolution, anthropologists like Bronislaw Malinowski (1884–1942) and A. R. Radcliffe-Brown (1881–1955) in England and sociologist/anthropologist Emile Durkheim and his colleagues in France declared a moratorium on speculations about cultural evolution unsupported by empirical evidence. All urged that research focus instead on living societies in order to collect precisely the kind of detailed empirical evidence that might one day enable the construction of a plausible theory of cultural evolution.

Malinowski set an example with his own field research in the Trobriand Islands. Not only was he a pioneer in modern participant-observation field methods, but he also set standards for the collection of ethnographic data that had a lasting influence on subsequent generations of anthropologists. His approach was to classify the customs and beliefs he learned about in the field in terms of the function each one performed in the satisfaction of what he called *basic human needs* (also discussed in Chapter 7). For this reason, his research program became known as **functionalism**. Malinowski's main goal in much of his ethnographic writing was to debunk contemporary stereotypes of "savage" peoples as irrational, compulsive slaves to their passions, and so he emphasized repeatedly how orderly and well organized Trobriand life was and how customs that appeared irrational to ignorant outsiders could actually be shown to play important functions in meeting the Trobriand Islanders' basic human needs.

The theoretical response of other British and French anthropologists was to focus not on the function of particular customs in meeting the needs of individual human beings but rather on their function in preserving the structure of the society itself. Hence, this school of thought came to be called **structural functionalism**. Heavily influenced by the writings of Durkheim, Radcliffe-Brown was its most tireless promoter in Britain. Structural-functionalists were concerned with what kept societies from falling apart (discussed in Chapter 6), and they could demonstrate that a variety of social practices described by ethnographers—witchcraft accusations, kinship organization, myths, and the like—performed this function.

In the mid-twentieth century, an antagonism developed between structural-functionalist British social anthropologists (as they called themselves) and North American cultural anthropologists. In retrospect, the antagonism seems rather trivial, but for many anthropologists at the time the issue was whether anthropology would be taken seriously as a science. As we have seen, British social anthropologists, via Radcliffe-Brown, who was influenced by Durkheim, took *society* as their defining concept. To them, human bodies arranged in space in particular configurations constituted the unquestionable reality that must be shaped by material laws of cause and effect operating in the social realm. North American anthropologists, however, focused on the concept of *culture*—the ideas, beliefs, values, and meanings that different groups of people developed to express their understanding of their lives and themselves.

For a British social anthropologist, nothing could be less material and thus possess less causal power than ideas, beliefs, and values. For the most outspoken of them, culture was a by-product, or a rationalization of material social arrangements that had nothing to do with culture but were instead the inevitable outcome of the operation of universal social laws (the necessity of maintaining social solidarity so that the social group endures over time) that automatically forced living human organisms into particular social configurations in particular circumstances. But North American cultural anthropologists countered such arguments by emphasizing the power of culture to shape all aspects of people's lives, including the ways they organized their societies.

To counter the **social determinism** advocated by some structural-functionalists, some cultural anthropologists proposed a form of **cultural determinism**. For example, A. L. Kroeber (1876–1960), one of Boas's students, argued that culture was a **superorganic** phenomenon (to be contrasted with inorganic matter and organic life). That is, although culture was carried by organic human beings, it existed in an impersonal realm apart from them, evolving according to its own internal laws, unaffected by laws governing nonliving matter or the evolution of living organisms, and essentially beyond the control of human beings whom it molded and on whom, in a sense, it was parasitic.

The views of social determinists and cultural determinists were so extreme in part because they completely rejected any explanation of society or culture that would locate its origins either outside human individuals in some unseen, immaterial, personalized force like God or within human individuals in the psychological structure of their minds. Durkheim, Radcliffe-Brown, and Kroeber, each in his own way, struggled to defend the view that sociocultural beliefs and practices constituted a distinct scientific subject matter that had to be explained in its own terms by specialists who understood how it operated—that is, by social (or cultural) scientists like themselves.

In North America, cultural anthropologists developed a series of theoretical perspectives based on their conviction that culture shaped human behavior, including the construction of particular forms of social structure. In the early twentieth century, inspired by the work of Ruth Benedict, they turned to psychology and attempted to apply what was understood about the configuration of individual human personalities to the **configurations of entire cultures**. Attempts to explain why adults from different cultures held different values and engaged in different practices promoted attention on child-rearing practices, leading to the development of what was called the **culture-and-personality school**.

12.4 Mid-Twentieth-Century Approaches

Developments in the study of language inspired other cultural anthropologists to borrow insights from linguistics in attempting to explain how culture worked. One outcome of this was the development of **ethnoscience**, a movement in cultural anthropology that involved borrowing the techniques perfected by descriptive linguists to elicit information about culturally relevant domains of meaning by studying how the members of a particular group classified objects and events in their environments. Ethnoscientists were extremely concerned that the taxonomies they elicited not be contaminated by the imposition of their own cultural perspectives. Therefore, they went to great pains to preserve the boundary between the culturally relevant categories of their informants, called **emic** categories, and the categories that were the product of anthropological theory, called **etic** categories (also discussed in Chapter 3).

Another rather different attempt to apply insights from linguistics to cultural analysis was developed by French anthropologist Claude Lévi-Strauss. Inspired by the so-called structural linguistics of Swiss scholar Ferdinand de Saussure (1857–1913, see Chapter 3), particularly its analysis of phonemic structures, Lévi-Strauss tried to see whether the same kinds of structural patterns might be found in other domains of culture. Lévi-Strauss first applied his structural analysis—later called **structuralism** or **French structuralism**—to the study of kinship systems, but he gained an international reputation both inside and outside anthropology for his structural studies of myth (myth is discussed in Chapter 4).

Lévi-Strauss collected multiple variants of numerous myths from indigenous societies in the Americas and appeared to be, on the surface at least, as interested in explaining cultural diversity as other contemporary cultural anthropologists. But he parted company with those anthropologists, such as ethnoscientists, who used linguistic methods to produce more detailed and accurate descriptions of culture but who still thought of culture as a historically contingent set of learned beliefs and practices. Instead, Lévi-Strauss saw surface diversity as the by-product of much simpler underlying processes of thought rooted in the structure of the human mind itself. Lévi-Strauss argued that, because all human beings were members of the same species, they possessed the same innate mental structures. The most obvious of these structures, he asserted, was the tendency to classify phenomena in terms of binary oppositions, like male–female, night–day, up–down, or mind–body. Lévi-Strauss argued that the diversity of cultural phenomena around the world was a surface diversity, the output produced by people with identical mental structures who were working with different kinds of natural and cultural resources. All people thus were engaged in a kind of cultural tinkering, what he called **bricolage,** in which they combined and contrasted elements of their experience in complex constructions rooted in a universal set of human mental structures.

Structuralism was immensely influential inside as well as outside anthropology. Literary critics, in particular, seized upon structuralism as a theoretical toolkit that could help them dissect the structure of literary or artistic work. But Lévi-Strauss and other structuralists also had their critics. Early criticism mostly concerned the validity of particular structural analyses of myths or other cultural phenomena. Different analysts, using what they thought were the same structuralist methods, frequently produced different analyses of the same cultural materials, leading critics to raise the question of just how "scientific" structural analysis actually was and how much it depended on the analysts' own interpretive style.

Later criticisms, which fed into postmodernism, pointed out that structuralists (not unlike the Chomskyan linguists mentioned in Chapter 3) assume that cultures are monolithic and that cultural products, like myths, can have only a single "correct" reading. Structuralists wanted their readings accepted as objectively valid, like scientific discoveries, but their critics argued that the attempt to reduce all the variants of a myth to a single underlying structure ignored the possibility that the variants themselves contained important information about the social, political, or historical self-understanding of the myth-tellers. Rather than simply being the vehicles through which myths worked themselves out across time and space, perhaps the members of each society who recounted the myth were agents attempting to use the resources of myth to make sense of specific concrete social experiences. By reducing all cultural forms to the innate structures of the human mind, structuralism appeared to some observers to be merely a new kind of biological determinism.

Structuralism is only one of a series of theoretical perspectives in contemporary cultural anthropology that have come under fire because of their apparent denial of human **agency** (defined in Chapter 6). An ongoing struggle in anthropology concerns the relationship of culture to the individual. While most contemporary parties to the struggle agree that culture is learned, they disagree concerning how much is learned, how important it is for human survival, and how far individuals can go in modifying or rejecting aspects of their cultural heritage.

A different and very influential approach to human action developed in anthropology in the 1960s. This is referred to as **symbolic anthropology,** or sometimes *interpretive anthropology*, because of its emphasis on systems of meanings rather than on innate structures of mind or on the material dimensions of human life. For symbolic anthropologists, human culture is a system of symbols and meanings that human beings create themselves and then use to direct, organize, and give coherence to their lives. The most prominent symbolic anthropologists of the last part of the twentieth century were Mary Douglas, Victor Turner, and Clifford Geertz.

The work of Mary Douglas (1921–2007) combined a commitment to Durkheimian functionalism with an emphasis on the ways in which cultural symbols both reflect and shore up particular social orders. In her most famous book, *Purity and Danger* (1966), she explored widespread beliefs about purity and pollution in different societies, arguing that pollution was best understood as "matter out of place" within a particular symbolic order. Douglas drew attention to the ways in which a particular society's ideas about purity and pollution were regularly based on a metaphoric connection between the human body and society. She argued, for example, that symbolic practices that appeared to be concerned with protecting vulnerable human bodies from pollution were actually concerned with keeping vulnerable social structures from falling apart. Social vulnerabilities were symbolically represented as bodily vulnerabilities as when the orifices of the body were seen to stand for points of entry into or exit from the body politic. Thus, food taboos designed to protect individual bodies from ingesting polluting substances could be understood as a symbolic way of protecting a vulnerable social order from dangerous outside forces. Douglas's work focuses on forms of symbolism that appear to be universal in human cultures, an emphasis that sets her apart from both Turner and Geertz, who both paid far more attention to the particular symbolic practices of specific societies.

Victor Turner (1920–83) was trained as a structural-functionalist in England but became dissatisfied with examining abstract social structure. Rather than emphasizing people's unthinking conformity to the underlying principles that ordered their society, Turner's work emphasized practice and performance. His work came to focus on *social dramas*: people's concrete interactions and conflicts in everyday social life. Turner showed how social dramas not only offered anthropologists insight into the structure of a given society but also revealed how people in that society made sense of their lives. Turner's interest in social dramas led him into studies of ritual (see Chapter 4), pilgrimage, and theater. In all of these studies, he was concerned with how the symbols of a particular group of people—those "things that stand for other things"—were used as stores of meaning and as resources for social action. For Turner, what mattered were not the symbols themselves but what they meant to specific people and how they led to action in specific social situations.

Like Turner, Clifford Geertz (1926–2006) was interested in symbols and their interpretation. For Geertz, culture was a system of symbols and meanings that are publicly displayed in objects and actions. Drawing on literary theory more than on drama theory, Geertz came to see cultures as made up of *texts*, "stories that people tell themselves about themselves." In his view, the anthropologist's job is to learn to read those texts, not the way natives did because it was impossible to get inside the natives' heads, but from within the same cultural context. Geertz proposed the phrase *thick description* for this process of finding the local meanings of cultural texts and in so doing drew attention to the fact that written texts were the typical product of ethnographic fieldwork. Beginning in the early 1970s, many anthropologists increasingly came to see that their task was to *write about* other societies, not merely to collect and analyze data, and that their ethnographies should be understood as texts to be read alongside the natives' own texts.

Both Geertz and Turner were influential outside of anthropology in such branches of the humanities as religious studies and literary theory. Indeed, a common complaint about Geertz's work was that by relying so heavily on the interpretive skills of the anthropologist, it made the field appear more like literary criticism than social science.

The mid-twentieth century also saw a revival of evolutionary thinking in North American cultural anthropology. The new evolutionary anthropology rejected biological determinism, together with the racist evolutionary scheme that went with it. At the same time, evolutionary anthropologists accepted current biological understandings of evolution by natural selection and argued that human biological evolution, like the biological evolution of all organisms, involved adaptation to the environment. If varying modes of human adaptation were not the outcome of variations in human biology, some anthropologists reasoned, then perhaps the environments themselves were responsible for human cultural diversity. Anthropologists who ask such questions today usually are described as doing one or another kind of **ecological anthropology** (see Chapters 6 and 7).

Ecologists and ecologically inclined anthropologists generally analyze particular human populations as parts of *ecosystems*; that is, they are one group of living organisms that, together with other organisms, make their living within a given environmental setting. This setting is called a *system* because it exhibits regularities in terms of the variety and size of different populations and the resources they depend upon to survive and reproduce. These regularities are usually described in terms of a patterned flow and exchange of energy. Stable ecosystems are ones in which each population occupies its own *niche*; that is, all coresident populations make their livings in different ways and do not compete with one another.

An important founder of ecological approaches in cultural anthropology was Julian Steward (1902–72). His analytic framework, which is called **cultural ecology**, studied the ways in which specific human cultures interacted with their environment. Steward was an evolutionary thinker: He argued that cultural change over time was conditioned by the specific kinds of cultural developments, particularly in subsistence technology, available in a given society and the ways in which members of that culture used their technology to obtain what they needed to survive from the particular environment in which they lived. As cultural systems changed the way they interacted with their environments, thus changing their adaptations, they evolved to new levels of sociocultural integration.

Steward did not accept the universal stages of cultural evolution supported by his contemporary Leslie White (1900–75). For White, cultural evolution was a general process encompassing all the cultures of humanity. White recast the major stages of cultural evolution proposed by nineteenth-century anthropologists (and by Karl Marx) in terms of how much energy per capita per year was captured by particular cultural systems. For White, cultures evolved as they captured more energy or as their technologies improved, or both. Using these criteria, White identified three major evolutionary turning points: (1) the domestication of plants and animals (the agricultural revolution of antiquity), (2) the beginnings of mechanization (linked to the "fuel revolution" at the beginning of the nineteenth century), and (3) the technological harnessing of atomic energy in the mid-twentieth century. Steward's approach to cultural evolution, by contrast, has been described as **multilineal evolutionism**. Steward focused not on global evolutionary trends but rather on particular sequences of culture change, showing how local, evolutionary trajectories in similar societies could go in different directions, depending on the society's overall culture, its technology, and the particular environment to which each society was adapting. Today, those evolutionary anthropologists who assign symbolic culture a key role in their explanations of human adaptations to their environments (for example, cultural inheritance theorists) are sometimes said to be continuing the practices of cultural ecology and multilineal evolutionism pioneered by Steward.

Research in ecological anthropology addresses debates about human agency because some ecological anthropologists argue that human adaptations are heavily circumscribed by environmental restrictions. In common with sociobiology, for example, **behavioral ecology** applies to human societies the same analytic principles that have been used to study the social behavior of animals, especially the social insects (for example, ants). Indeed, sociobiology-inspired behavioral ecological anthropologists claim that, over the millennia, natural selection operating on individuals in particular environments not only has selected for genes responsible for the physical and behavioral traits of *individuals* but also has operated to increase the frequency in individuals of genes that control our *social* behavior.

Behavioral ecologists thus argue that we have been programmed to respond to others in stereotypical (but individually adaptive) ways that neither cultural conditioning nor individual willpower can modify. Put another way, behavioral ecology stresses that natural selection has produced human beings programmed to automatically find ways of maximizing their own individual self-interest, which in evolutionary terms means getting as many of one's genes into the next generation as possible (see Chapter 7). Some versions of behavioral ecology have little or no role for symbolic culture in their accounts of human adaptation because acting in terms of arbitrary symbol systems could potentially mislead individuals into acting in ways that go against their own self-interest, such as taking risks for others with no obvious gain for oneself (or one's genes). If environmental curbs are as extensive as some behavioral ecological anthropologists claim, they would appear to restrict human agency just as much as the kinds of biological programming claimed by the biological determinists.

By drawing attention to ecological factors that affect cultural adaptations, ecological anthropologists have attempted to show the inadequacies of cultural theories that take no account of the material conditions of human life. Three other theoretical movements in the latter half of the twentieth century, each rather different from the ecological approaches described previously, also tried to argue for theories of culture that take the material world into account.

One such attempt was the **cultural materialism** of Marvin Harris (1927–2001), a theoretical perspective rooted in Harris's idiosyncratic readings of Marx, Engels, White, and Steward. He tries to tame what he sees as the extravagant claims of cultural determinists by pointing out the material constraints with which any cultural adaptation must come to terms. He attempts to show that particular customs that shock or disgust us today, such as warfare, cannibalism, or infanticide, were invented to ensure human survival in some past habitat. Although these are cultural inventions, their inventors are no more conscious of why they are doing what they do than are the human beings described by some behavioral ecologists. In both cases, moreover, the same kinds of self-interest calculations are said to govern the selection of particular practices. Indeed, both behavioral ecology and cultural materialism take an essentially **utilitarian** approach to the explanation of the evolution of cultural diversity: In any given case, behaviors are selected because they confer the greatest good for either a particular individual (behavioral ecology) or the group (cultural materialism).

A second brand of materialism that has been influential in recent cultural anthropology is the **historical materialism** based on the writings of Karl Marx and his followers. The main feature distinguishing Harris's cultural materialism from Marxian historical materialism is the role of the material forces of history. Whereas Harris's approach explains cultural adaptation or evolution in terms of local conditions, the Marxian approach explains cultural evolution in world-historical terms; after all, Marx was another nineteenth-century unilineal evolutionist. But the ways in which he differed from other unilineal evolutionists made him an inspiration for anthropologists dissatisfied with accounts of culture change that did not take into account social and political conflict, domination, and inequality (discussed in Chapters 6, 7, and 10). Marx attributed large-scale sociocultural change to the working out of material contradictions within the organization of society (its relations of production). Ecological constraints are less important than the social constraints and contradictions generated by a particular, culturally constructed mode of production (for example, between landowners and the people who own no land and so must rent from the owner). Marxian ideas were also attractive because, in at least some of his writings, Marx suggested that human beings could exercise agency—could "make history"—albeit not under conditions of their own choosing. The material constraints of history limited the action they could take, limited even the alternatives they could imagine to the present order, but did not necessarily turn them into puppets unable to affect their cultural surroundings. Although the political hopes inspired by historical materialism have dimmed considerably with the end of the Cold War, Marx's crucial insights into the workings of capitalism and the mechanisms of domination continue to offer theoretical inspiration to some anthropologists.

A third attempt to develop a theory of culture that takes the material world into account may be seen in **political ecology.** As we noted in Chapter 6, political ecologists draw attention to the ways in which human groups struggle with one another for control of (usually local) material resources. They frequently provide ethnographic accounts that show why a particular local group's economic difficulties are due not to the backwardness of their cultural ecological practices but rather to the fact that political interventions by outsiders have deprived them of the resources they once could count on to help them secure their subsistence. Some political ecologists have pointed out that the material deprivation experienced by some local social groups is occasionally the result of their own decision to live with deprivation rather than succumb to political domination; this choice has been called an *adaptation of resistance*. In the past, many political ecologists were inspired by Marxian approaches to political and economic issues (see Chapter 7).

Today, a number of political ecologists describe themselves as "post-Marxists" who reject Marx's deterministic account of the evolution of modes of production. However, even post-Marxist political ecologists in anthropology continue to value the attention that Marx and his followers drew to economic inequality and political oppression, especially in a globalizing world where struggles to control the environment and its resources are multiplying. Many political ecologists believe that anthropologists have much to contribute to help resolve issues of environmental management. Some are active in environmental movements and collaborate with indigenous groups and others in pursuit of environmental justice.

12.5 Late-Twentieth-Century Debates

At the beginning of the twentieth century, cultural anthropologists wanted to create a science of culture. By the beginning of the twenty-first century, cultural anthropology had split into two camps divided not only over whether a science of culture is possible but also whether science itself, as traditionally conceived, is possible. One camp consisted of those who defended the traditional understanding of science, which many call *positivism* (see Chapter 1). They were committed to the view that universal, objective truth can be discovered by rational methods, that scientific explanations involve reducing complex effects to their simpler determining causes, and that these procedures ultimately will unify knowledge from all domains of experience in one grand "theory of everything."

The other camp took very seriously the critique of modern science embodied in *postmodernism* (see Chapter 11). Its members regarded the universalizing, reductionist approach of positivist science as inadequate and distorting when applied to the study of culture. For them, taking symbolic culture seriously required a reflexive, interpretive approach in which the details of specific cultural realities are not eliminated, in which people's individual voices and their unique understandings are not silenced by generalizations.

TABLE 12.1   Some Key Theoretical Positions in Anthropology

LATE NINETEENTH CENTURY	FIRST HALF OF TWENTIETH CENTURY	MID-TWENTIETH CENTURY	LATE TWENTIETH CENTURY
Unilineal evolution	Historical particularism	Ethnoscience	Symbolic anthropology
Diffusion	Functionalism	Structuralism	Behavioral ecology
	Structural functionalism	Ecological anthropology	Cultural materialism
	Cultural determinism	Cultural ecology	Postmodernism
	Culture-and-personality approach	Multilineal evolutionism	Political ecology
			Science studies

They call into question the supposed universal truths of "scientific anthropology." (Table 12.1 lists the key theoretical positions in anthropology.)

Since the late 1980s and early 1990s, many anthropologists have realized that, for all their political attractiveness, extremist positions are unsatisfactory. The issues are complex, however, because some kinds of progressive politics, such as the condemnation of genocide, seem to rest squarely on the assumption that all human beings everywhere are bearers of universal human rights that *nobody* can be permitted to ignore. It is precisely in the area of human rights that the critics of interpretivism have made their most powerful argument. If all action is culturally relative, they argue, then one has no grounds for international condemnation of leaders of nation-states who persecute their own citizens. If postmodernists have their way, they conclude, and all forms of culture are assumed to be equally valuable, then the grounds for moral outrage at genocide evaporate. Indeed, the leaders of genocide campaigns frequently attempt to silence international critics by defending their actions as culturally appropriate for their societies, and they accuse their critics of ethnocentrism or imperialism. Some cultural anthropologists are quite open about the stopping points beyond which their analysis cannot go. For those of a traditional positivist bent, it may be deterministic theories that attempt to construct scientific bases for racism or sexism or other forms of social inequality. For those of an interpretivist bent, it may be forms of relativism that would explain away, say, poverty or violence against women.

One of the reasons why many contemporary anthropologists insist on walking the narrow line between positivism and interpretivism is that they realize that there is no simple relation between a particular set of knowledge claims and a particular political agenda. Claiming that women are "natural peacemakers," for example, might be a justification for placing women in high political office but has more often been used (at least in the West) as a justification for keeping women outside of politics because of their supposed incapacity to make war. Responsible scholarship (as well as responsible politics) thus requires paying more attention to what Donna Haraway (1944–) calls the *situated knowledges* produced by differently oriented observers engaged in different forms of knowledge production. Taking the orientation of observers into account also makes for better theory. For example, recent work on the history of anthropology has brought to light the significance of intellectual precursors whose work has been overlooked in past histories of the field but whose contributions to the ongoing development of anthropology have been vital. They range from Karl Marx and Max Weber to W. E. B. Du Bois and Zora Neale Hurston.

Attention to the position of situated observer—to his or her *standpoint*—builds on the insights that emerged when cultural anthropologists began to pay attention to the reflexive dimension of fieldwork. They recognized that making clear the historical, social, cultural, political, and economic contexts within which scholarly research is conducted can actually *increase*, rather than decrease, our ability to recognize where a particular set of knowledge claims are strongest and where they are weakest. For example, ethnographer A's observations about the culture of the X people may be based on fieldwork he conducted exclusively among adult males because young people and women refused to talk to him. Suppose that ethnographer A then writes an ethnography about the X people based on this research. The knowledge claims he makes about the culture of the X people will be stronger if he makes it clear from the outset that they are based on situated knowledge: that his information came exclusively from adult males. A different ethnography based on research only among adult females of the X people would be based on differently situated knowledge. The portraits of the X people that are produced by these two ethnographies may be at odds with one another in a number of respects. But readers would not have to decide that only one ethnography was telling the "true story"; perhaps no single ethnography can capture the "whole truth" about any way of life. If each ethnography clearly identifies the specific kinds of situated knowledge on which it is based, readers might expect them to offer different representations of the way the X people live their lives. People who occupy different standpoints within the same society are unlikely to understand their society in exactly the same way, but distinctly situated points of view can still offer excellent access to *some* of the truths about life in that society. And if these partial truths constructed from different standpoints are not easily reconciled, this may be an accurate reflection of contradictions in the society itself. These days, after all, few anthropologists expect any society to be neatly bounded, internally harmonious, or functioning smoothly.

This same approach has also led anthropologists to question the assumption that anthropological categories—ritual or kinship, for example—are timeless, universal structures that are not dependent on historical contingencies for the ways in which they are expressed among specific groups of people. The strengths of much recent work in cultural anthropology lie in continuing commitment to ethnographic particularities that frequently resist assimilation into predictable theoretical categories. Much contemporary ethnography relates macroprocesses of globalization with the microlevel of specific people's everyday life. This work, cultural anthropologists often discover, calls into question both positivist and postmodern positions because it focuses on the often unpredictable ways people come to terms with these processes as they construct meanings in the historical and cultural contexts of their own changing lives. This enduring commitment to recognizing the reality of other perspectives and taking them seriously keeps cultural anthropology a vibrant, exciting, and compelling discipline with great potential for allowing human beings to come to know and understand themselves better.

12.6 New Directions in the Twenty-First Century

There are no unambiguous rules for how to walk the line between the extremes of determinism (whether biological, cultural, ecological, or historical) and the extremes of relativism; in the wake of the postmodern critique, cultural anthropologists have committed themselves to a range of different projects. Probably no form of cultural anthropology being practiced today is carried out in ignorance of or indifference to global interconnections that have been brought into existence since the end of the Cold War. But such interconnections can be studied in many ways.

Some cultural anthropologists root their ethnography among a given local "indigenous" population in a particular location and focus on the way global processes and institutions have come to affect the lives of that local population. For example, work by ethnographers working in sites from the Amazon lowlands to highland Papua New Guinea has documented the arrival of miners, loggers, and other outsiders who turn up and challenge local people for access to their resources. Sometimes the ethnography chronicles the destruction left in the wake of such encounters; often ethnographers use their special relationships with the threatened indigenous groups to become their advocates and defenders in a variety of different settings, from the media to courts of national and international law. This work may include involvement in national and international social movements as ethnographers and those with whom they work join together with like-minded activists and allies on the local, national, or international level to prevent environmental destruction or to protect cultural or human rights. In these kinds of settings, various forms of collaborative research and ethnographic writing are becoming increasingly common.

Some anthropologists prefer to focus their attention on the international political and economic processes that dispossess some populations of their homes and ways of life and push them into new territories as immigrants or refugees. Ethnographers follow the movements of such groups and their resettlement, temporary or permanent, in new locations ranging from refugee camps to neighborhoods in cities in different nation-states or continents. One result has been an increasing number of ethnographies carried out in the United States and Europe among newly arrived groups of all kinds, who engage in the complex work of constructing relationships with new neighbors even as they continue to manage relations with those they have left behind. Groups like undocumented migrants and homeless people have also become a focus of ethnographic research motivated by ethnographers' concerns for social justice.

Studies of the international political economy from ethnographic and historical points of view also continue to be produced. Contemporary ethnographers have little patience with ethnographic accounts of contemporary ways of life that ignore history and assume that local affairs have always been the way they were the day the ethnographer first began fieldwork. At a time when numerous global processes are undoing cultural identities and practices before everyone's eyes, many ethnographers find it important to document the way those identities took shape over time and to identify processes that promote current changes. In many parts of the world, this requires paying attention to European colonial conquest, noting carefully the precolonial, colonial, and postcolonial regime changes that have regularly remade the circumstances with which particular populations have had to cope. Such concerns prompt the continuing direction of historical ethnographic attention to European cultural practices in the colonial setting as well as to the cultural responses of colonized peoples.

At the beginning of the twenty-first century, cultural anthropology has become well established in many parts of the world; distinct "schools" of Mexican, Brazilian, and Indian anthropology are stronger than ever. Theory and practice have been decentered from institutions in Europe and the United States, and Euro-American cultural practices are fully accepted as viable ethnographic research topics.

For example, anthropological studies of science and technology have become increasingly numerous and influential (see Chapter 11). Beginning in the late 1970s and early 1980s, scientific laboratories, clinics, and hospitals became increasingly important as settings for ethnographic research. Such work has had an important impact in medical anthropology, especially studies focusing on bioscience and biotechnology. This work is concerned with not only scientific theories and practices, such as stem cell research, but also scientific apparatuses and procedures that may directly intervene in people's lives, such as infertility treatments, new imaging technologies, advances in organ transplantation, and the production of sophisticated artificial implants or prostheses. The unprecedented nature of these developments regularly raises ethical issues about the appropriateness of the research or the procedures as well as how it will be funded, who will benefit from it, and what its negative impacts are likely to be. Developments in biotechnology also blur the boundaries between "nature" and "culture," encouraging ordinary people who have experienced in vitro fertilization or organ transplantation, for example, to refashion the way they understand their own biological and cultural identities. Many anthropologists are concerned with understanding and documenting such changes and their potential social, political, and economic consequences.

Insights from science studies have been influential among anthropologists whose interests are only tangentially concerned with science and technology themselves. In some cases, this is because certain concepts originally developed in the context of the anthropology of science and technology seem to illuminate the ethnographic materials the anthropologist is studying. For example, some work in science studies has drawn attention to the role of *distributed agency* in the production of scientific knowledge. This work argues that successful scientific projects and successful technologies are both *heterogeneous assemblages of components, human and nonhuman, living and nonliving,* all of which exercise some degree of agency, thereby contributing to the final outcome. Despite their often divergent interests, these components have been brought together in a way that allows them to work as one. The loss or breakdown of any component removes its agency, withdraws its contribution, and may destabilize the entire assemblage, whether it be a smoothly functioning piece of technology or the structure of knowledge claims in a particular scientific field.

The notion of a heterogeneous assemblage characterized by distributed agency has been important to some anthropologists who trace the emergence and development of new kinds of social, economic, and political structures in the context of globalization. A good illustration is Anna Tsing's recent analysis of rainforest destruction and environmental activism in Indonesia, presented in her book *Friction: An Ethnography of Global Connection* (2005). Tsing recounts how, for a short time in the late 1980s and early 1990s, local villagers, "nature-loving" university students, a handful of national bureaucrats concerned with burnishing their "modern" environmentalist credentials, and international environmental movements were able to forge an alliance that successfully kept international loggers out of a particular part of the Indonesian rainforest. This short-lived alliance was surprising, both because it took hold when Indonesia was ruled by a dictatorship and because it held firm even though different allies at different levels had very different understandings of what the alliance was all about. When the dictatorship ended, the alliance fell apart. These complex global assemblages, described in Chapter 10, represent alliances between players and institutions that forge global connections with one another despite the sometimes extremely divergent interests that otherwise divide them. Such forms are theoretically interesting because of the way they contrast with complex hierarchical forms of social organization that have historically been the focus of much theoretical work in the social sciences.

For Further Reading

THEORY

Behar and Gordon 1996; Bernard 2000; Darnell 2001; Geertz 1973; Harrison and Harrison 1999; Knauft 1996; Kuper 1996; McGee and Warms 2011; Moore 1997; Moore and Sanders 2006; Rosaldo 1989

Appendix:
Reading Ethnography

In Chapters 1 and 2, we explored ethnographic research and considered how ethnographic fieldwork is done. In this appendix, we will consider how to read the result of that work. As we saw earlier, an ethnography is a scholarly work about a specific way of life. It is based on the author's lived experience with a specific group of people over a period of time, ideally at least a year. Ordinarily, an ethnography is based on knowledge of the other way of life that is both deep and broad—anthropologists try to learn as much as they can about as much of their hosts' way of life as possible. The anthropologist may then write a general description of the way of life or (as is more common today) explore a particular problem of importance in anthropology from the perspective of the people whom he or she knows. Ethnography is therefore a kind of *writing*; it is not just a straightforward reporting of "the facts." Some of the same techniques that readers have learned for reading in other genres can be applied to reading ethnography. An ethnography is an exercise in representing a set of beliefs and practices, and this raises issues of ethics, politics, and interpretation. In this appendix, we offer you some suggestions for getting as much as possible from your reading of ethnographies.

The Parts of an Ethnography

How is an ethnography put together? While each ethnography has its own unique characteristics, there are several stylistic features that many ethnographies share. Ethnographies generally begin with a preface, in which the author may "set the scene," introduce him- or herself, explain how the field research to be reported came about, and thank a set of people for their help. The preface can be useful to a reader even if he or she doesn't recognize any of the names at the end. It can give the reader an idea about the purpose of the ethnography and why the author wrote it. The reader can learn if the ethnography is a revision of the author's doctoral dissertation or a new work, written after the author received his or her doctorate. It can give the reader an idea of how long ago the author was in the field and perhaps what theoretical directions the author might take.

The preface is usually followed by an introductory chapter that tends to have two major parts: an entrance narrative and the academic context of the work. The entrance narrative dates back to the earliest classic ethnographies in anthropology—both Malinowski's *Argonauts of the Western Pacific* (1922) and Raymond Firth's *We, The Tikopia* (1936), for example, begin with entrance narratives that are well known in anthropology. In the entrance narrative, the author invites the reader to join him or her in experiencing the first impressions of the field—what things looked like at the beginning, sounded like, smelled like; what the local people looked like and how the anthropologist was received at first; and how he or she lived. This narrative is useful in several ways: it gives the reader a sense of the author as a person, acquaints the reader with the author's field situation, and orients the reader to the ethnography. At the same time, it also serves as a way for the author to establish a kind of complicity with the readers, to introduce them to the author's legitimacy as a trustworthy source—to convince readers that they can have confidence in what the author will argue in the rest of the book. At the most basic level, this is the equivalent of saying, "I was there. Trust me."

The other part of the introductory chapter can be difficult for nonspecialists to get through. In a sense, what makes an ethnography an ethnography is that it is part of an ongoing debate within anthropology. Ethnographers do not just write about their experiences—their work is ordinarily intended to address current issues within the discipline of anthropology. Writing an ethnography that is not just for classroom use, then, obliges the author to spell out where his or her work fits in cultural anthropology: Who are the other scholars who have influenced him or her? What are the theoretical issues that the author plans to address? These issues are dealt with early in an ethnography and take the form of a section in which the author reviews (1) the regional and theoretical literature, indicating the strengths and weaknesses of work by other scholars among the same or related people, and (2) the strengths and weaknesses of theorists who have addressed similar issues. This can be challenging for nonspecialists because they usually do not have very much experience with the theoretical issues involved, nor do they recognize any of the names that are being cited by the author (for other anthropologists, this section is very important because it provides hints and clues as to the directions that the author will take in the rest of the ethnography). A further difficulty is that the author may choose to use a highly elaborated theoretical language in this section. You need to ask yourself (or your instructor) how much of this section is required reading. At the very least, you might want to try to apply the theoretical approaches discussed in Chapter 12 in order to put the arguments that the author is making into a theoretical context. It is not necessary to memorize the names of other scholars that are cited in this part of the text, but it is useful to try to follow the argument that the author is making. This section may be one of the points that your instructor will choose to discuss in lecture to help the class make sense of the key issues to be raised in the ethnography.

The style of most ethnographies now changes abruptly as the author shifts to the presentation of data and interpretation of those data. Here is the heart of the ethnography as the author presents a set of descriptions and analyses that will simultaneously represent aspects of a way of life and make an argument about their meaning. Here, the author has carefully and intentionally chosen the order and topics of the chapters. A book is always composed—some material included, other material left out—to make the points that the author wants made. Part of your job as an intelligent reader is to try to figure out why the author has structured the book in *this* particular way.

In some cases, of course, the author tells the readers in the preface or the introduction why the chapters are in the order in which they are found, but sometimes readers have to try to figure out the logic. Sometimes the sequence of chapters is chronological, following a ritual, agricultural, or calendrical cycle, or based on the anthropologist's own acquaintance with the community. More common, perhaps, is a sequence of chapters based on the complexity of the topics to be raised, beginning with the most straightforward and ending with the most complex, or where the topics of later chapters require information that can only be presented in earlier chapters.

Another common format is to begin with the environmental setting or history of the community or people who are the subjects of the ethnography, and then once the historical and ecological background is established, the author turns to the social and cultural worlds of the community. In other cases, authors may choose to arrange their chapters by the emotional difficulty or cultural unfamiliarity of the topics presented. Authors may feel that all the details of their arguments must be presented first before getting to material that their readers might find difficult to accept without the necessary background. Alternatively, they may have concluded that their readers need to know and sympathize with their informants before readers are introduced to aspects of informants' lives that might be difficult for readers to understand or accept.

There are many other ways to structure an ethnography, but in all cases that structure is something to which the author has given considerable thought. This doesn't mean that the author is always successful, by the way. Once they have figured out the logic, readers may decide that the author has not presented the material in a way that convinces them, satisfies them ("I wish she had written in greater detail about . . . "), or explains to them what the author wanted them to know ("I still don't understand why the people in the ethnography do . . . "). Sometimes authors may have omitted material that readers consider important. Sometimes there may be too much material that readers find tangential or that becomes overly repetitive. In other cases, readers may have had experiences that differ so much from the ethnographer's interpretation that they cannot accept either the accuracy of the ethnography or the universality of the claims ("I was in high school at the same time the author was doing his research in a high school. We did things very differently. Maybe what the author found was true in that school because it was not like other high schools.").

Following the body of the ethnography is the conclusion. Here, the style often changes again, as the author attempts to tie up the loose ends, summarize, and connect the body of the work with the theoretical issues, which are set out in the introduction, that motivated him or her. This is also a place where authors may return to a style that resembles the style of the first chapter because they wish to situate their work in the context of other work on similar topics: There may be more discussions of theory, more citations of work by other scholars, and an attempt to make a statement that is more general and abstract than anything in the preceding chapters. Here, your job is to try to figure out where the concluding remarks come from. Do they seem justified, based on what has been presented before, or does the author go too far or not far enough? Does the author connect the ethnographic chapters to the conclusion in a way that makes sense to you? Having finished the book, do you feel that you know something about the world that you had not known before? That you have gotten a sense of "being there"?

The Use of Indigenous and Local Terms

One of the most distinctive stylistic features of ethnographic writing is the use of indigenous or local terms. Readers of ethnography may have been taken aback and perhaps puzzled by this ethnographic usage; they may even find it makes reading the ethnography more difficult. There are several reasons why ethnographers may use many indigenous or local terms. At one level, it is further proof to the readers that authors know what they are talking about—they have learned the language that the local people use and they can demonstrate this in their writing. Also, there may be other people who speak that language who read the book. Whether the language in question is the Kiriwinian that Malinowski learned in the Trobriand

Islands in 1915–18 or the German that Daphne Berdahl used in the small town of Kella in the 1990s, scholarly professionalism requires that ethnographers record information about the languages of research as accurately as possible so that other fluent speakers will be able to recognize how the ethnographer has made sense of the language. Such linguistic accuracy is further proof that the authors can be trusted.

In a way, this is the equivalent of "showing your work" in a math class. But more important, it is a reflection of one of the fundamental assumptions in anthropology—that other people create through their languages coherent and meaningful ways to look at the world and that the language used to live those worlds *does not map perfectly onto English*. Using indigenous or local terms becomes a way of signaling dimensions of a way of life that are different from that of the ethnographer. Part of the ethnographer's job, as Bruce Knauft (2004, 18) puts it, is "learning and conveying concepts that are important to other people even when they exceed our initial understanding." For all of these reasons, then, the use of indigenous or local terms can be seen as a characteristic of the style of writing we call *ethnographic*. So, in reading ethnography, readers should not panic over the many indigenous or local terms that appear—it's unlikely that your instructor expects you to memorize all of them!—but should use the terms as indicators of important points of entry into understanding a way of life that is different from their own.

The Photographs

Many ethnographies are illustrated, usually with photographs. This is also an area that should draw the reader's attention. Photographs have been part of ethnographic writing since the first ethnographies—Malinowski's *Argonauts of the Western Pacific* (1922) contains 66 photographs, and he was following a guide to field photography first published in 1899. It is likely the case that the use of the camera in early ethnography was based on the idea that the camera was a tool of "scientific" recording, and it is certainly the case that Malinowski was very thorough in his use of cameras in the Trobriand Islands (see Young 1998). But it is well worth the reader's time to examine the photographs in any ethnography that he or she is reading and think about why they are there and what they contribute to the ethnography. After all, it adds to the expense of publishing a book to include photographs, and so they are not there just because the author thought it would be nice to include a few. First, the photographs are yet another way for the ethnographer to establish credentials—the photographs, especially when taken by the ethnographer or spouse, are a testimony to the fact that the ethnographer was there; often they signify that the author was well accepted by local people (many ethnographies have at least one image of the author interacting with local people). In both cases, the message is "I was there. You can trust what I am telling you."

Second, the photographs can set the scene, moving the reader from imagining the scene to having a picture of the scene. Sometimes even the most vivid writing cannot express the distinctive reality that the ethnographer wishes to convey. The photographs can help by giving the readers a visual reference for the ethnographer's descriptions and analyses. The photographs can also communicate details of the social and physical environment that the ethnographer may have neglected or found excessively complex to describe. Indeed, the photographs can allow readers a kind of complicity with the author by allowing them to check their interpretation of a scene against the author's. Third, the photographs can humanize the people with whom the ethnographer lived. For example, a tightly composed portrait that fills the photographic frame with a face is not a very useful photograph for seeing the social and physical world in which people live, but it is very effective at establishing the common humanity of subject, photographer, and viewer. Finally, from the use of captions and references in the text to the photographs, the ethnographer can create a dialogue between the text and the photographs that will allow the reader to understand better the world that the ethnographer is trying to evoke.

It must be said, however, that photographs have sometimes been used to exoticize the people in them. Some ways of drawing attention to costume, facial or body painting, body mutilations, ritual postures, activities, housing, or material objects can portray people as so alien that readers viewing the photos may see them as being socially or culturally abnormal or inferior or may see only differences, losing sight of the commonalities that they may share. For example, a text that includes photographs of people only in "traditional" costume can leave the impression of quaintness or exoticism: that this is how people dress on a daily basis, even when the traditional costume is only worn once a year or just for photographs. In recent years, anthropologists have critically examined the use of photographs in ethnography and consider very carefully the photographs they include with their own work. It is important to remember that photographs do not speak for themselves. Photographs are ambiguous, which is why they are given captions or discussed in the text of the ethnography itself.

As you read an ethnography with photographs, you might ask yourself some questions about the way that these images are treated. Are there extensive captions? Do the captions refer to the text, and does the text refer to the photographs? Are the photographs of people? Places? Both? How much of the scene is included in the photographs (that is, are most of the photographs close-ups of people, or are the people always surrounded by their environment)? Do the photographs draw you into the society or do they distance you? Are there things in the text that you wish were illustrated with a photograph? Can you figure out why the author chose the photographs that appear in the book? Do the photographs make you want to go where the ethnographer has been? Do you feel that you know the society better having seen the photographs?

Why Are You Reading This Ethnography (and How Should You Read It)?

Even before you open an ethnography, you should ask yourself (and perhaps your instructor, too) why you are reading it because why you are reading it will affect *how* you read it. The goal of reading an ethnography is not to memorize the multitude of details that are found within it. Frequently, the goal of reading an ethnography is to get a sense of a way of life very different from your own as well as to learn how the people described in the ethnography make sense out of their lives. The explicit focus of the ethnography might be economic activities or kinship reckoning, but your first goal ought to be to look for overall patterns rather than to remember details like the term for "Father's-Sister's-Daughter marriage" or the exact sequence of events in spirit possession.

You might be asked to read more than one ethnography in order to compare the ways of life of peoples on different continents or with different ways of making a living, or to find out what has happened to people whose ancestors used to farm but who now work in a factory in Malaysia or Mexico. You might also be reading an ethnography set in your own world, and the instructor's goal may be to get you to think about the ways in which your way of life, like that of other people elsewhere, is also a social and cultural construction. Even if your instructor has not told you why you are being asked to read this ethnography or specifically what to look for, you can often figure this out if you think about what the instructor has been discussing in class or where this ethnography is placed on the course syllabus.

In all cases, you should read actively and with paper and pencil handy. As noted above, all writing in anthropology is part of an ongoing dialogue within the field, and you should make yourself part of that dialogue: Reading is active, not passive. If you don't understand what the author is saying, make a note either on paper or in the margin of the book (only if it's yours, of course!). If you don't agree with something that the author has written, make a note. If you are really impressed with something that the author has written, make a note. If you want to know more about something the author has written, make a note. You and the author are in this together, and what you write in (and about) the book becomes part of the text.

Although it is difficult to do, especially when you are just starting out, think about what the author may have omitted or not discussed. Does the author not write about men? Or women? Does the author talk about globalization or the effects that nation-building efforts may have had on the people about whom you are reading? Does the author ignore or pay attention to conflicts within the group the ethnography is about? Are there topics that you would like to know more about? Is there anything that would make this book speak more directly to you?

One final set of questions to ask has to do with the ethnographer him- or herself. How does the ethnographer appear in the book? What role does the ethnographer take? Does the ethnographer give the impression of being a detached, outside observer, or does the ethnographer take a political position? Was the ethnographer an advocate for the people or working in an applied way with or for a group of people? Does the ethnographer take a position about any of the issues that are raised? What does the ethnographer reveal about him- or herself? About the purposes of the research? About how it came about? About who paid for it? About the nature of his or her interactions with the people in the study? In some cases, particularly in older ethnographies, the author appears as a character in the entrance narrative and then never makes another entrance. In other cases, the ethnographer is one of the characters in the book, sometimes as an observer, sometimes as a narrator, sometimes as someone whose experiences become part of the data being collected. More recently, ethnographers and their informants have begin to cowrite ethnographic texts based on the fieldwork that they did together. It will be valuable to you to think about the effect these strategies have on your reading and on the ethnography more generally.

It has been a long time since ethnographies were taken at face value. Contemporary ethnographers are aware as never before that their texts are not innocent documents—they are not simply objective reports of the heaps of data that the ethnographer collected like ripe fruit on the trees of knowledge. They are part of an ongoing debate within the discipline of anthropology; they are based on an unequal, carefully negotiated relationship between the ethnographer and the set of people with whom he or she worked; they are necessarily partial (there were subjects left unstudied and events that the ethnographer did not or was not allowed to see); and they have political implications. They can be used by governments, by political groups within the society, and by scholars in other fields for purposes not intended by the ethnographer. As a result, ethnographers have become increasingly diligent about positioning themselves and their research in explicit contexts. They make clear who they are, how they were received both personally and politically, who they were able to spend time with, who paid for their research, how it was managed and carried out, and what parts of it may have been used by or objected to by local people of various kinds. They do this so that the significance of their data will be neither under- nor overestimated. Knowing who collected the data, how they were collected, from whom, and how they were interpreted makes the significance of ethnography stronger and more precise.

That said, it is important not to lose sight of the fact that a key factor motivating ethnography itself is an undeniable fascination with the varied ways of life people continue to make for themselves in different geographical, historical, political, and cultural settings. Ethnographies reveal the sometimes surprising inventiveness and resilience of people facing challenges of many kinds. Reading ethnography is an excellent pathway into the richness of the human experience. Enjoy!

Bibliography

Abu-Lughod, Janet. *Before European Hegemony: The World System A.D. 1250–1350*. New York: Oxford University Press, 1989.

Agar, Michael. *Language Shock: Understanding the Culture of Conversation*. New York: Morrow, 1994.

———. *The Professional Stranger*. 2nd ed. San Diego: Academic Press, 1996.

Akmajian, Adrian, et al. *Linguistics: An Introduction to Language and Communication*. 6th ed. Cambridge, MA: MIT Press, 2010.

Alland, Alexander. *The Artistic Animal*. New York: Doubleday Anchor, 1977.

Anderson, Benedict. *Imagined Communities*. London: Verso, 1983.

Anderson, Richard L. *Calliope's Sisters: A Comparative Study of Philosophies of Art*. 2nd ed. Upper Saddle River, NJ: Pearson Prentice Hall, 2004.

Appadurai, Arjun. *Modernity at Large: Cultural Dimensions of Globalization*. Minneapolis: University of Minnesota Press, 1996.

Arens, W., and Ivan Karp. *Creativity of Power: Cosmology and Action in African Societies*. Washington, DC: Smithsonian Institution Press, 1989.

Asad, Talal. *Formations of the Secular: Christianity, Islam, Modernity*. Palo Alto, CA: Stanford University Press, 2003.

Ashmore, Wendy, and Robert J. Sharer. *Discovering Our Past: A Brief Introduction to Archaeology*. 5th ed. New York: McGraw-Hill, 2009.

Askew, Kelly, and Richard R. Wilk, eds. *The Anthropology of Media: A Reader*. Malden, MA: Wiley–Blackwell, 2002.

Baer, Hans, Merrill Singer, and Ida Susser, eds. *Medical Anthropology and the World System*. 2nd ed. Westport, CT: Praeger, 2003.

Baker, Lee D. *From Savage to Negro: Anthropology and the Construction of Race, 1896–1954.* Berkeley: University of California Press, 1998.

Becker, Gaylene. *The Elusive Embryo: How Women and Men Approach New Reproductive Technologies.* Berkeley: University of California Press, 2000.

Behar, Ruth, and Deborah Gordon, eds. *Women Writing Culture.* Berkeley: University of California Press, 1996.

Bernard, Alan. *History and Theory in Anthropology.* New York: Cambridge University Press, 2000.

Bernard, H. Russell. *Research Methods in Anthropology: Qualitative and Quantitative Approaches.* 5th ed. Lanham, MD: AltaMira Press, 2011.

Biehl, João. *Will to Live: AIDS Therapies and the Politics of Survival.* Princeton, NJ: Princeton University Press, 2007.

Biersack, Aletta, and James B. Greenberg. *Reimagining Political Ecology.* Durham, NC: Duke University Press, 2006.

Blackwood, Evelyn, and Saskia E. Wieringa, eds. *Female Desires: Same-Sex Relations and Transgender Practices across Cultures.* New York: Columbia University Press, 1999.

Blount, Ben G., ed. *Language, Culture, and Society: A Book of Readings.* 2nd ed. Prospect Heights, IL: Waveland Press, 1995.

Blum, Susan. *Making Sense of Language: Readings in Culture and Communication.* New York: Oxford University Press, 2009.

Boellstorff, Tom. *Coming of Age in Second Life: An Anthropologist Explores the Virtually Human.* Princeton, NJ: Princeton University Press, 2008.

Bohannan, Paul. *How Culture Works.* New York: Free Press, 1995.

Bonvillain, Nancy. *Women and Men: Cultural Constructs of Gender.* 4th ed. Upper Saddle River, NJ: Pearson Prentice Hall, 2006.

———. *Language, Culture, and Communication: The Meaning of Messages.* 5th ed. Upper Saddle River, NJ: Pearson Prentice Hall, 2008.

Bowen, John, ed. *Religions in Practice: An Approach to the Anthropology of Religion.* 4th ed. Needham Heights, MA: Allyn & Bacon, 2008.

Bowie, Fiona. *The Anthropology of Religion: An Introduction.* 2nd ed. Malden, MA: Wiley–Blackwell, 2006.

Boyd, Robert, and Peter J. Richerson. *Culture and the Evolutionary Process.* Chicago: University of Chicago Press, 1985.

Bradburd, Daniel. *Being There: The Necessity of Fieldwork.* Washington, DC: Smithsonian Institution Press, 1998.

Breckenridge, Carol, Sheldon Pollock, Homi Bhabha, and Dipeesh Chakrabarty, eds. *Cosmopolitanism*. Durham, NC: Duke University Press, 2002.

Brenneis, Donald, and Ronald Macaulay, eds. *The Matrix of Language: Contemporary Linguistic Anthropology*. Boulder, CO: Westview Press, 1996.

Brettell, Caroline B., and Carolyn F. Sargent, eds. *Gender in Cross-Cultural Perspective*. 5th ed. Upper Saddle River, NJ: Pearson Prentice Hall, 2008.

Brosius, J. Peter, et al. *Communities and Conservation: Histories and Politics of Community-Based Natural Resource Management*. Walnut Creek, CA: AltaMira Press, 2005.

Bunten, Alexis. 2006. "Commodities of Authenticity: When Native People Consume Their Own 'Tourist Art.'" In *Exploring World Art*, ed. Eric Venbrux et al. Long Grove, IL: Waveland Press, 2006.

Burling, Robbins. *The Talking Ape: How Language Evolved*. New York: Oxford University Press, 2005.

Caldwell, Melissa L. "Domesticating the French Fry: McDonald's and Consumerism in Moscow." In *The Cultural Politics of Food and Eating: A Reader*, eds. James Watson and Melissa L. Caldwell. Malden, MA: Blackwell, 2005.

Campbell, Christina J., et al., eds. *Primates in Perspective*. New York: Oxford University Press, 2006.

Carrier, James G., ed. *A Handbook of Economic Anthropology*. Northampton, MA: Edward Elgar 2006.

Carsten, Janet, ed. *Cultures of Relatedness: New Approaches to the Study of Kinship*. Cambridge: Cambridge University Press, 2000.

———. *After Kinship*. Cambridge: Cambridge University Press, 2003.

———. *Ghosts of Memory: Essays on Remembrance and Relatedness*. Malden, MA: Wiley–Blackwell, 2007.

Chambers, Erve. *Native Tours: The Anthropology of Travel and Tourism*. 2nd ed. Long Grove, IL: Waveland Press, 2010.

Clifford, James. *The Predicament of Culture*. Cambridge, MA: Harvard University Press, 1988.

Coe, Sophie, and Michael Coe. *The True History of Chocolate*. London: Thames & Hudson, 1996.

Collier, Jane Fishburne, and Sylvia Junko Yanigasako, eds. *Gender and Kinship*. Stanford, CA: Stanford University Press, 1987.

Colloredo-Mansfeld, Rudi. *The Native Leisure Class: Consumption and Cultural Creativity in the Andes*. Chicago: University of Chicago Press, 1999.

Contemporary Issues Forum: Race and Racism. *American Anthropologist* 100, no. 3 (1998).

Counihan, Carole, and Penny Van Esterik. *Food and Culture: A Reader.* 2nd ed. New York: Routledge, 2008.

Counihan, Carole M. *Around the Tuscan Table: Food, Family, and Gender in Twentieth Century Florence.* New York: Routledge, 2004.

Daniel, E. Valentine, and John Knudsen, eds. *Mistrusting Refugees.* Berkeley: University of California Press, 1995.

Darnell, Regna. *Invisible Genealogies: A History of Americanist Anthropology.* Lincoln: University of Nebraska Press, 2001.

Das, Veena, Arthur Kleinman, Margaret Lock, and Mamphela Ramphele. *Remaking a World: Violence, Social Suffering, and Recovery.* Berkeley: University of California Press, 2001.

DeWalt, Kathleen M., and Billie R. DeWalt. 2nd ed. *Participant Observation: A Guide for Fieldworkers.* Lanham, MD: AltaMira Press, 2010.

Di Leonardo, Micaela, ed. *Gender at the Crossroads of Knowledge: Feminist Anthropology in the Postmodern Era.* Berkeley: University of California Press, 1991.

Dirks, Nicholas B. *The Scandal of Empire: India and the Creation of Imperial Britain.* Cambridge, MA: Harvard University Press, 2010.

Douglas, Mary. *Purity and Danger.* London: Routledge and Kegan Paul, 1966.

———. "Introduction." In *Witchcraft Confessions and Accusations,* ed. Mary Douglas. London: Tavistock, 1970.

Duranti, Alessandro. *Linguistic Anthropology.* Cambridge: Cambridge University Press, 1997.

———, ed. *Linguistic Anthropology: A Reader.* Malden, MA: Blackwell 2001.

———, ed. *A Companion to Linguistic Anthropology.* Malden, MA: Wiley–Blackwell, 2006.

Durham, William H. *Coevolution: Genes, Culture, and Human Diversity.* Stanford, CA: Stanford University Press, 1991.

Edelman, Marc, and Angelique Haugerud, eds. *The Anthropology of Development and Globalization: From Classical Political Economy to Contemporary Neoliberalism.* Malden, MA: Wiley–Blackwell, 2005.

Errington, Shelly. *The Death of Authentic Primitive Art and Other Tales of Progress.* Berkeley: University of California Press, 1998.

Ervin, Alexander M. *Applied Anthropology: Tools and Perspectives for Contemporary Practice.* 2nd ed. Upper Saddle River, NJ: Pearson Allyn & Bacon, 2004.

Farmer, Paul. *Pathologies of Power: Health, Human Rights, and the New War on the Poor*. Berkeley: University of California Press, 2003.

Fassin, Didier, and Mariella Pandolfi. *Contemporary States of Emergency: The Politics of Military and Humanitarian Interventions*. New York: Zone Books, 2010.

Featherstone, Mike, ed. *Global Culture: Nationalism, Globalization, and Modernity*. London: Sage, 1990.

Fiddis, Nick. *Meat: A Natural Symbol*. London: Routledge, 1991.

Firth, Raymond. *We, The Tikopia*. Boston: Beacon Press, 1966 [1936].

Fischer, Edward, and Peter Benson. *Broccoli and Desire*. Stanford, CA: Stanford University Press, 2006.

Fox, Richard G., and Barbara J. King, eds. *Anthropology Beyond Culture*. Oxford: Berg, 2002.

Fried, M. H. *The Evolution of Political Society*. New York: Random House, 1967.

Galison, Peter. *How Experiments End*. Chicago: University of Chicago Press, 1987.

———. *Image and Logic: A Material Culture of Microphysics*. Chicago: University of Chicago Press, 1997.

Gamst, F. C., and E. Norbeck, eds. *Ideas of Culture*. New York: Holt, Rinehart & Winston, 1976.

Gardner, Katy, and David Lewis. *Anthropology, Development and the Post-Modern Challenge*. London: Pluto Press, 1996.

Geertz, Clifford. *The Interpretation of Cultures*. New York: Basic Books, 1973.

Gershon, Ilana. "Email My Heart: Remediation and Romantic Break-Ups." *Anthropology Today* 24 (2008): 13–15.

Ginsburg, Faye, and Rayna Rapp. *Conceiving the New World Order: The Global Politics of Reproduction*. Berkeley: University of California Press, 1995.

Ginsburg, Faye D., Lila Abu-Lughod, and Brian Larkin, eds. *Media Worlds: Anthropology on New Terrain*. Berkeley: University of California Press, 2002.

Gmelch, Sharon. *Tourists and Tourism: A Reader*. 2nd ed. Long Grove, IL: Waveland Press, 2010.

Good, Byron, et al. *A Reader in Medical Anthropology: Theoretical Trajectories, Emergent Realities*. Malden, MA: Wiley–Blackwell, 2010.

Goodale, Mark. *Human Rights: An Anthropological Reader*. Malden, MA: Wiley–Blackwell, 2009.

Goodman, Alan H., and Thomas Leland Leatherman, eds. *Building a New Biocultural Synthesis: Political–Economic Perspectives on Human Biology*. Ann Arbor: University of Michigan Press, 1999.

Goody, Jack, and Stanley Tambiah. *Bridewealth and Dowry*. Cambridge: Cambridge University Press, 1973.

Graburn, Nelson, ed. *Readings in Kinship and Social Structure*. New York: Harper & Row, 1971.

Gudeman, Stephen. *The Anthropology of Economy: Community, Market, and Culture*. Malden, MA: Wiley–Blackwell, 2001.

Gutmann, Matthew. "Trafficking in Men: The Anthropology of Masculinity." *Annual Review of Anthropology* 26 (1997): 385–409.

Gwynne, Margaret A. *Applied Anthropology: A Career-Oriented Approach*. Upper Saddle River, NJ: Pearson Allyn & Bacon, 2003.

Hackett, Edward J., et al. *The Handbook of Science and Technology Studies*. 3rd ed. Cambridge, MA: MIT Press, 2008.

Halperin, Rhoda H. *Cultural Economies: Past and Present*. Austin: University of Texas Press, 1994.

Hannerz, Ulf. *Transnational Connections: Culture, People, Places*. London: Routledge, 1996.

Haraway, Donna. *Simians, Cyborgs and Women: The Reinvention of Nature*. New York: Routledge, 1991.

———. *Modest-Witness@Second-Smillennium.Femaleman-Meets-Oncomouse: Feminism and Technoscience*. New York: Routledge, 1997.

Harris, Olivia, ed. *Inside and Outside the Law: Anthropological Studies of Authority and Ambiguity*. New York: Routledge, 1997.

Harrison, Ira, and Faye Harrison, eds. *African-American Pioneers in Anthropology*. Champaign: University of Illinois Press, 1999.

Herdt, Gilbert, ed. *Third Sex, Third Gender: Beyond Sexual Dimorphism in Culture and History*. New York: Zone Books, 1994.

Hicks, David, ed. *Religion and Belief: Readings in the Anthropology of Religion*. 3rd ed. Lanham, MD: AltaMira Press, 2010.

Hill, Jane, and Judith Irvine, eds. *Responsibility and Evidence in Oral Discourse*. Cambridge: Cambridge University Press, 1992.

Hinton, Alexander Laban. *Annihilating Difference: The Anthropology of Genocide*. Berkeley: University of California Press, 2002.

Hirsch, Jennifer S., and Holly Wardlow. *Modern Loves: The Anthropology of Romantic Courtship & Companionate Marriage*. Ann Arbor: University of Michigan Press, 2006.

Hobsbawm, Eric, and Terence Ranger. *The Invention of Tradition*. Cambridge: Cambridge University Press, 1992.

Hodgson, Dorothy L. *Once Intrepid Warriors: Gender, Ethnicity, and the Cultural Politics of Maasai Development*. Bloomington: Indiana University Press, 2004.

Hughey, Michael. *New Tribalisms: The Resurgence of Race and Ethnicity*. New York: New York University Press, 1998.

Inda, Jonathan Xavier, and Renato Rosaldo, eds. *The Anthropology of Globalization: A Reader*. 2nd ed. Malden, MA: Wiley–Blackwell, 2007.

Inhorn, Marcia Claire. *Local Babies, Global Science: Gender, Religion, and in Vitro Fertilization in Egypt*. New York: Routledge, 2003.

Kahn, Susan Martha. *Reproducing Jews: A Cultural Account of Assisted Conception in Israel*. Durham, NC: Duke University Press, 2000.

Karkazis, Katrina. *Fixing Sex: Intersex, Medical Authority, and Lived Experience*. Durham, NC: Duke University Press, 2008.

Kearney, Michael. "The Local and the Global: The Anthropology of Globalization and Transnationalism." *Annual Review of Anthropology* 24 (1995): 547–65.

———. *Reconceptualizing the Peasantry: Anthropology in Global Perspective*. Boulder, CO: Westview Press, 1996.

Kedia, Satish, and John van Willigen, eds. *Applied Anthropology: Domains of Application*. Westport, CT: Praeger, 2006.

Kelty, Christopher M. *Two Bits: The Cultural Significance of Free Software*. Durham, NC: Duke University Press, 2008.

Kiefer, Christie W. *Doing Health Anthropology: Research Methods for Community Assessment and Change*. New York: Springer, 2007.

Kleinman, Arthur, Veena Das, and Margaret Lock, eds. *Social Suffering*. Berkeley: University of California Press, 1997.

Knauft, Bruce. *Genealogies for the Present in Cultural Anthropology*. New York: Routledge, 1996.

——— *The Gebusi*. New York: McGraw-Hill, 2004.

Kuhn, Thomas S. *The Structure of Scientific Revolutions*. 3rd ed. Chicago: University of Chicago Press, 1996.

Kuper, Adam. *Anthropology and Anthropologists: The Modern British School*. 3rd ed. London: Routledge, 1996.

———. *Culture: The Anthropologists Account*. Cambridge, MA: Harvard University Press, 1999.

Labinger, Jay A., and H. M. Collins. *The One Culture? A Conversation About Science*. Chicago: University of Chicago Press, 2001.

Lambek, Michael, ed. *A Reader in the Anthropology of Religion*. 2nd ed. Malden, MA: Wiley–Blackwell, 2008.

Lancaster, Roger N. *Life Is Hard.* Berkeley: University of California Press, 1992.

Lancaster, Roger N., and Micaela Di Leonardo, eds. *The Gender/Sexuality Reader: Culture, History, Political Economy.* London: Routledge, 1997.

Latour, Bruno. *Science in Action: How to Follow Scientists and Engineers Through Society.* Cambridge, MA: Harvard University Press, 1987.

———. *We Have Never Been Modern.* Cambridge, MA: Harvard University Press, 2007.

Latour, Bruno, and Steve Woolgar. *Laboratory Life: The Construction of Scientific Facts.* Princeton, NJ: Princeton University Press, 1986.

Lee, Richard B. *The Dobe* Ju/'hoansi. 3rd ed. Belmont, CA: Wadsworth, 2002.

Levine, Nancy. *The Dynamics of Polyandry: Kinship, Domesticity, and Population on the Tibetan Border.* Chicago: University of Chicago Press, 1988.

Lewellen, Ted C. *Dependency and Development.* Westport, CT: Bergin & Garvey, 1995.

———. *The Anthropology of Globalization: Cultural Anthropology Enters the 21st Century.* Westport, CT: Bergin & Garvey Paperback, 2002.

———. *Political Anthropology: An Introduction.* 3rd ed. Westport, CT: Praeger, 2003.

Lewin, Ellen. *Feminist Anthropology: A Reader.* Malden, MA: Wiley–Blackwell, 2006.

Li, Tania. *The Will to Improve: Governmentality, Development, and the Practice of Politics.* Durham, NC: Duke University Press, 2007.

Littlefield, Alice, and Hill Gates, eds. *Marxist Approaches in Economic Anthropology.* Lanham, MD: University Press of America and Society for Economic Anthropology, 1991.

Lock, Margaret M., and Vinh-Kim Nguyen. *An Anthropology of Biomedicine.* Malden, MA: Wiley–Blackwell, 2010.

Malinowski, Bronislaw. *Argonauts of the Western Pacific.* Long Grove, IL: Waveland Press. 1984 [1922].

Malkki, Liisa H. "Refugees and Exile: From 'Refugee Status' to the National Order of Things." *Annual Review of Anthropology* 24 (1995): 495–523.

Mankekar, Purnima. *Screening Culture, Viewing Politics: An Ethnography of Television, Womanhood, and Nation in Postcolonial India.* Durham, NC: Duke University Press, 1999.

Marcus, George. "Ethnography in/of the World System: The Emergence of Multi-Sited Ethnography." *Annual Review of Anthropology* 24 (1995): 95–117.

Marcus, George, and Michael Fischer. *Anthropology as Cultural Critique: An Experimental Moment in the Human Sciences.* Chicago: University of Chicago Press, 1986.

McDonald, James H. *The Applied Anthropology Reader.* Upper Saddle River, NJ: Pearson Allyn & Bacon, 2001.

McElroy, Ann, and Patricia K. Townsend. *Medical Anthropology in Ecological Perspective.* 5th ed. Boulder, CO: Westview Press, 2008.

McGee, R. Jon, and Richard Warms. *Anthropological Theory: An Introductory History.* 4th ed. New York: McGraw-Hill, 2007.

Merry, Sally Engle. *Human Rights and Gender Violence: Translating International Law into Local Justice.* Chicago: University of Chicago Press, 2006.

Messer, Ellen. "Anthropology and Human Rights." *Annual Review of Anthropology* 22 (1993): 221–49.

Miller, Barbara Diane, ed. *Sex and Gender Hierarchies.* Cambridge: Cambridge University Press, 1993.

Miller, Daniel. "Consumption and Commodities." *Annual Review of Anthropology* 24 (1995): 141–61.

———. "Coca-Cola: A Black Sweet Drink from Trinidad." In *Material Cultures: Why Some Things Matter,* ed. Daniel Miller. Chicago: University of Chicago Press, 1998.

Miller, Daniel, and Don Slater. *The Internet: An Ethnographic Approach.* Oxford: Berg, 2000.

Mintz, Sidney W. *Sweetness and Power: The Place of Sugar in Modern History.* New York: Penguin Books, 1985.

———. *Tasting Food, Tasting Freedom: Excursions into Eating, Culture, and the Past.* Boston: Beacon Press, 1996.

Moore, Henrietta L., and Todd Sanders. *Anthropology in Theory: Issues in Epistemology.* Malden, MA: Wiley–Blackwell, 2006.

Moore, Jerry D. *Visions of Culture: An Introduction to Anthropological Theories and Theorists.* Walnut Creek, CA: AltaMira Press, 1997.

Morgan, Marcyliena. *Language, Discourse, and Power in African American Culture.* Cambridge: Cambridge University Press, 2002.

Moro, Pamela, and James Myers. *Magic, Witchcraft, and Religion.* 8th ed. New York: McGraw-Hill, 2010.

Murthy, Dhiraj. "Muslim Punks Online: A Diasporic Pakistani Music Subculture on the Internet." *South Asian Popular Culture* 8 (2010): 181–94.

Myers, Fred. *Painting Culture: The Making of an Aboriginal High Art.* Durham, NC: Duke University Press, 2003.

Nader, Laura. *Law in Culture and Society*. Berkeley: University of California Press, 1997.

Nagata, Judith. "Beyond Theology: Toward an Anthropology of 'Fundamentalism.' " *American Anthropologist* 103 (2001): 481–98.

Nagengast, Carole. "Violence, Terror, and the Crisis of the State." *Annual Review of Anthropology* 23 (1994): 109–36.

Nardi, Bonnie A. *My Life as a Night Elf Priest: An Anthropological Account of World of Warcraft*. Ann Arbor: University of Michigan Press, 2010.

Netting, Robert. *Smallholders, Householders: Farm Families and the Ecology of Intensive, Sustainable Agriculture*. Stanford, CA: Stanford University Press, 1993.

Netting, Robert, Richard Wilk, and E. J. Arnould, eds. *Households: Comparative and Historical Studies of the Domestic Group*. Berkeley: University of California Press, 1984.

Ong, Aihwa. *Flexible Citizenship: The Cultural Logics of Transnationality*. Durham, NC: Duke University Press, 1999.

Ong, Aihwa, and Stephen J. Collier. *Global Assemblages: Technology, Politics, and Ethics as Anthropological Problems*. Malden, MA: Blackwell, 2005.

Ortner, Sherry. *Anthropology and Social Theory: Culture, Power, and the Acting Subject*. Durham, NC: Duke University Press, 2006.

Ottenheimer, Harriet Joseph. *The Anthropology of Language: An Introduction to Linguistic Anthropology*. 2nd ed. Belmont, CA: Wadsworth, 2009.

Ottenheimer, Martin. *Kinship: An Introduction to the Anthropological Study of Family and Marriage*. Belmont, CA: Wadsworth, 2006.

Padilla, Mark, et al. *Love and Globalization: Transformations of Intimacy in the Contemporary World*. Nashville, TN: Vanderbilt University Press, 2007.

Park, Michael Alan. *Biological Anthropology*. 6th ed. New York: McGraw-Hill, 2009.

Parkin, Robert. *Kinship: An Introduction to Basic Concepts*. Oxford: Blackwell, 1997.

Parkin, Robert, and Linda Stone, eds. *Kinship and Family: An Anthropological Reader*. Wiley–Blackwell, 2004.

Peletz, Michael. "Kinship Studies in Late Twentieth-Century Anthropology." *Annual Review of Anthropology* 24 (1995): 343–72.

Pels, Peter. "The Anthropology of Colonialism: Culture, History, and the Emergence of Western Governmentality." *Annual Review of Anthropology* 26 (1997): 163–83.

Pickering, Andrew. *The Mangle of Practice: Time, Agency and Science.* Chicago: University of Chicago Press, 1995.

Pickering, Andrew, and Keith Guzik. *The Mangle in Practice: Science, Society, and Becoming.* Durham, NC: Duke University Press, 2008.

Plattner, Stuart, ed. *Economic Anthropology.* Stanford, CA: Stanford University Press, 1989.

Pospisil, Leonard. *Anthropology of Law: A Comparative Theory.* New York: Harper & Row, 1971.

Rabinow, Paul. *Reflections on Fieldwork in Morocco.* Berkeley: University of California Press, 1977.

Relethford, John. *The Human Species: An Introduction to Biological Anthropology.* 8th ed. New York: McGraw-Hill, 2009.

Robbins, Richard H. *Global Problems and the Culture of Capitalism.* 3rd ed. Upper Saddle River, NJ: Pearson Allyn & Bacon, 2004.

Rosaldo, Renato. *Culture and Truth: The Remaking of Social Analysis.* Boston: Beacon Press, 1989.

Sacks, Karen. *Sisters and Wives.* Westport, CT: Greenwood Press, 1979.

Sahlins, Marshall. *Stone Age Economics.* Chicago: Aldine, 1972.

Salzmann, Zdenek. *Language, Culture, and Society: An Introduction to Linguistic Anthropology.* 4th ed. Boulder, CO: Westview Press, 2006.

Savage-Rumbaugh, Sue, et al. "Spontaneous Symbol Acquisition and Communicative Use by Pygmy Chimpanzees (Pan Paniscus)." *Journal of Experimental Psychology: General* 115 (1986): 211–35.

Schieffelin, Bambi, Kathryn Woolard, and Paul V. Kroskrity, eds. *Language Ideologies: Practice and Theory.* New York: Oxford University Press, 1998.

Schiller, Nina Glick, and Georges Fouron. "Long-Distance Nationalism Defined." In *The Anthropology of Politics,* ed. Joan Vincent. Malden, MA: Blackwell, 2002.

Schneider, David. *American Kinship.* Englewood Cliffs, NJ: Prentice Hall, 1968.

———. *A Critique of the Study of Kinship.* Ann Arbor: University of Michigan Press, 1984.

Scheper-Hughes, Nancy. *Death Without Weeping: The Violence of Everyday Life in Brazil.* Berkeley: University of California Press, 1992.

Schuler, Sindey Ruth. *The Other Side of Polyandry.* Boulder, CO: Westview Press, 1987.

Schultz, Emily. *Dialogue at the Margins: Whorf, Bakhtin, and Linguistic Relativity.* Madison: University of Wisconsin, 1990.

Scott, James. *Weapons of the Weak.* New Haven, CT: Yale University Press, 1987.

———. *Domination and the Arts of Resistance.* New Haven, CT: Yale University Press, 1992.

———. *Seeing Like a State: How Certain Schemes to Improve the Human Condition Have Failed.* New Haven, CT: Yale University Press, 1998.

Service, Elman. *Primitive Social Organization.* New York: Random House, 1962.

———. *Origins of the State and Civilization.* New York: Norton, 1975.

Shapin, Steven. *The Scientific Revolution.* Chicago: University of Chicago Press, 1996.

———. *Never Pure: Historical Studies of Science as If It Was Produced by People with Bodies, Situated in Time, Space, Culture, and Society, and Struggling for Credibility and Authority.* Baltimore, MD: Johns Hopkins University Press, 2010.

Shapin, Steven, and Simon Schaffer. *Leviathan and the Air-Pump: Hobbes, Boyle, and the Experimental Life.* Princeton, NJ: Princeton University Press, 1985.

Sharma, Aradhana, and Akhil Gupta. *The Anthropology of the State: A Reader.* Malden, MA: Wiley–Blackwell, 2006.

Sharp, Lesley. *Strange Harvest: Organ Transplants, Denatured Bodies, and the Transformed Self.* Berkeley: University of California Press, 2006.

Singer, Merrill, and Hans Baer. *Introducing Medical Anthropology: A Discipline in Action.* Lanham, MD: AltaMira Press, 2007.

Smedley, Audrey. *Race in North America.* 2nd ed. Boulder, CO: Westview, 1999.

Smith, Valene L. *Hosts and Guests: The Anthropology of Tourism.* 2nd ed. Philadelphia: University of Pennsylvania Press, 1989.

Stein, Rebecca, and Philip L. Stein. *Anthropology of Religion, Magic, and Witchcraft.* 2nd ed. Upper Saddle River, NJ: Pearson Allyn & Bacon, 2008.

Stoler, Ann Laura. *Carnal Knowledge and Imperial Power: Race and the Intimate in Colonial Rule.* Berkeley: University of California Press, 2002.

Stone, Linda. *Kinship and Gender: An Introduction.* 4th ed. Boulder, CO: Westview Press, 2009.

———, ed. *New Directions in Anthropological Kinship.* Lanham, MD: Rowman & Littlefield, 2001.

Strathern, Marilyn. *Reproducing the Future: Anthropology, Kinship, and the New Reproductive Technologies.* New York: Routledge, 1992.

Suggs, David, and Andrew Miracle. *Culture and Human Sexuality.* Pacific Grove, CA: Brooks/Cole, 1993.

Tambiah, Stanley. *Leveling Crowds: Nationalist Conflict and Collective Violence in South Asia.* Berkeley: University of California Press, 1997.

Tsing, Anna Lowenhaupt. *Friction: An Ethnography of Global Connection.* Princeton, NJ: Princeton University Press, 2005.

van Willigen, John. *Applied Anthropology.* 3rd ed. Westport, CT: Bergin & Garvey, 2002.

Venbrux, Eric, Pamela Sheffield Rosi, and Robert L. Welsch. *Exploring World Art.* Long Grove, IL: Waveland Press, 2006.

Vincent, Joan. *The Anthropology of Politics: A Reader in Ethnography, Theory, and Critique.* Malden, MA: Wiley–Blackwell, 2002.

Vogel, Susan M. *Baule: African Art Western Eyes.* New Haven, CT: Yale University Press, 1997.

Wallace, Anthony F. C. *Religion: An Anthropological View.* New York: Random House, 1966.

Watson, James L. *Golden Arches East: McDonald's in East Asia.* 2nd ed. Stanford, CA: Stanford University Press, 2006.

Watson, James L., and Melissa L. Caldwell. *The Cultural Politics of Food and Eating: A Reader.* Malden, MA: Blackwell, 2005.

Weatherford, Jack. *The History of Money.* New York: Crown, 1997.

Weismantel, Mary. *Food, Gender, and Poverty in the Ecuadorian Andes.* Prospect Heights, IL: Waveland Press, 1998.

Welsch, Robert L. "The Authenticity of Contemporary World Art: Afterword." In *Exploring World Art,* ed. Eric Venbrux et al. Long Grove, IL: Waveland Press, 2006.

Weston, Kath. *Families We Choose: Lesbians, Gays, Kinship.* New York: Columbia University Press, 1991.

———. "Lesbian/Gay Studies in the House of Anthropology." *Annual Review of Anthropology* 22 (1993): 339–67.

Wiley, Andrea S., and John S. Allen. *Medical Anthropology: A Biocultural Approach.* New York: Oxford University Press, 2009.

Wilk, Richard R., and Lisa Cliggett. *Economies and Cultures: Foundations of Economic Anthropology.* 2nd ed. Boulder, CO: Westview Press, 2007.

Williams, Brackette. "A Class Act: Anthropology and the Race to Nation across Ethnic Terrain." *Annual Review of Anthropology* 18 (1989): 401–44.

Winzeler, Robert L. *Anthropology and Religion: What We Know, Think, and Question.* Lanham, MD: AltaMira Press, 2008.

Wolcott, Harry F. *The Art of Fieldwork*. 2nd ed. Lanham, MD: AltaMira Press, 2004.

———. *Ethnography: A Way of Seeing*. 2nd ed. Lanham, MD: AltaMira Press, 2008.

Wolf, Eric. *Peasants*. Englewood Cliffs, NJ: Prentice Hall, 1962.

———. *Europe and the People without History*. Berkeley: University of California Press, 1982.

———. *Envisioning Power: Ideologies of Dominance and Resistance*. Berkeley: University of California Press, 1999.

Yan, Yunxiang. "Of Hamburger and Social Space: Consuming McDonald's in Beijing." In *The Cultural Politics of Food and Eating*, ed. James Watson and Melissa L. Caldwell. Malden, MA: Blackwell, 2005.

Young, Michael W. *Malinowski's Kiriwina: Fieldwork Photography 1915–1918*. Chicago: University of Chicago Press, 1998.

Zentella, Ana Celia. *Growing Up Bilingual: Puerto Rican Children in New York*. Malden, MA: Wiley–Blackwell, 1997.

Index

Key terms are defined on boldfaced page numbers

269